CONFLICT WITHOUT CHAOS

*A Look Back at Conflict Intervention Initiatives
During the Nation's Early Civil Rights Era*

HAMPTON PRESS COMMUNICATION SERIES
COMMUNICATION AND SOCIAL ORGANIZATION
Gary L. Kreps, series editor

CONFLICT WITHOUT CHAOS

A Look Back at Conflict Intervention Initiatives During the Nation's Early Civil Rights Era

Bob Greenwald

HAMPTON PRESS, INC.
CRESSKILL, NJ 07626

Printed in the United States of America

Library of Congress Cataloging-in-Publication Data

Greenwald, Bob
  Conflict without chaos : a look back at conflict intervention initiatives during the nation's early civil rights era/Bob Greenwald.
    p. cm. -- (Communication series (Hampton Press). Communication and social organization.
  Includes bibliographical references and index.
  ISBN 978-1-57273-764-8 (hardbound) -- 978-1-57273-765-5 (paperbound)
1. Mediation--United States. 2. Conflict management--United States. 3. Dispute resolution (Law)--United states. I. Title.
  KF9084.G73 2008
  303.6'9--dc22
                                        2007042201

Hampton Press, Inc.
23 Broadway
Cresskill, NJ 07626

CONTENTS

FOREWORD

As I write this foreword to Bob Greenwald's preeminent book on conflict resolution, I feel some bit of embarrassment. Over the past twenty-five years or so, I have done a lot of talking about alternative dispute resolution (ADR) and have written sporadically to encourage its use. Because I happened to be among the first Texans to speak openly about ADR, I picked up the title of "father" (or more recently, "grandfather") of the Texas ADR movement.

My embarrassment on this occasion arises out of the fact that Bob Greenwald was the first individual I had met who was actually engaged professionally in mediation practice. As I recall, it was in the late 1970s when we first crossed paths as a result of our concurrent involvement with our respective cities—Houston and Dallas, where we were each working toward the establishment of a community mediation center. He was by then already amply experienced in "doing his thing" as a third party neutral, in Texas and beyond. Bringing disputants to the negotiation table to settle their differences was already part and parcel of his modus operandi as regional mediator for the U.S. Department of Justice's Community Relations Service.

So it occurs to me now that if Bob was not the father of ADR in Texas, he had a substantial impact on its early development and should, at the very least, bear the moniker of "*godfather* of Texas ADR!"

Before 1980, Texas ADR was mostly talk. In those days few lawyers or judges were familiar with the concept of mediation, except perhaps in the context of labor-management dispute settlement. Often the term was confused with the very distinguishable practice of arbitration. In 1979, then Texas Supreme Court Chief Justice Joe Greenhill returned home from a judicial seminar carrying with him the notion that mediation might be a way to reduce overcrowded court dockets. In a casual discussion with me and a colleague, Charles R. Dunn, he sought to encourage the Houston Bar Association to look into the possibility of establishing what by then was generically referred to as a "*neighborhood justice center* to serve as a peoples' mediation forum."

The rest of the story, as the saying goes, is history. In 1980, Houston opened its doors to people who needed a relatively quick and inexpensive way to get their disputes resolved. The parallel Dallas project was set in motion shortly thereafter. Since then, the neutral intervention process in dealing with intergroup and interpersonal conflict has taken root. From our initially tentative beginnings in Texas (having joined with the few earlier pioneers already in operation elsewhere in the country), has emerged a remarkable new framework in the nation's conflict settlement system. Community-based mechanisms today, providing neutral intervention services, often as an alternative to litigation, can be found not only in most metropolitan centers, but in many smaller towns all across the land.

The use of mediation as a tool to overcome diversity has found its rightful place in the contemporary environment. A whole new career field has developed, preparing young aspirants to serve a cause that has much to contribute to a more stable society and to improved human relations.

Frank G. Evans, Founding Director
The Frank G. Evans Center for Conflict Resolution
Chief Justice (retired), Texas First Court of Appeals

PREFACE

This book is not intended as a memoir, although it is largely an account drawing upon my years as a federal mediator with the Community Relations Service (CRS) of the U.S. Department of Justice. Some will find it a fertile reference source for assisting dispute settlement practitioners in the application of a particular genre of mediation process or technique. A primary goal is to offer a plea for greater attention to a well-established conflict resolution methodology among those who find themselves responsible for overcoming intergroup dissension. It is written with the hope of creating a fresh perspective that will add appreciably to currently available literature dealing with mediation and other nonjudicial measures to relieve discord.

A compelling case can be made for the phenomenal increases since the early 1970s in broad applicability and recognized viability of conflict management as a methodology that can help avoid needless litigation, improve human relationships, and even save lives. True, the neutral third-party intervenor model has been in favor for a very long time. It has been the centerpiece of resolving labor-management polemics since the early 1900s. It has been a staple for centuries in the arena of international diplomatic affairs. But it has emerged as a more universal strategy only in recent decades. In the world of interpersonal and intergroup conflict resolution it has impacted the professional employment market and has come to influence related practitioners with a vigor and implacability seldom seen in the realm of human services.

Yet it is my contention that the use of alternatives to litigation in resolving disputes has not as yet delivered on its greater promise. Disputants of every stripe are still drawn to legal remedies in ever-increasing numbers, often heedless of excessive costs in money, time, and energy. Overt confrontation with law enforcement or other governmental authority still haunts the streets and public squares of this nation and around the globe. Hostilities between nations, religious sects, and government ideologies, more often than not are still settled under the aegis of force.

Negotiation and civilized discourse are the instruments for overcoming contention. Are not fairness and reason the marks of honorable character? Why wouldn't the notion of an impartial intervention to bring about the resolution of rancor and antagonism find wide appeal and acceptance?

It is true that opportunities for exposure and access to mediation and other intermediary roles have become more available. An ever-increasing number of universities, and even secondary schools, have opened their curricula to student interest in this relatively new discipline.

Perhaps even more significant in the emergence of dispute settlement resources has been the creation of local community centers to assist families, neighbors, businesses, landlords and tenants, employees, churches, and organizations with problem solving between parties in conflict. Today, in my home state of North Carolina alone, a recent count showed twenty-three member centers in a statewide network of such organizations, utilizing more than 2,500 volunteer mediators. According to the National Association for Community Mediation, there are well over 500 such conflict resolution agencies throughout the United

States, many privately funded with small paid staffs and large cadres of trained volunteer intermediaries.

The Better Business Bureaus of this country have also pioneered programs designed to help businesses and their customers address and overcome problems through the use of mediation techniques and other good office practices. For decades, they have facilitated procedures through which parties can settle disputes at low cost and without need to engage the legal system.

And then, of course, we can consider the fact that most of us use one or another form of negotiation in the normal course of our lives. How often in dealing with others do we articulate a position or opinion, attempt to persuade another toward our view, and reach a mutually satisfactory accommodation? Probably more often than we realize. Our contender may be a spouse, a supervisor, a business associate or competitor, or a professional colleague. Sometimes it is a friend or relative with whom you are about to share an experience or responsibility. It might be a television repairman, a sales clerk, or a revenue agent. In fact, hardly an interaction occurs without some form of negotiation at work. It can be fleeting and subtle or it can be sustained and of considerable substance.

Therefore we might conclude that negotiation has something of a universal interest and application. We as individuals seeking to be successful negotiators in our daily relationships can likely benefit from examining the definitive concept presented here—the resolution of intergroup conflict through third-party neutral intervention—primarily within a framework of the relatively narrow process we call mediation. I will on these pages try to set forth the parameters within which a somewhat formalized intermediary procedure can contribute significantly to the narrowing of diverse perceptions, to the facilitation of effective communication between adversaries, and ultimately to the reduction or elimination of differences among parties with opposing viewpoints, objectives, or values.

This book is also written for those who would revisit the crescendo days of the civil rights movement with an eye toward ways in which turbulence was moved toward productive dialogue and resolution. It is intended to attract the interest of those who would examine a slice of our history that was, in many respects, a treasure trove of experimentation in the human condition. If the past is prologue, it should also be of special interest to present-day professionals who engage in third-party assistance in helping to resolve ruptured domestic relations, neighborhood antagonisms, individual allegations of discrimination, and other types of interpersonal and collective discord.

This account is intended to offer new insights into contemporary intergroup belligerency and the resulting tensions that arise when one group's interests and welfare are perceived to be incompatible with those of another group. Because the field experiences described in this chronicle are drawn from the watershed years of civil rights ferment, the lessons it produced were taken from a context of racial unrest and a national preoccupation with self-examination in coping with diversity. For purposes of developing insights and drawing comparisons, however, it is clear that the mediation concepts and processes in this milieu are very closely akin to the practice of mediation in other settings and circumstances. It is with that recognition in mind that those readers who are involved in parallel applications of third party intervention are invited to examine the group conflict model found here.

It is our tangent purpose in this work to assess the impact of new approaches to dispute settlement that, during its years of incubation, for the most part escaped public attention. This is about an experimental undertaking that did not capture widespread or sustained media interest and so was carried out in relative obscurity. At most, these developments were only at the periphery of public awareness. It is a relatively unfamiliar civil rights chapter that unfolded in the midst of a vast array of mostly government-sponsored new programs, new promises, and new challenges, thus relegating it even further behind the unseen shadows of innovation and change.

Much of the inspiration and virtually all of the practical learning in preparation for this project arose out of a nineteen-year career (1965-84) as a conciliator and later a mediator for the Community Relations Service (CRS) of the U.S. Department of Justice. It was an experience that would reveal to me many unfamiliar aspects of conflict resolution. It would mold my attitudes and convictions about intergroup and interpersonal discord. It would be the incubator for developing insights regarding the balance among humans between benevolence and malevolence. It would finally lead me to a full recognition of the potential available for helping to overcome the intergroup alienation that seems so commonplace today in virtually every society.

The setting of these accounts is during a period when our country was accommodating and adjusting to a new law of the land—the Civil Rights Act of 1964. This legislative harbinger of a changing social order was certain to create tensions and divisions. It called upon community, political, and economic institutions to implement substantial reforms and it struck forcefully at interracial attitudes and behavior in a way that would change the nation's mores forever.

To achieve its primary objective, this book will help reawaken interest and stimulate renewed investigation into an important apparatus for improving human relationships, moderating contention and bringing new insights into our combative natures and self-serving inclinations. In contrast to most other published works in this genre, the message here will be conveyed through the lessons of actual field experience rather than academic discourse.

ACKNOWLEDGMENTS

To my wife, Pat, who endured with patience and understanding the too frequent solitude and neglect of spousal authorship. When discouragement jeopardized progress, she provided the stimulus to sustain momentum. Her keen eye for the misplaced word or faulty syntax made the early editing considerably less burdensome;

and

To my son, David, a wordsmith of some repute and always eager to take his father to task, applied his language skills in the early going to help enhance expression and readability;

and

To dear friend, Peggy Collins, whose own publishing adventure concurrent with mine offered a model of inspiration and encouragement with her showing of dedication to her craft and with her generous sharing of ideas.

and

A special word of thanks to the many who participated in the diverse case experience reported on these pages. Among those who responded to this project with particular interest and contribution: Frank G. Evans, founding director of the Frank G. Evans Center for Conflict Resolution in Houston and retired chief justice of the Texas First Court of Appeals; George Dibrell, former city manager of Port Arthur, Texas.

ABOUT THE AUTHOR

Few careers offer the opportunity to open doors to a new frontier. The author was one of the fortunate few to be so advantaged.

Circumstances arising out of the nation's era of civil rights reform brought with it intriguing prospects for innovation in the resolution of intergroup conflict. It was the introduction in the early 1970s of the mediation process with regard to moderating inter-racial/ethnic discord that gave this writer a vehicle to follow an uncharted course. Somewhat unwittingly, he became a pioneer in an unexplored corner of the racial divide.

Bob Greenwald spent a total of twenty-two years in federal service, most of it with the Community Relations Service of the U.S. Department of Justice, an agency created by the landmark Civil Rights Act of 1964. Following three years of military service, he spent almost twelve years of his earlier career in chamber of commerce management positions in Texas and Oklahoma, and as a senior administrator for a social service agency. Born in Jamaica, New York, he is a graduate of The George Washington University with a degree in government.

After leaving federal service in 1984, not ready for full retirement, Bob and his wife Pat spent some five years establishing and operating a niche publishing business, creating and marketing booklets for use by realtors and corporations in helping families cope with the exigencies associated with relocation. Later, the author's retirement was postponed again for almost another five years when he took on the task of organizing and managing a national trade association for owners of short-term corporate housing properties.

The author's first book, published in 1998 by Career Press, was titled *50 Fabulous Planned Retirement Communities for Active Adults.* Unrelated to his mediation work, the appearance of that book coincided with, and was motivated by, a family relocation from Dallas, Texas to Hendersonville in western North Carolina. It is there that he and his wife reside today in blissful retirement.

INTRODUCTION

*The notion that most people want black-robed judges,
well-dressed lawyers, and fine paneled courtrooms
as the setting to resolve their disputes is not correct.
People with problems, like people with pain, want relief,
and they want it as quickly and inexpensively as possible.*

—Warren E. Burger, former Chief Justice (1977)
United States Supreme Court

The Civil Rights Act of 1964 was created in a maelstrom of unprecedented underclass discontent and turmoil. Conflict issues of the day centered on racial and ethnic minorities who saw themselves as having been denied access to the fruits of equal opportunity in a nation of plenty. Their disquiet had gradually won understanding, and their causes acquiescence, from an increasing number of Americans. The nation's elected representatives responded.

Among the various mechanisms created to implement the resulting legislation was an inconspicuous agency of the U.S. Department of Justice called the Community Relations Service (CRS).[1] Its primary mission was to help communities resolve ". . . disputes, disagreements or difficulties relating to discriminatory practices based on race, color or national origin . . ."

The work of the Community Relations Service in conflict resolution experimentation, especially during its early years, largely escaped public attention. It was a relatively unfamiliar civil rights federal resource in the midst of a vast array of new programs, new promises, and new challenges. Moreover, the relatively confidential and behind-the-scenes nature of its modus operandi often required avoidance of media attention whenever circumstances permitted. At best, case practice was only at the periphery of any broad public awareness.

From its inception, CRS engaged essentially in two categories of activity: (a) crisis *resolution* (initially through *conciliation*, a process of facilitating *communication* between

---

[1]Established under Title X of the 1964 Civil Rights Act, the creation of a federal mechanism to provide third party intervention under conditions of racial-ethnic conflict was the vision of President Lyndon B. Johnson. Initially, until April 1966, CRS was a part of the U.S. Department of Commerce.

adversaries, and later through *mediation*, a process of *negotiation*), and (b) crisis *prevention*—a programmatic approach aimed at eliminating the root causes of social discord. It is the first of these dual mandates to which this work is primarily devoted.

Particularly since the 1950s and following decades, confrontation among diverse community groups was a familiar characteristic of conflicting values, perceptions, and objectives. Issues revolved around alleged, demonstrated, and sometimes imagined inequities in education, housing, law enforcement, employment, health care, welfare, and government services. Positions of opposing parties were generally quite predictable. On the one hand were those who sought resolution of grievances perceived to be discriminatory, illegal, or worse. On the other were those who had the authority and/or responsibility to make decisions in response to the alleged transgressions. In the vernacular of the day, it was "the establishment" versus those who saw themselves as its victims.

This was a period when our country was in the midst of accommodating and adjusting to a new law of the land—the Civil Rights Act of 1964. This legislative harbinger of a changing social order was certain to create tensions and divisions. It called upon major community, political, and economic institutions to consider and implement substantial reforms, striking forcefully at interracial attitudes that had been part of our society since its beginnings. The new reforms would transform the very cultural moorings that shape our everyday lives.

Federal authority had mobilized and instituted a variety of agencies and functions to implement provisions of the new civil rights legislation. Virtually all were created as enforcement or administrative mechanisms responsible for implementing programs. The Community Relations Service was uniquely distinguished as an agency that would deliver a new approach to facilitating change. It would offer resources to stimulate and support constructive and **voluntary** channels of reconciliation. It would promote resolution of conflict through the use of conciliation and later in its development, through the more structured process of mediation.

MORE QUESTIONS THAN ANSWERS

During its early years of operations, CRS relied heavily on the trouble-shooting experience of trained conciliators who were often called upon to enter volatile confrontations and use their powers of reason and persuasion to help maintain or restore community stability. As conflicts grew more complex, stridency tended to be supplemented by more sophisticated complaint documentation and legalistic bills of particulars. New approaches to the effective resolution of racial and ethnic conflict began to emerge.

Early in 1972, CRS assigned a small task force to explore and formulate alternative concepts in conflict resolution. It had become apparent to some within the agency, myself included, that racial unrest and related community discord might be ameliorated through use of a negotiation format somewhat similar to the well-established and successful industrial collective bargaining model that had contributed so much to the relief of labor-management unrest.

Given a new forum for bringing culturally and economically diverse parties together to resolve differences, could there be a reasonable expectation of success? Could racial-ethnic conflicts involving high school and university student agitation of the day be diminished through intensive, professionally assisted dialogue? Could problems of police-citizen alienation be mitigated through a process of structured communication? Could such a process make federal, municipal, and other public funding disputes less apt to result in acrimony if evaluated under conditions of mutual examination and understanding? And most importantly, would disadvantaged parties and their adversaries be able to face one another across a table, in good faith, on a relatively level playing field? Would not institutional resources of the respondents likely be so intimidating as to be inconsistent with reaching such objectives?

The answers to these and other questions of equal uncertainty were soon forthcoming. The agency's first five years of experimentation produced surprising insights and unexpected dividends.

One of the earliest CRS initiatives was a series of personal contacts with federal judges. Notions about mediation as a promising option for court referral were heard first hand by scores of selected jurists. Several heeded our initial invitation to consider referral of potential litigants still in pretrial stages.

The first, Judge E. Gordon West of the United States District Court for the Middle District of Louisiana, put before our agency the question of whether we would be willing to try to apply our experiment to several core issues underlying a series of lawsuits initiated by inmates against administrators of the Louisiana State Penitentiary at Angola. We accepted, recognizing that if we wished to test the flexibility and adaptability of mediation as an alternative to legal recourse, there could be no better circumstance under which to demonstrate it.[2]

DON'T TELL IT TO THE JUDGE

Racial turmoil in the United States had impacted the judiciary in unprecedented ways. The courts, from state to federal levels of jurisdiction, were being inundated with litigation that caused serious backlogs. Prison inmates with access to institutional law libraries were aggressively pursuing broad prison reforms. Civil rights organizations were pounding on courthouse doors, seeking relief from inequities in education, employment, law enforcement, housing and public accommodations. Barriers to equal opportunity in these crucial conditions of citizenship, all granted under the sweeping federal legislation of 1964 and later years, became the bedrock for claims of noncompliance with the laws of the land. The courts, under considerable docket strain, were highly motivated to examine innovation and nontraditional remedies.

Added to the judicial malaise was a growing recognition that too many parties to legal action were not being well served by the generally slow and costly process of litigation. There was an emerging call for developing imaginative programs to divert petitioners from conventional dispute resolution systems. A chorus of voices, some from within the legal profession itself, began calling for alternatives to courtroom adjudication. Pilot projects were being explored to establish community mechanisms for helping disputants reach common ground through nonjudicial, nonadversarial proceedings.

There was ample precedent for such sentiment. For many years the Federal Mediation & Conciliation Service had used the "third-party neutral" approach to seeking labor-management accord. In the private sector, the American Arbitration Association had likewise established a similarly well-deserved reputation as a resource for settling labor relations differences.[3] Universities were beginning to examine and evaluate the need for academic

---

[2]The experience at Angola is fully presented in Chapter 5.
[3]The National Center for Dispute Settlement, a pioneering program of the American Arbitration Association in Washington, DC, was among the first nongovernmental organizations devoted to community dispute resolution, using the mediation process. Other noteworthy private sector initiatives operating in the late 1960s and early 1970s included the Institute for Mediation and Conflict Resolution (New York City), the Department of Law, Justice and Community Relations of the United Methodist Church (Washington, DC), and the Community Crisis Intervention Center (St. Louis, Missouri).

offerings in conflict management. A few had already established such programs, having sensed the potential for a new professional genre in the making.

Until these developments unfolded, the focus of dispute settlement initiatives had been primarily on the collective bargaining model. Little attention had been given to bringing about a mechanism to relieve the interracial and interethnic tensions threatening the nation's sociopolitical stability.

TALK IS CHEAP

By the early 1980s, mediation as an alternative to traditional methods of dispute resolution had taken on a life of its own, impacting a variety of professional disciplines. Social workers and family counselors were scrambling for mediation training, visualizing a new tool to help clients in domestic relations squabbles. Environmental issues were also at the center of some impressive strides in this new framework of deliberative dialogue. Soon, mediation was being mandated in certain municipal and county courts (juvenile, domestic relations, small claims, etc.) before seeking a judicial remedy.

Many attorneys in civil practice, however, were turning a wary eye toward the fledgling voluntary settlement process. Early on, there was skepticism of, and resistance to, the widespread application of mediation as a dispute settlement device. Many lawyers, at first exposure, felt threatened. They saw this upstart movement as an intrusion on their turf, if not an outright threat to their livelihoods. Some resented what they perceived to be an attempt to side-step their rightful professional domain and as an intention to subvert the legal process. There were cries of "justice denied."

But over time, mediation began to take hold and become better understood as an alternative to litigation. Leadership surfaced from the American Bar Association and from many local and state bar organizations, mostly taking positions in support of mediation and encouraging attorneys to explore ways in which they could become involved in it. Eventually, there was a significant influx of lawyers enrolled in various mediation training programs springing up around the country. A growing number of lawyers were trading courtroom advocacy for the more pacific calling of the neutral intervenor, with the promise of a "win-win" outcome and with lower levels of acrimony and stress.

Some began to integrate the mediation option into their practices. Others found the new calling so appealing that they began devoting themselves to it full time, relinquishing entirely their traditional roles as jurisprudence professionals and advocate counselors.

Inevitably, a dichotomy developed. On the one hand there were those who viewed legal orientation and practice as incompatible with neutrality. After all, they contended, lawyers are necessarily advocates by the essential nature of their attorney-client relationship. It is their mission and obligation to help one party prevail over another by taking advantage of whatever the law will allow. By training, and more often than not by temperament as well, the attorney prepares his/her client for combat. Was that not the antithesis of the mediator's third-party neutrality? Would it not be expecting too much for the tiger to change its stripes? They would make poor neutrals, went the reasoning.

On the other side of the coin, legal practitioners pointed out that no other profession was better equipped to deal with adversaries and bring them to settlement without recourse to litigation. Very often, they emphasized, the pretrial phase of litigation results in just that outcome. Furthermore, knowledge of the law would be crucial in framing agreements designed to hold parties to their commitments, whereas the enforcement of voluntary agreements might in some instances ultimately rely on statutory recourse. Finally, went the counter-reasoning, lawyers were adept at negotiating between adversaries, helping them prepare positions and protect their legal rights, important considerations even in connection with a nonbinding procedure.

With startling momentum, the popularity of this new dispute settlement concept grew until it became clear that it was more than merely an abstract invention. Within a relatively few years it had become a legitimate alternative for bringing belligerents to less contentious and more rewarding negotiated settlement.

Contemporary society is prone to controversy with little enough provocation. Conflict has been basic to human relationships since the arrival of our species on the planet. It has shown itself to be just as inherent in interpersonal and intergroup relations as the quest for security or the need for love and acceptance. The problems that arise in our everyday lives are for the most part deficiencies in communication. They are found in families, in relationships among friends and neighbors, in the business and professional world, and on just about any plane of social interaction.

FUNDAMENTAL UNDERLYING ASSUMPTIONS

It is my contention that at the core of American life are certain conceptual values and structural systems that support voluntary negotiation to resolve conflict. Among them:

- That there is virtue merely in the pursuit of peaceful dispute settlement through forthright, honest, and open-minded dialogue between adversaries. This maxim is illustrated, as already noted, by the largely successful history of labor-management relations in this country since the early 20th century.
- That the democratic legislative process itself, upon which this nation's government was founded, is the very embodiment of the principles of negotiation. Our judicial system, at least in its purest and most ideal context, also embraces such principles.
- That the great majority of the nation's citizenry are reasonable people of goodwill who will act with moral probity and practical enlightenment if given the opportunity to do so in a setting free of duress.

With these preliminary observations, a clarification of intent is in order. There is no presumption that the specific techniques, definitions, procedures, and practices set forth on these pages necessarily should be applied universally to the many modes of mediation found in today's diverse practice environment. Clearly, however, the neutral intervention role in one milieu has meaningful parallels to those found in a different setting. Nuances drawn from one scenario bring worthwhile insights to another, regardless of the dissimilarities of the parties and circumstances. This book proposes to offer the professional intervenor or conflict manager the benefit of such analogies.

1

A CONFLICT PERSPECTIVE

*It's a most important thing for people who have power and money—who've made it—
to be sensitive to the intensity of the needs and feelings of those who haven't made it.
People who have power don't have to give it up. But they must share it. It is one of the
most important issues of these times*

McGeorge Bundy, President (1969)
The Ford Foundation

OUR HERITAGE OF MALEVOLENCE

Notwithstanding the civilizing of our species, peace, goodwill, and brotherhood have been elusive throughout the ages. We have produced an array of religious faiths, persistently and convincingly proclaiming morality, love, and compassion. Our heritage and our mores, in this and in most societies, call for the best in human inclinations.

Where then were we taught that self-interest is an acceptable pursuit? How do we come to regard aggressive competition and achievement at the expense of others as commendable objectives? Why do we find it so difficult to perceive without bias? Why, long after reaching the age of accountability, do we hold on to the values of our parents, or others around us, without examining those values for their intrinsic worth by reasonably humane standards?

Look around. In this age of world-wide, almost instantaneous reporting of news (and conflict, it seems, is given the highest priority of newsworthiness) we are constantly reminded of the pervasiveness of discord. There is conflict everywhere among individuals and the institutions they create. Contentiousness and stridency seem more commonplace, more relevant to the order of life, than does harmony. One might conclude that many of our socioeconomic, religious, and political inventions thrive on dissonance.

In the world of commerce, who would deny that progress for one enterprise is often made at the expense of another? Is that not a fundamental characteristic of the private enterprise system? Most businesses must fight for market share sufficient to sustain themselves, at the very least. But if the entrepreneur is motivated to reap maximum return, it is all too often necessary to go beyond any "do unto others . . ." limits that might readily apply in another compartment of life. The business environment is not infrequently a battlefield upon which to confront and vanquish a foe. As in all wars, tactics can become harsh, if not violent. Ethics diminish. There are ready rationalizations easily within reach to justify an all-out attack on an adversary. Let the weaker competitor beware. Succeed and prosper; fail and perish.

What evidence is there that conflict infects the family unit? To the extent that each family member has his or her own set of interests, value parameters, spheres of influence, and sources of satisfaction, is it not predictable that contention may threaten peaceful coexistence? There is no need to cite statistics for divorce, child and spousal abuse, desertion, and family instability. They are all too familiar. Most clergymen will confirm that a significant share of their ministries is devoted to family counseling and salvaging relationships. Psychologists and psychiatrists, social workers, marriage counselors, and a host of other professional advisors are among the growing army of those who, during and between crises in their own lives, are sometimes able, and invariably willing, to grapple more successfully with other people's problems than with their own.

Which among our institutions designed for accomplishment escape our rugged individualism or our conditioned group loyalties and opposing alliances? The church? The political party? The social agency? The university, public school system, hospital, fraternity, professional organization? How many of them elude internal dissension or conflict for any sustained period of time? Does there not too often arise the struggle to dominate or the will to impose? No matter how homogeneous its members, diversity is more the nature of any group when we consider the emergence and maintenance of leadership, control, and influence. Personalities emerge to exercise dominance, often at the expense of fairness or equity and in contradiction to reason. Perceptions are too dependent upon individual life experiences to allow for consensus, especially with regard to those issues involving emotional response, conditioned attitudes, or long-nurtured prejudices.

And then there is the community of nations. The 20th century, perhaps more than at any other time in history, produced a dismal global account of the international forfeiture of peaceful rapprochement and a profound disrespect for ethnic differences. As we move into the early decades of a new century there seems to be little evidence of our having learned and profited from the past. Surely, we should by now have learned the futility of xenophobia and the deception of nationalistic or religious zealotry.

If we can assume that nations are led by the more intelligent and benevolent of our species, or the more sensitive, or the more practical (assumptions that can be readily contested, to be sure), then prospects for a peaceful and beneficent world are remote. The United Nations, noble experiment that it is, has demonstrated with too much consistency that people of all races, creeds and nationalities suffer the same vulnerabilities. Fealty is typically defined by accident of birth, class or location. It is virtually beyond human comprehension, it seems, to identify with and embrace the interests of the larger good of humankind.

Group antagonisms are so familiar that they tend to be ignored or so taken for granted that they are all but invisible. The "we-they" syndrome is inherent in the social order. We divide ourselves into artificial allegiances.

Perhaps the most perplexing and yet widespread manifestations of this propensity for establishing opposing group loyalties is found in the religious life of virtually every society. The practice of worship, even among those following the same or parallel belief systems, often divides followers into subgroups, each of which subscribes to relatively minor variations, but upon which the ultimate group identity is forged.

The outcome of divisions brought about by religious differences is not infrequently cataclysmic. We have only to reflect upon the world news of recent years to wince at the factions of Northern Ireland that have devastated one another over the schism between their Protestant and Catholic faiths. The Christian-Moslem feuds in the Middle East and elsewhere have smoldered and erupted for generations. The willingness of one sect within the very same theological foundation to revile and even annihilate those of another sect has been demonstrated with appalling consistency. That they find inspiration and spiritual guidance from the same sacred scriptures and worship the same deity is not, as we might expect, the tie that binds. The Arab-Israeli bitterness, although not entirely a matter of theological incompatibility, has its roots in alien cultural and religious fundamentals. In Africa, in South America, in India and neighboring Pakistan, men have killed their unknown enemy—all in the name of some holier deity, more legitimate tribalism, or political ideology. Even our Canadian neighbors, seemingly endowed with a generous share of civility, have difficulty moderating tensions between cultural antagonists (mixed perhaps with a generous portion of ancestral nationalistic pride, but revealing the same symptomatology).

Former United Nations Secretary General Kofi Annan, in commenting on the corrupting use of religion and the violence it has been known to spawn, had this to say:

> Religion, sadly, has been misused throughout history in the cause of division, discrimination and even death. From antiquity through the Crusades to the present day, religion has been distorted, turned from a personal matter of faith and sustenance into a weapon of power and coercion. The cry of the soul for meaning, and for God, has been drowned out by the battle cry of those claiming to have God on their side.[1]

GET THEE BETWEEN

During the third decade of the 20th century, the United States endured unprecedented economic stress. The struggle for survival among large numbers of blue-collar workers led to pervasive violence over the right of employees to collectively organize and to negotiate with their employers on issues of compensation, benefits, and working conditions. There were no effective mechanisms to deal with the growing strife between labor and management. Out of spreading turmoil came legislative action that eventually brought corresponding instruments of government into being, charged with providing alternatives to bitter confrontation. The Federal Mediation and Conciliation Service, among other agencies offering ancillary labor-management services, administers what is today a complex third party machinery that provides neutral intermediaries to help adversaries settle their differences at the collective bargaining table. Similarly, the American Arbitration Association in the private sector has for decades garnered an enviable reputation for providing industrial conflict resolution mechanisms. Unions and employers have had their freedom to abuse one another significantly curtailed. The bloody yesteryear street battles seem mostly relegated to a bygone era.

Perhaps the most convincing evidence that human relationships are too often characterized by dissension is found in our judicial system. Our social order has created an enormous network of professions and institutions through which most interpersonal and intergroup differences can be resolved, or at least contested, with a degree of probity. A whopping number of attorneys and judges (to say nothing of their satellite functionaries) is required to maintain a reasonable state of equilibrium in determining who among antagonists shall prevail—another reflection of our dilemma.

---

[1] The Tanenbaum Center for Interreligious Understanding (web site: www.tanenbaum.org/programs/conflict resolution).

No consideration of our propensities for conflict can suffice without going to the deep well of racism and other forms of intolerance. In no other segment of our lives do we so cling to the bosom of estrangement. How comforting, how convenient, to be able impulsively and intuitively to mark another human being as our adversary. No matter that he is entirely unknown to us. There he is, easily distinguishable by his skin color, his features, his language or dialect—perhaps even by his dress, manner, or grooming.

There are theories enough to explain our proclivity for racial/ethnic chauvinism and related characteristics. A hedge against Anglo-Christian insecurities? The need to feel superior to others, without examination? The search for scapegoats for our own ancestry? Rationalizations perhaps for a sinful history of intolerance and enslavement? It scarcely matters. It is here today, as it has been for centuries.

THE PERCEPTION PREDICAMENT

We have learned, if we are willing to acknowledge it, that the basis for our grievances against others is frequently a product of our imagination. We find it much easier to hate or fear a group of nameless people than an individual who bears the group traits we reject but who may strike us as a redeeming human being if we look closely. We paint our enemies with a collective brush. Many warped perceptions go well beyond racial, ethnic, or religious bias. Our objects of disdain may be directed toward members of a political party, alcoholics, or homosexuals. It might even be motorcyclists in black leather jackets who inspire our derision. We give them no opportunity to register their worth as individuals. We see them as antagonists by virtue of their group identities. A climate for conflict is created.

Then, we chance to come upon a member of the discredited group who doesn't at all fit our biased expectations. Puzzled and dismayed, our preconception is shattered. The individual doesn't conform to the mold so long and carefully nurtured.

Even social workers, government employees, bankers, trade unionists, elected officials (the ignobly characterized "politician"), musicians—and let's not forget lawyers and used car salesmen—find themselves labeled by those who would judge their worth or the nature of their character, based entirely on occupational happenstance. Such stereotyping, even when operating at a subconscious level, is likely to plant the seeds of contention.

Consider, if you will, the theater of international politics. Within a relatively short period of time, a president of the United States can transform a foreign leader from an infamous despot to a trusted partner. The friend in the diplomatic world, after all, is the one who is most likely to serve our purposes at a moment in history. No matter that we may have earlier called upon a younger generation to sacrifice life and limb in order to save us from the evil intentions of this same official (or his erstwhile collaborators) just a relatively few years before.

All of this is to suggest, simply, that conflict is often at least illogical, if not contrived. It can arise out of a wide assortment of human needs and foibles. Seldom will it stand the test of reason. And yet, we see that it pervades our personal and group relationships. There is little that is rational in this seemingly universal madness. It has been that way since the beginning of recorded history, some would say, and is likely to remain forever thus. Not a very hopeful outlook.

Is the irrationality of these excesses and indulgences indicative of our basic nature? Does it reveal our incapacity to create meaningful fraternity? Are we fated for eternal alienation from those whom we see as being unlike us?

If not, if escape from conflict is possible, then there is an urgent need to develop mechanisms that would facilitate better communication and, as a result, better understanding and disposition to accommodation. And this must occur particularly at the level that touches most of us in our everyday lives—within the institutions we create to help us function productively, and upon which we rely to help order our existence.

To a degree beyond the expectations of those among us who participated in the early days of searching for conflict remedies, there has been remarkable progress. Processes have been devised, refined, and applied for the peaceful settlement of conflict issues to an extent unprecedented in the annals of human relationships. Throughout the civilized world, inventive mechanisms have been created to help resolve disputes and to reduce interpersonal and intergroup antagonisms among adversaries of virtually every description.

A WAVE OF CONFLICT REMEDIES

Well before the end of the 20th century, alternative dispute settlement resources, especially at the local and state levels, were widely available. County and district courts throughout the land, and at the federal level to some extent as well, have come to rely increasingly on private intermediary organizations and practitioners to whom they can refer appropriate litigants. An increasing number of state governments have established various types of dispute resolution mechanisms to handle issues confronting programs and agencies within their jurisdictions.

Choosing mediation as a means of avoiding the judicial process (and thereby saving time and money for the contesting parties as well as for taxpayers) and of resolving issues through mutual assent rather than through arbitrary declaration has become a significant part of the negotiated settlement landscape.

Many times parties are in litigation because there was never an opportunity for honest, in-depth, good faith communication. We have noted that conflict can be the consequence of perceptual differences, misunderstandings, or simple ignorance. Fact and fancy can all too easily combine to feed dissent and increase divisiveness. Parties seeking a voluntary settlement have obvious advantages over those who are cast in the adversarial positions of litigants for whom antagonisms typically grow stronger as issues are pursued.

Long before it embraced mediation with a degree of enthusiasm, the legal profession was contributing significantly to improving communication between litigants and in offering alternatives to legal action. In first resort courts, judges not uncommonly act as brokers for a voluntary settlement. In many respects, they are some of the nation's most experienced mediators, if without benefit of title. At times they find, as do the attorneys representing clients before them, that relief is sought under conditions that hold little promise for a *de jure* or sanctioned remedy.

THE EMERGENCE OF COMMUNITY-BASED
DISPUTE SETTLEMENT PROGRAMS

One of the most significant developments in conflict resolution has been the establishment of community-based organizations devoted to settling disputes. In the early 1970s there was just a handful of such programs in the entire country experimenting with and demonstrating the promise of the mediation concept. In New York City the Institute for Mediation and Conflict Resolution was among the few with an established program to help curb the widespread social upheaval of the day and to help relieve the overloaded judicial system. It was to that enterprise, among others, that CRS turned for the early staff training of its small band of budding mediators.[2]

Among other notable precursors to modern community mediation were several exemplary prototypes, broadly identified as "neighborhood justice centers," located in Los Angeles, Columbus, Ohio, Atlanta, Boston, Kansas City, San Francisco, and Rochester, New York. It was the Ford Foundation that provided early funding initiatives in support of training programs that would help elevate the new discipline to a level of professional standing.

Within the next two decades countless more conflict management organizations came into being throughout the nation. The movement was already spreading to Canada and any number of other countries. Some of these agencies were private nonprofits, whereas others were funded and operated by municipal or state governments. By the mid-1990s there was estimated to be some 150 community-based programs. According to the National Association for Community Mediation (http://www.nafcm.org/pg5.cfm), ten years later there were over 550 such centers involving almost 20,000 trained volunteer mediators processing nearly 100,000 case referrals annually. Today, New York, Michigan, and North Carolina are among the states with the proportionately highest concentrations of local dispute resolution service facilities.

Cases handled by these organizations typically involve disputes among family members (often when divorce or estrangement creates conflict over child custody/visitation rights, financial support arrangements, child-parent dissension, etc.), or between neighbors, landlords and tenants, consumers and vendors, or various other groupings in which disagreements often arise. In some communities, local court referrals make up a substantial portion of the case load.

OTHER PLAYERS JOIN THE PARADE

Faith-based peacemaking has been on the world stage for generations. Most roles of religious leadership have been connected to worldwide conflicts, many of them in Africa, the Near East, and Central America. But several religious groups, most prominent among them the Quakers and the Mennonites, true to their respective traditions as peace-makers, were some of the earliest activists to devote energy and resources to the notion of *community* mediation. It was Dr. James Laue, director of research for our agency, who encouraged the Mennonites to start both a domestic conciliation and peace-building program at the international level. Since then, many other denominational groups and church-related organizations devoted to helping resolve conflict have come on the scene. They have been joined by a much larger array of nonreligious, nonprofit citizen groups with parallel programs and objectives. Many church leaders have long held to the notion that their theistic values outside their congregational domains can be best fulfilled through ministering to the vicissitudes of individuals in their daily lives. The role of the third-party neutral intervenor in helping to overcome trouble at the family or neighborhood level was often seen to be an activity consistent with creedal tenets and worthy of pursuit. So it is that the religious community has been resolutely drawn to the new challenges of converting enmity to harmony.

---

[2]Other agencies from which CRS sought training assistance were the Federal Mediation and Conciliation Service and the American Arbitration Association, both of which had a wealth of experience in providing negotiated settlements between adversaries in the labor-management field, but neither of which had any involvement with civil rights issues (although AAA did partner with the federal Law Enforcement Assistance Administration in 1968 to launch the National Center for Dispute Settlement in Washington, DC, which is generally acknowledged to have been the prototype model for the local centers that followed).

In another societal segment, institutions of higher learning have responded enthusiastically to the opening of a new field of professional opportunity rapidly gaining in popularity and clamoring for training resources. Many colleges and universities offering well-established courses in peace studies and conflict resolution concentrate on international relations and diplomacy, but an increasing number are now including studies in multiple interdisciplinary components designed to prepare students for careers in conflict management, mediation, and negotiation. Academic interest in these types of programs has grown and with it the need for development and refinement in theory and practice, moving the field toward higher levels of professionalism. Future practitioners would need credentials, standards of competence, and perhaps a certification requisite for licensing purposes.

One of the early national surveys to examine the various dimensions of teaching conflict resolution in higher education was conducted by sociologist Paul Wehr in 1986. Among 500 universities surveyed, 294 offered at least one course. Over 50% of the courses surveyed were taught in schools of law, government/political science, sociology/anthropology, business/commerce and management/organization. By 1999 there were at least 20 programs in the United States offering graduate certificates, master's or doctoral degrees in dispute resolution or its equivalent, with many more known to be under development. In more recently published compilations, there was reported to be over 50 universities in some 32 states and the District of Columbia in which graduate programs are in place. An almost equal number were identified by the Conflict Research Consortium (2004) at locations outside the United States, with the largest concentrations found in Canada and Europe.

One of several other reports on such programs from the same source (http://www.gradschools.com/program/peace_studies.html), lists 49 graduate schools in the United States with 18 certificate (nondegree), 40 master's programs, and 11 doctoral degrees along with 60 more postgraduate schools outside this country with similar curricula. Another listing of universities and other educational nonprofits offering conflict resolution training (http://www.peacemakers.ca/education) shows 27 such in the United States, 15 of which do not appear in the other compilation. Undergraduate programs too have proliferated in this country and around the world. Presumably, because growth development in this field is so vigorous and ongoing, these data are inevitably incomplete, there being any number of programs unknown to the researchers in these investigations at any given point in time.

Higher education pioneers in the development of postgraduate domestic alternative dispute resolution and conflict transformation studies include Nova Southeastern University in Fort Lauderdale, Florida (where all three advanced levels of certificate, master's, and doctoral programs are offered), the University of Colorado, Harvard, George Mason University in Fairfax, Virginia, Wayne State University in Detroit, the University of Baltimore, Kennesaw State University in Kennesaw, Georgia, Woodbury College in Montpelier, Vermont, Stanford, Eastern Mennonite University in Harrisburg, Virginia, and the University of Denver.[3]

ANOTHER COMPLAINANT INTERVENOR

Ombudsmanship is yet another alternative system designed to overcome discord and facilitate reconciliation. Used largely by governments at the local, state, regional, and federal levels, and by sizable corporations and institutions, the concept was pioneered in Sweden (1809) and New Zealand among Commonwealth nations (1962), later gaining a degree of

---

[3]A complete list of such academic programs is found in addendum DD.

acceptance and practice in many European countries, as well as in Canada and the United States (Hawaii, in 1967, was the first state to sanction an ombudsman office). By the turn of the 21st century, the concept had been adopted by an estimated 86 countries in every corner of the globe.

The term "ombudsman" is derived from the Swedish word meaning "entrusted person." Responsibilities, in general, involve overseeing the activities of public authorities, investigating citizen complaints of malfeasance, recommending corrective action in redressing grievances found to have merit, and publishing their findings. Ideally, those appointed to the ombudsman position enjoy the freedom to act independently of political influence. In its classic and strongest form, derived from the Swedish model, the office is created legislatively, thus avoiding having to serve at the whim of a new executive administration or coming under undue domination by newly elected officials.

The ombudsman concept has had notable application outside the public domain in a variety of manufacturing and service industries that are particularly susceptible to chronic consumer dissatisfaction, among them automobile companies, funeral homes, health insurance providers, telecommunications products manufactures, and nursing care facilities. Many hospitals, institutions of higher learning, and other large enterprises in the nonprofit sector with sizable constituencies have also created offices to deal exclusively with patron/client complaints.

The *United States Ombudsman Association* (USOA) (http://usombudsman.org/) is the national organization for public sector ombudsman professionals. It is strongly committed to the establishment of programs that incorporate characteristics such as legal/legislative authority, a free hand with investigative processes, an environment conducive to uninhibited criticism of governmental agencies within its jurisdiction, the authority to recommend appropriate corrective action, the power to issue public reports of its work, and sufficient independence to operate effectively.

NONSTRUCTURED OPTIONS
FOR DISPUTE SETTLEMENT

It is well at this point to examine briefly the alternatives for dealing with conflict resolution other than by means of the structured processes that have been discussed thus far.

Probably the most common method used to settle dissension between individuals, and to some extent between groups, is short-term, informal, direct, voluntary and spontaneous dialogue. It takes a degree of maturity on the part of the participants, and something of a sense of practicality, for such interaction to be fruitful. Yet it is commonly applied in our everyday lives, frequently with satisfying results. When it works, it has the great advantage of being without cost in terms of time, expense, or the need for professional assistance.

More tempting, and perhaps most frequently adopted by disputants who feel no great urgency to settle their differences, are the options of rejecting or avoiding the issues at hand. No action is favored over confrontation or other unpleasantness. The parties choose to let time dispose of the quarrel. They are willing to accept the consequences of inaction.

For those with grievances against governmental bodies, and sometimes institutions as well, the only redress may be a willingness by the respondent (often required by law, policy or practice, or otherwise) to grant the complainant a hearing, whether public or private. An alternative might be agreement to conduct an inquiry or to "study the problem" in order to determine the validity of the allegations. Whatever course is offered, the outcome must rely on the integrity of the accused to proceed without prejudice or a preconceived mindset in examining the issues and reaching conclusions. It is ultimately an arbitrary outcome.

During the early days of the civil rights movement and continuing to this day, various forms of duress are drawn upon to wage protest. Among the most common, and often the most effective, are those conflicts in which the disaffected mobilize street demonstrations. Typically intended as peaceful, but sometimes turning to violence, such demonstrations have drawn sufficient public attention to ultimately impact the nation's legal parameters and even some of its most deeply embedded attitudes. The largely successful protest struggles by African-Americans, Latinos, Native Americans, and other minorities for equal treatment under the law requires no recounting here.

The boycott is a parallel form of direct action by organized dissidents, designed to soften an adversary's position toward change or compliance with the petitioner's objectives. Like public protest, it sometimes succeeds in bringing respondents to a more receptive posture with regard to some type of negotiated settlement.

Yet another device for creating a more conducive climate for negotiation is the artful manipulation of the media in an attempt to influence public opinion and thereby bring an otherwise reluctant respondent to a more consenting position. To garner such attention, of course, depends a great deal on the nature of the issues contested and the degree to which newspapers and/or broadcasters see the dispute to be of legitimate newsworthiness or human interest value.

CONVENTION DIES HARD

Change, it is said, is inevitable. There are those irresistible forces that demand it, but there are those inexorable influences that inhibit and restrain it. Whenever social change has come resulting in a shift in power or control relationships, it has generally involved a weighing of alternatives. Organization leadership responding to the challenge of protest is likely to react in whatever manner it perceives to be in the best interest of its constituency.

In the milieu of corporate and institutional protest, too often there are overly cautious response mechanisms at work. In both the public and private sectors, legal and public relations advisors, as well as executive officers and other responsible administrators, are inclined to "play it safe." How to keep from "rocking the boat" is the order of the day. Understandably so. Their superiors may see any conflict as a sign of weak management. Negative publicity can damage the reputation of the organization.

But the lessons of experience tell us that such "safe" strategies can be costly indeed. The ostrich with its head in the sand puts its entire being at risk. The organizational respondent who tries to escape dealing with adversaries, whether they are angry employees, customers, clients, or an irate segment of the general public, is opening the door to the worst of consequences. Concealing information, berating or ignoring hostile parties, and avoiding communication in the long run can create a regrettable deterioration in conditions and relationships.

The notion that institutions give undeserved legitimacy to their detractors by agreeing to meet with them to resolve grievances has been shown consistently to be without merit. A perceived problem allowed to fester is more apt to raise tensions, harden positions, and create a climate for more drastic hostile action than is typically recognized.

The employer will grant wage concessions or other benefits to its work force if it believes that in doing so, at least in the long run, it will produce greater employment stability and, of course, productivity and profitability. The federal, state, or local legislative body will enact laws to protect consumers at the peril of offending powerful special interests only if popular support is strident enough to threaten political survival. The public agency will more likely reform its policies and practices at the cost of exposing favored alliances if there is a more probable threatening alternative to be contemplated. An example might be the fear or anticipation of an investigative reporter shining the light of inquiry on unexposed misdeeds.

And so it is across the spectrum of group relationships. Respond to the lesser evil. Accede to the more threatening duress.

The following three chapters deal with the nuts and bolts of a mechanism that has been shown to be an effective antidote to intergroup conflict. Its promise of greater utilization is largely a matter of bringing greater public attention to its potentials. This book is devoted to that end.

THE SHAPE OF MEDIATION

A Federal Model

*An association of men who will not quarrel with one another
is a thing which has never yet existed, from the greatest confederacy
of nations down to the town meeting or a vestry.*

Thomas Jefferson

MERE SEMANTICS

It was in Dallas in the late 1970s, at a Southern Methodist University symposium on community development, as I recall, that special guests were being introduced to a large luncheon audience. I was flattered to be among those recognized. The mistress of ceremonies, an uncommonly gracious woman, was calling off the names and identities of honorees from the list placed on the lectern before her, giving each an appropriate comment, as if to justify the basis for their having been singled out for notice.

When it came my turn to stand and be acknowledged, the voice at the microphone heralded my moment of cherished recognition by introducing me as a highly regarded *meditator* with the U.S. Department of Justice southwest regional office! Revealing no sign of having made any faux pas, she dutifully went on with her scripted biographical sidebar about how I had contributed much to the establishment of a local dispute mediation center, then being created in Dallas.

My wife and I may have been the only ones in the entire ballroom assemblage to enjoy the humor of it all. Was there, after all, that much distinction between a mediator and a meditator? Later, in reflecting upon the occasion, it did bring to mind the fact that the general public, in the 1960s and 1970s, was largely unaware of the impact this third-party intervention process had begun making as an alternative to litigation in resolving disputes. Few could foresee that the concept would very soon take on a vastly more universal role in resolving interpersonal and family conflict, as well as issues with community-wide implications.

THE SCENARIO

Mediation is more an art, less a science. It is shaped more by the individual style, capabilities, and personality of the mediator than by any instructional manual or finite or codified rules of procedure. It is *not* synonymous with compromise. Its basic premise is that legitimate objectives cannot be reached without agreement. In theory, at least, the parties are not expected to sacrifice their purpose for something less than remedy.

When the Community Relations Service (CRS) embarked on its statutory mission to bring a measure of relief to the nation's widespread community unrest, its principal thrust was as a catalyst to help implement available programs that would further sensitivity and understanding among diverse and often antagonistic cultures. It wasn't until several years after CRS was launched that mediation as one of the agency's working programs was introduced and developed.

There were few academicians to turn to for theoretical or practical guidance in establishing a training framework. The novice intermediary, in those early days of creating the CRS conflict intervention program, often had to learn his/her role through trial and error. Insights were borrowed from related disciplines (drawn not only from lessons out of the labor relations experience, as already noted, but from family counseling and international diplomatic negotiations as well). Invariably, there were troublesome dissimilarities, an absence of legal/procedural controls and safeguards, and a paucity of precedents from which to develop sound approaches to third-party problem solving. In short, there had been little contribution to the influencing of professionalism or to the codification and measurement of expectations and results. The lessons of success and failure remained largely the property of those who had both enjoyed achievement and suffered mistakes after having plunged into the murky waters of community conflict resolution.

It was recognized by CRS at the outset that many community disputes could be and were being resolved without the assistance of an imported third party. Not infrequently there were local resources available to serve as intermediaries. Local municipal or private human relations agencies, legal or clergy coalitions, and various ad hoc citizen groups were among those who sometimes could mobilize the necessary ingredients and engender a neutrality acceptance by the disputing parties. Such efforts sometimes succeeded notwithstanding lack of training and preparation among those who donned the mediator's hat.

Among the difficulties faced by local intervenors, however, was the probability of being seen by the parties to be biased in favor of one side or the other. As products of the community in which the contention was centered, it was an unusual resource that could be accepted and trusted by the opposing parties as being truly impartial, as well as competent, to bring about resolution.

The CRS mediator, too, carried some weighty baggage. Approaching conflict parties with an offer of assistance faced a variety of reactions, some positive, some negative. Those representing a responding agency or institution were sometimes reluctant to see their wrangle with malcontents given elevated significance or magnitude by virtue of intervention by the United States Department of Justice. Reactions also often included the feeling that the presence of a federal agency would tend to legitimize the protest issues, given the weight of authority implied by such participation. Some saw the entry of CRS, even wearing the mantle of neutrality, as an unnecessary and unwelcome intrusion by the federal government in local affairs. Perhaps of greatest concern was the anticipated escalation of media attention to the dispute at hand, a development normally looked upon as a highly undesirable consequence.

On the other side of the ledger, of course, there were strong motivations at work that tended to favor CRS intervention, sometimes among the very persons who feared it most.

First, and perhaps foremost, was the recognition that nonadversary proceeding were clearly preferable to litigation (if that possibility was considered likely). The opportunity to remove the polemics from tension and confrontation to a climate of "civilized" discourse was, for many, an appealing prospect. Respondents often saw such a course as one that would, at long last, prepare the complainants to deal more realistically with the issues. Further, it would force opponents to face the nature of obstacles in the way of solutions and thereby develop a better understanding and appreciation of why remedies might be limited rather than fully unattainable or even entirely without practical solution.

Protest participants typically were less likely to resist the introduction of a federal resource in the intermediary role. The Justice Department, after all, was identified with enforcement of civil rights legislation. Even though it was made clear that CRS had nothing whatever to do with enforcement activity, more often than not, they saw such involvement as something of a security blanket—an authority that might assure protection against an abusive antagonist who could otherwise overpower them with the sheer weight of superior human and material assets at their disposal. At the very least, it might pave the way in getting the attention of a previously unresponsive adversary.

Not infrequently, both sides of a controversy to be mediated would welcome the opportunity to communicate and respond to clearly identified spokespersons representing the opposition. That dynamic came into play when either or both sides had been frustrated by the fact that they were continually having to relate to new personalities, and where lines of authority and responsibility were not clearly drawn as to who should be representing each constituency.

Finally, it was not unusual to find both sides of the conflict yearning for greater stability in their capacities to communicate with one another effectively. Complainants typically perceived rigidity, deception, and evasiveness by the opposition. Respondent/institutional parties frequently complained about mindless rhetoric, questionable motives and tactics and sinister objectives. The idea of bringing the opposing sides together in the presence of a neutral third party to pursue honest dialogue and equitable resolution of differences tended to ameliorate each side's cynical perspective of the other.

MAXIMS OF MEDIATION

There are precepts regarding the mediation process that deserve emphasis if the intermediary role is to succeed. Foremost among them are the following:

- No party to negotiation can be expected to be brought to unconditional surrender. A conflict party cannot be expected to agree to its own undoing.
- A claim that is enforceable only under law is not generally suitable for mediation. The negotiation process has its best utility where conflicts are not responsive to resolution through the legal system.
- If a party to mediation assumes a win-lose posture and cannot be dissuaded from such an outlook, there is little to be accomplished through negotiation.
- It is of great importance for the mediator to understand the political and social controls within the organizational structure of a group disputant. Leadership groups and individuals often have fragile influence within constituencies. Perceptions of their behavior and effectiveness in the mediation process are often challenged from within and/or from external sources of community or institutional pressures. Militancy can escalate in inverse proportion to the organizational leadership's security and in direct proportion to the effective resistance to meaningful change by those who hold institutional power.

- Socioeconomic change typically involves the sharing or transfer of power. History teaches that such a transition is rarely serene.
- Parity is an essential ingredient of mediation. It requires: (a) the existence of a relationship between the parties, (b) recognition of the neutrality of the intervenor, (c) acceptance of the mediation process, and (d) a relatively uniform perception of a "level playing field" upon which participants negotiate.

TERMS DEFINED

By the mid 1970s the CRS conflict resolution program was operating in something of a bipolar mode. Conciliation and mediation were the two principal elements. It was important for reasons of both internal administration/training and community perception to distinguish clearly between them.

DICTIONARY DEFINITIONS:

CONCILIATION: "to *overcome the distrust or hostility* of . . . win over . . . to make compatible . . . *reconcile* . . ."

MEDIATION: (International Law): "an attempt to effect a *peaceful settlement* between disputing nations through the friendly *good offices* of another power . . . process for bringing about agreement or reconciliation between opponents in a dispute . . . *implies deliberation* that results in *solutions that may or may not be accepted by the contending parties* . . ."

The key words above in bold italics provided some basis for working definitions that CRS would adopt in the field:

CONCILIATION: A process wherein CRS, upon invitation by one or several disputants, or upon its own initiative, facilitates *communication* between intergroup conflict parties in order to:

1. reduce the likelihood of disruption or violence; and/or
2. lessen the effects of intergroup tension, suspicion or distrust; and/or
3. broaden the perceptions of disputants to a degree that they are willing to effect an early or eventual accommodation of differences and/or termination of hostilities.

MEDIATION: A more structured process whereby CRS, upon invitation or consent of disputants, facilitates *voluntary, good faith, face-to-face NEGOTIATION* between willing parties in order to achieve a documented settlement of issues in contention; includes use of agency-established procedures and techniques to bring about *full examination* of opposing views and the creation of a *written agreement*, signed by the parties, with adequate *provision for enforcement.*[1]

---

[1]Enforcement of compliance by the parties to provisions of such documents was, in some cases, given legal substance as a written *contract*, subject to statutes in the applicable jurisdiction. Agreements executed in court-ordered cases could be made enforceable by order of the referring jurist.

In the CRS model, the mediation stage of intervention often followed an earlier period of conciliation effort. A liaison may have first been established between the adversaries by a CRS representative other than the mediator—typically a conciliation specialist or a fact finder. Elements of the dispute may already have been identified and possible remedies considered. Other prenegotiation matters (e.g., identification and acknowledgment of party spokespersons, ascertaining of the historical aspects of the conflict, interpretation of opposing party positions, etc.) may have been examined and analyzed during a conciliation phase of case development and before the mediation option was proposed.

As a footnote to these definitions, it is well to call attention to a third form of conflict intervention—the process known as arbitration, given extensive application in labor-management relations. Under that procedure, the intervenor (arbitrator) is given the authority and responsibility, by agreement of the parties or sometimes under court order, to make a *binding decision*, following a hearing, *as to who shall prevail* and under what circumstances. It is a delegated final disposition of matters in contention and in many respects has the effect of a judicial remedy. Some perceive the arbitrator's role to be inconsistent with the mantel of sustained, long-term neutrality, however, because the arbitrator, by the very nature of the process within which he functions, creates winners and losers.

It is well to take note of the fact that dispute settlement between organized labor and corporate management is subject to legislated limitations—a legal framework—whereas community disputes seldom are. At the community level, the parties are typically unaffected by statutory parameters.

There are other distinctions to be drawn in comparing the two conflict settings. Perhaps most important is the fact that positions, attitudes, and strategies common to the industrial model include recognition of mutual interests, interdependence and lawfully mandated power sharing. Modern collective bargaining is unlikely to allow one party to threaten the organizational legitimacy, or the very existence, for that matter, of the other (not an uncommon scenario in the earliest days of industrial relations).

Arbitration can be seen to require the parties to forfeit their opportunity to negotiate a settlement, thereby sacrificing a significant degree of control over the fate of their objectives. It was not considered to be a prerogative within the CRS mandate, nor to be consistent with its mission, to offer an arbitration option. Such a policy was seen as necessary in order to safeguard the perception of the agency's neutrality.

ILLUSTRATED CRS FIELD ACTIVITY— CONCILIATION

Because conciliation, in the CRS format, was sometimes a prelude to mediation, often carried out by different personnel, it is appropriate to provide examples of both types of activity. It is also useful to show their important interrelatedness.

Conciliation activity could be described in any of a variety of case scenarios. These are somewhat typical examples:

1. An Afro-American protest group plans to march on city hall for a public rally and then to picket the municipal building for two days prior to expected city council action on a controversial zoning issue which affects their community. CRS intercession included:
   - Separate meetings with appropriate city officials and protest spokespersons to familiarize them with CRS roles and resources, including prospects for utilizing the mediation option;

- Attendance at several public meetings and private briefings to assess possible third-party courses of action;

- Arrangements for protest leadership to consult directly with police and other officials regarding logistics for the march and subsequent picketing, thus reducing the possibilities for miscalculation of intentions and possible violence;

- Consultation provided for protesters regarding self-policing procedures in cooperation with the local police department;

- Arrangements proposed and implemented for contingency planning to deal with rumor control; possible mass arrests (transportation of arrestees, temporary detention facilities, availability of legal assistance, emergency judicial procedures, etc.); police deployment, tactical projections, and guidelines governing the use of force; public address equipment use; and protection at rally and crowd dispersal.

- Monitoring demonstration scene, maintaining ongoing communication with leadership figures, heading off unanticipated problems before they become inhibiting to a peaceful conclusion.

2. A group of Indian (Native American) students withdrew from classes in a rural public school system in protest over dress codes alleged to have denied them reasonable adaptation of traditional hair styles and clothing. Interracial relationships have been severely strained due to escalating emotionalism in both the minority and nonminority communities. CRS conciliation activity includes:

- Meetings with representatives of both sides of the issue, producing agreement to have school board members and the superintendent come to the Indian Cultural Center to hear directly for the first time about the problems expressed by affected students and their parents, in a nonhostile setting and in the presence of a third party neutral;

- Arrangements for protesters to consult with an out-of-state tribal Indian education specialist known to have had successful experiences in dealing with similar dress code problems in other parts of the country;

- Subsequent persuasion of school authorities to amend dress code regulations to accommodate objectives of petitioning students;

- Introduction to the parties of a responsible federal agency official with the Indian education credentials to examine other issues of discontent and work toward attainable solutions before other further serious confrontation develops.

3. Spanish-surnamed tenants in a public housing project have initiated a rent strike after repeatedly unsuccessful attempts to influence changes in management policy that they believe would improve living conditions. CRS entry centers on:

- Review of grievances with tenants and assistance to them with framing and documenting problems for later presentation to housing administrators;

- Meeting with housing authority board and staff for commitment to a fair and full hearing of complaints;

- Chairing of meeting at which parties gather at a conference table to communicate feelings, discuss issues, interpret perceptions, and consider available remedies and limitations (an ad hoc gathering for spontaneous exchanges without introducing a formalized mediation process which would take considerably more preparation and orientation before bringing the parties together).

The foregoing examples of conditions and response activity under which CRS conciliation was typically conducted by no means reflect the full extent of possible settings or circumstances that could, and often did, arise during the period covered by this account. Virtually all such field activity had little consistency in terms of party characteristics, the issues in dispute, or potential for resolution. Still, these examples provide a general idea of the kind of work in which CRS conciliators were involved and the sort of circumstances that often led the parties to consider mediation as a viable option in search of long-term results in moderating dissidence.

ILLUSTRATED CRS FIELD ACTIVITY—MEDIATION

In contrast to conciliation, mediation calls for a more predictable predetermined process. Although institutional settings may be as diverse as they are in conciliation cases, the mediator employs techniques and procedures with greater consistency. The following example, with minor variations, illustrates a typical procedural sequence in an atypical case scenario: Black inmates in a state prison have petitioned the federal courts for relief from alleged discriminatory treatment by corrections authorities, said to violate certain constitutional protections. CRS response includes:

- Joint exploratory meetings with the referring judge, inmate counsel, and prison administrators to explain the mediation process and determine mutual willingness to pursue good faith negotiations;
- Enlistment of corrections resource specialist/consultant to provide technical assistance to both teams during mediation;
- Series of meetings with inmates and prison officials to determine how negotiating teams are to be selected and later, after such teams are chosen, to arrange for documentation of grievances and preparation of a mediation agenda;
- Briefing of negotiation teams for both sides regarding detailed mediation ground rules;
- Orientation of prison line employees and management staff (not participating in mediation) as to the nature of mediation, the background of its development in the present case, and the urgency of their understanding and cooperation in assuring a constructive result;
- Chairing of all mediation sessions, facilitating step-by-step agreement on those issues for which resolution can be reached, moving toward realistic settlement goals;
- Preparing the final agreement instrument for party signatures.

THE MEDIATOR IN A NEUTRAL ROLE

Mediators are primarily impartial facilitators. Their strength lies in the limitations imposed of them. There is no power to command. There is no intrinsic authority to bring about change. The art of persuasion and the largely attitudinal images projected to facilitate mediation are tools of the trade. Such attributes might include among others: (a) a firm commitment to a thorough process orientation of the parties to help avoid later procedural misunderstandings that could threaten productive interaction; (b) a disciplined attention to detail in arranging for a negotiation site (e.g., optimal amenities to ensure a neutral, comfortable, and convenient environment conducive to effective communication); (c) a deliberative effort when meeting separately with the parties to avoid the appearance of providing one side or another with favored information or other advantage; (d) scrupulous care in dealing with the media to avoid judgmental commentary or any apparent breach of confidence.

The intervenor provides the parties with a process through which there can be joint examination of issues, recognition of common objectives, and insights into opposing perspectives. The contestants are prepared for orderly negotiation by consulting with them on their agenda and advising them on position documentation, enlistment of resource assistance on technical matters, and establishment of ground rules for productive dialogue. As a neutral, the mediator can help probe and dispel areas of misunderstanding, encouraging a climate conducive to good faith problem solving. Often it requires laying the groundwork for settlement, performing as a courier, interpreter, catalyst, and gentle persuader. When appropriate, the mediator can play the devil's advocate in separate consultations with participating teams, helping them recognize differing perceptions and values likely to be held by their adversaries. Simply *clarifying* the issues and helping to *document* them, can be among the most meaningful functions the mediator performs.

Implicit in virtually all mediation is the influence exerted by the mediator in bringing about "a level playing field." When a complainant is facing an adversary who is in a position of obviously greater power, resources, or influence, it is sometimes necessary for the mediator to bring about a perception by the respondent that acknowledges the protesting party's legitimacy. It is likely that the mediator has already established a relationship with the aggrieved party and, in the course of preliminaries with the respondent, may be in a position to lend credibility to the reasonableness and constructive intentions of the less enabled opposition. Simply to establish a willingness to enter into negotiations, or sometimes even merely to establish a dialogue, can in itself confer legitimacy upon the weaker side.

There are times when the mediator's role calls for creating a suitable climate for effective negotiations. This can be accomplished by providing a variety of ways, the essentials of which are set forth on pages to follow. It may involve such relatively unimposing matters as helping to select an appropriately neutral site at which negotiations can be conducted with the fewest impediments.

The activities of the federal mediator in community disputes are varied and not readily cataloged. He or she may be called upon to play a discreet but critically supportive function between the parties, outside the parameters of the officially acknowledged context. Much of what is done may overlap with activities performed during the conciliation process—resource identification, interpreting issues and positions, fact-finding, serving as a courier, consultation with law enforcement or other governmental authorities, influencing parties to maintain "good faith" positions, providing a "federal presence," and so on.

Those functions that are more specific and germane to the preparation and execution of negotiations include:

1. Instructing the parties regarding the concepts of negotiation and mediation and assuring their understanding of the obligations and responsibilities entailed in the process;
2. Establishing recognition of opposing spokespersons and negotiating team participants;
3. Helping the parties to understand and assess their own authority to negotiate and to conclude agreements on issues, as granted by their constituencies;

4. Presiding over negotiation sessions; establishing and explaining procedural matters (e.g., establishment of priorities; advice in the preparation of documentation to support or refute allegations, positions, or issues; guidance in dealing with the media; explanation of caucus/recess and other negotiation procedures, etc.); suggesting possible areas of accord or alternative approaches to the settlement of a point or issue; utilizing caucus and recess techniques to the fullest advantage in assuring effective communication within and between disputing parties;

5. Acting in a consultative capacity to help the parties review and modify their positions or adjust rationale; maintaining a level of trust with all principals so as to assure confidence in privileged communication;

6. Assisting and advising with the preparation of a final instrument of agreement;

7. Proposing and/or arranging for an appropriate mechanism with which to assure follow-up implementation of any agreement reached.

One of the most challenging requirements put upon the mediator is the matter of gaining initial acceptance from the contesting parties. The parties must be fully aware that the mediator serves at their bidding and that the entire mediation process is completely voluntary and subject to termination at the will of either party. They must understand that there will be no attempt to dictate terms or remedies and that nothing will be imposed without consent. Above all, of course, there must be confidence that the mediator will perform his/her role with sensitivity, fairness and objectivity. There must be a sense of trust that, when required, they can depend upon the mediator to honor confidentiality.

Frequently during joint negotiation sessions there is need for the mediator to narrow, clarify, define, and redefine issues and points of contention. At times, one party or the other will assume a rigid posture largely because there has been a misunderstanding of the opponent's viewpoint. Perceptions of issue validity, party images, motives, and past behavior patterns can be loaded with emotional baggage. The mediator, as the neutral standing between opposing forces, is likely to be the only resource able to bring about modification of such perceptions and bring movement toward resolution. Through skillful questioning and analysis without compromising neutrality, the intermediary with sufficient patience, persistence, and a modicum of good fortune, can bring about a basis for accord.

Contesting forces in a community dispute seldom meet as equals.[2] It is the mediator who can establish a climate of equality around the negotiating table. Very simply, the mediator treats all principals equally, without regard for differences in social, economic, educational, or other status. The hearing/witness/judgment syndrome of litigation is rejected. The parties are given to feel a sense of control over the final outcome and so are relieved of the anxieties associated with an arbitrary determination of winners and losers.

USE OF OUTSIDE RESOURCES

It was not unusual, in the CRS model, for circumstances to call for the mediator to become an agent for identifying and enlisting resources that might help bring information and insights to the parties in order to shed light on sometimes complex or controversial issues. Expertise was drawn from any number of professional and specialized fields, depending on the nature of matters to be brought to the table—legal considerations, institutional educa-

---

[2] For example, a major corporation responding to a single employee or small group of unorganized employees; a lone parent confronting a large school district; a disgruntled citizen appearing without counsel before a governmental agency hearing board, etc.

tion practices and precedents, corrections/law enforcement administration/training, urban planning, finance/accounting procedures, or whatever body of knowledge was seen to be appropriately introduced. Often it was the parties' different *perceptions of what the facts were* that lay at the core of their opposing positions. A detached, reputable authority from outside the environment in which the dispute was centered, could sometimes bring a wholly new, objective, and reliable parcel of information to the dialogue. Or at least such input could raise questions or shed light on conflicting perspectives and positions between the parties that were impeding progress in negotiations.

In some respects, such a resource was seen as comparable to an expert witness at trial. Only in this instance, the expertise was brought to the proceedings in behalf of not one party or the other, but for the benefit of *both* parties, and usually at the suggestion and facilitation of the mediator.

As mediators representing an agency of the U.S. Department of Justice, we clearly enjoyed a significant advantage with regard to accessing resources. For one thing, we had a reasonably flexible budget that would allow payment of travel expenses for resource specialists when necessary. (Rarely did we pay a fee for service or otherwise compensate those called upon to assist. Typically, such persons, or their superiors, viewed the mission as a worthwhile voluntary contribution to a legitimate societal need.) In some quarters, we were seen as a request source that carried a degree of lawful authority, tending to favor a willing affirmative response.

Designed to enlarge the body of information available to the participants in order to reach sound conclusions, this introduction of outside unaligned specialists was found to be compatible with the neutrality of the third-party role. Of some significance was the fact that if the mediator was perceived by the parties as a "resource expander," it could help motivate their basic decision to accept or invite mediation. In some cases, it was just the incentive needed to give the intermediary process a chance to work.

On occasion, disputants recognized the need for objectivity and disassociation from any vested interest in uncovering facts and in assessing their relative validity and significance. Sometimes it was critical that tensions between the parties be seen from a somewhat detached perspective. The gathering of documentation to reveal pertinent information regarding contested issues could be extremely important to the intermediary in formulating strategies to build trust as an unbiased catalyst in the search for fairness and equity.

As just one example of reliance upon such extraneous sources of assistance, we can envision a dispute involving different interpretations of fact regarding the financial accounts of an institution. The respondent administrators may contend that their budget does not allow for the expenditure of funds to correct a complainant's charges of neglect or malfeasance. The accusers may or may not have an accurate perception of the budgetary capacity of the institution to provide remedies. The use of an objective, qualified professional accountant (hopefully one with whom both sides can feel comfortable and can see as an impartial fact-finder) to examine pertinent documentation and to make a reality determination can go a long way in progress toward resolution.

In other scenarios, legal questions may arise that can be best clarified and settled through enlistment of mutually acceptable expertise from a competent outside attorney. Health issues may call for reliable opinion from medical professionals. Allegations of unnecessary use of deadly force by a law enforcement officer can be examined with more likelihood of bilateral acceptance if negotiating teams can turn to one or more firearms or police training specialists who can be seen by both the parties to be unbiased in their evaluations and recommendations.

Conditions under which outside resources can contribute substantially to the negotiation process are almost limitless. As has been stated, the major hurdle in introducing this procedural refinement is the identification of expertise that is seen by disputants on both sides of the table as being without prejudicial inclinations favoring one party or the other.

Sometimes differences in selection criteria can be overcome by inviting input from more than one consultant. Occasionally, it is necessary to bring in as many as three experts on a given subject of inquiry—one selected by each of the opposing parties and one by the mediator. If the mediator enjoys a high level of trust from both negotiating teams, there is also the possibility of a willingness to accept the mediator's selection.

The introduction of external, independent resources to help achieve movement toward settlement was further favored by some CRS mediators because of the variety of conflict settings in which they found themselves emersed. A large percentage of cases were in the public education and law enforcement fields. But there were disputes centering on low-income housing and other landlord-tenant clashes. Issues dealing with media relations with the minority community, allegations of discrimination in employment and consumer protections, health care and welfare inequities, and challenges to a whole range of government provided services (community control of funded programs, child care, land use, transportation, recreation, etc.) were prominent features of the conflict landscape.

Given our penchant for advocating outside technical assistance, it was incumbent upon the CRS mediator to know how to identify and enlist a whole host of such resources—governmental and private—national, regional, and local. We were challenged repeatedly to gain timely access through the maze of federal, state, and local government agencies that might provide specialized information or funding options. A significant number of private organizations were typically easier to reach and sometimes more responsive. Nonprofit organizations and professional associations offering legal aid, low-income housing assistance, employment training and/or placement, neighborhood development programs, and any number of other services at the local level, contributed much to the mix of help available.

The mediator, as the only neutral at the table, no matter how experienced and knowledgeable, could not be expected to have the specialized or technical background necessary to help formulate reliable theses or to reach valid conclusions. Such input could only be provided by appropriate expertise from someone who, like the mediator, was perceived by the parties as a neutral and in whom both sides could have confidence as a source of objective reaction to proposals and agenda issues under consideration.

There is no suggestion here that resource assistance is an anticipated ingredient in all or even in most mediation cases. But in some instances, such a device could make an enormous contribution. Sometimes successful resolution can seem entirely out of reach without vital resource counseling and the funding availability provided by CRS to support such assistance.

MEDIATION GUIDELINES

Before Coming to the Table

In times of crisis, talk is action.

—Winston Churchill

No process designed to manage human interaction should be encumbered by inflexibility. The procedural guidelines set forth here for dealing with intergroup conflict resolution are generally applicable to most cases. None is to suggest mandatory policy parameters. Because of the infinite varieties of dispute scenarios, it is not realistic to codify mediation practices with any real sense of universal application.

CONTACT WITH THE PARTIES

Initiation of contact to explore or implement mediation was brought about in any of several ways. Sometimes a member of the protesting or respondent party was aware of CRS intermediary services, leading to initial contact. More often, one party to a dispute (or sometimes two or more) would establish contact with CRS as a result of referral from a secondary source such as a federal or state court, a government official or agency, a civil rights advocacy group or individual, or a professional colleague who had previous knowledge of CRS. On other occasions, CRS initiated first contact upon learning of the existence of the conflict and the appearance of conditions that were consistent with the CRS mandate based on preliminary evidence that there was some prospect for reaching settlement through third party intervention.

Under ideal circumstances, a biracial or multiethnic CRS team would engage the parties and, when possible, continue participation in the mediation process.[1] The mediator was the leader or chair of any such agency unit and one or more other staffers would play sup-

---

[1]Typically, the mediator carried out his/her task without staff assistance (other than technician specialists when circumstances required). Budgetary considerations made multiple member teams difficult to justify without compelling demonstration of need.

port roles as resource specialists, research assistants, or in other support functions in response to encountered needs. All other things being equal, there was ample evidence to show that gaining entry and establishing rapport with the disputants could be greatly enhanced through the use of intermediary teams matching the race/ethnicity of the parties in conflict.

INITIAL CONSULTATION

Under typical circumstances, the mediator would arrange for separate meetings with dispute representatives of both sides. It was important that everything possible be done to assure that those who met with the mediator represented the recognized and legitimate party principals. The primary purpose of these initial meetings was to explain the general concepts of mediation and to ensure understanding of its concomitant obligations, responsibilities, limitations and possible rewards. Included among the specific matters normally covered were:

1. An explanation of:
   (a) the mediator's background and the authority/responsibility of the Community Relations Service regarding its conflict resolution mission;
   (b) how the mediator had become involved in the present dispute;
   (c) the nature of the mediation process in general (as set forth elsewhere in this chapter) and the mediator's role in particular;
   (d) the importance of each party recognizing the legitimacy of opposing spokespersons and participants in the proposed negotiations;

2. Understanding of the projected requirements for the selection of the negotiation teams (i.e., the number to serve on each side, abilities and conditions considered essential for participants to serve effectively, anticipated team member time demands/projected time frame to complete the proposed negotiations process, constituencies represented, etc.);
3. Identity and role of any resource specialists who, by mutual consent of the parties, could be made available for consultation at the negotiation table in order to provide technical assistance on appropriate issues and, in some instances, to act as a sounding board for problem interpretation and solution;
4. With the protest team: review of issues, examination of position rationale, and "devil's advocate" probing to assure thorough understandings of strengths, weaknesses, and legitimacy of principal grievances; evaluation of the need for documentation related to the issues and positions proposed to be negotiated;[2]
5. Review and discussion of a proposed agreement instrument, its format and purpose; consideration of the appropriateness of ratification by respective constituencies;
6. Discussion of the obligations and advantages of preparing proposed solutions to problems, along with well-conceived and documented statements as to the nature of the issues;

---

[2]Seldom was there a written statement already prepared by the aggrieved party, and when such a document was provided, it was prepared in a manner that made it difficult for the respondents to fully understand, all too often resulting in faulty perceptions and avoidable negativism.

7. Discussion and concurrence regarding procedures for responding to any media attention during negotiations;

8. Consideration of the effect of the initiation and outcome of negotiations on possible future legal action, if applicable; effects on maintaining the viability of other protest options in pursuit of remedies (e.g., media exposure, demonstrations, political action/legislative lobbying, boycotting, compliance review by a regulatory agency, etc.);

9. Explanation of prospects for postmediation follow-up provisions, including possible CRS review and evaluation of implementation progress, to be provided within an appropriate period of time; availability of an enforcement mechanism (e.g., court-ordered consent decree, submission to arbitration of unresolved issues, institutional advisory body to deal with later possible difficulties over interpreting or implementing the agreement, etc.) should such a device be needed;

10. Consideration of rumor problems/repercussions, if applicable, and possible precautions to be taken to control their harmful effects;

11. Explanation and evaluation of the use of nonparticipating observers during negotiation sessions;

12. Consideration of mediation site selection and physical conditions of the meeting place; site neutrality implications, if likely to be a factor.

THE ROLE OF NEGOTIATOR

If mediation ground rules are to be observed—and that's critical to successful negotiations—those who participate in the process must be carefully and fully informed as to the parameters within which they will be expected to function. It falls to the mediator to deliver to each negotiating team clear and specific mandated requirements. Such prerequisite conditions may vary among intermediaries and their sponsoring agencies and are not infrequently modified to accommodate specific disputants and the particular issues being confronted. In the instance of CRS case practice, these were among the generally applicable conditions:

1. It is imperative that a negotiation team know its authority and responsibility as viewed by those it purports to represent. Whatever that relationship, whether delegated by vote, by established and acknowledged leadership reputations, or otherwise, the basis for their assumption of that representation should be clearly understood by all who are designated to participate. The extent to which substantive matters can be decided upon without constituency ratification, is also of special importance.

The process by which negotiation team spokespersons and participants are selected can be of considerable consequence.

2. Each participant in the mediation process must recognize the demands to be made upon them in terms of personal time allocations (especially if the nature of the conflict is complex and likely to require extended negotiations), emotional investment, and adherence to one's commitment to a good faith goal of equitable resolution.

3. The question of how decisions will be made during negotiations should be determined in advance. Matters of final agreement content may be subject to

a majority or greater consensus vote by team members whereas lesser decisions may be left to the discretion of the team chair after consultation with associates.

4. The role of the mediator as a neutral must be recognized by the parties as being external to the mediation process insofar as decision making is concerned, but it should also be made clear that the parties are free to call upon the intermediary as a facilitator, a resource expander, a sounding board, or as an interpreter of influences on the decision-making process.

5. In order to establish workable conditions for negotiation, the parties at the table must recognize and accept limitations placed upon them by the ground rules that prohibit their responding to media inquiries during the period when active negotiations are in progress and before a final agreement is reached or negotiations terminated. (This will be further expanded upon later in this chapter.)

6. A further time commitment is required in order to prepare respective cases before coming to the table (if indeed that has not already been done). Such preparation would normally include a written statement of positions with regard to each issue expected to be submitted to mediation. Such documents may not necessarily reflect the total dimensions of the final agenda, but they should be representative of the core grievances and, where appropriate, the presumed positions of the respondent party (to the extent they are aware of the allegations).

THE NEGOTIATING TEAMS

Success or failure in mediation is influenced by many factors. None is more critical than the proper selection of the negotiating team members and their subsequent preparation to go to the table. These are some of the more important considerations:

1. As a general rule, there should be no more than five active negotiators on each team, plus no more than two attorneys or advisors who, if circumstances warrant, may be seated at the table to consult with principals, but are typically excluded from dialogue participation. A larger number is likely to weaken the effectiveness of dialogue and prospects for productive exchange is diminished, to say nothing of hampering decision making. A smaller number, perhaps no more than three on each side, might be ideal but may also limit the breadth of representation of the respective constituencies.

If a legalistic approach is to be avoided, it is important to discourage allowing the team's counsel to become the principal negotiator or spokesperson as he or she would in the courtroom.

2. If discriminatory practice allegations are at issue, the racial/ethnic/gender composition of the teams should reflect a reasonable balance, proportionate to that found in the group or organization represented.

3. Negotiator alternates, of whom there are usually as many on each team as there are principal negotiators, can serve in several important ways:

    (a) They attend all sessions as observers but participate as negotiators only when taking the place of an absent primary team member;

    (b) They are allowed and encouraged to take part with the primary team members in caucus or recess deliberations, thereby providing, in some cases, for wider input from representative constituencies or divergent points of view;

    (c) They expand communication linkage with constituents and other interested parties, based on first-hand exposure to the negotiation proceedings;

    (d) They may be called upon by their team chairperson to comment during negotiations in connection with any specialized information or expertise they may possess;

    (e) Their ongoing presence makes them especially useful in performing limited research or information gathering tasks that can be done while sessions are in progress, thus avoiding unnecessary recesses or other delays in the proceedings.

Sometimes it is desirable to widen representation on a negotiating team by utilizing a type of rotation whereby one group of five may be the team principals during the first several meetings, followed by an alternate group. One group of five, for example, may be the team principals during the first or several early meetings, followed by an alternate group during the next session or group of sessions, continuing to rotate throughout the term of mediation. In effect, members of the second group become active principals instead of alternates, as previously described.

Such an arrangement does have a down side, however. Clearly, there is something to be sacrificed in the way of continuity. There is also the risk of losing a singular line of authority or responsibility. In essence then, this option was considered only when the scope of representation was a crucial component of the team selection process.

4. Each team selects its own chairperson and vice chair. These individuals become the principal contacts for communications between the mediator and the parties during off-hours and particularly during recess and caucus adjournments. They are responsible for leadership, direction, and control of their team members. They notify their associates of the date, time, and place for meetings and related information. They abide by adopted procedural rules and, in general, help maintain an orderly process.

5. Under some circumstances, it is desirable for negotiators to be voted upon for election by their constituencies in an acceptable balloting procedure. In any event, it is imperative that those who serve as negotiators have the delegated authority to make final decisions at the mediation table when they do, in fact or in claim, represent others who are not participating in the negotiations. Reaching effective resolution of conflict can be severely hampered if the school superintendent who chairs the team of institutional negotiators must obtain step-by-step concurrence from the school board before an agenda item can be resolved.

The same applies to the protest team chairperson who must go back to his/her organization for approval before action can be taken on each issue under consideration. This, of course, is not to say that either team chair is prohibited from calling for a recess in order to contact one or more associates, whether those individuals are authority figures or simply a source of needed information.

When necessary and appropriate, the decision can be made in advance to have the entire finalized agreement subject to ratification by all party constituents, whether they be an institutional policy board, a student body coalition, an Indian Tribal Council or some other group represented in negotiations.

PREMEDIATION TEAM PREPARATION

1. In premediation separate orientations, the negotiating teams should be given the same full information that was provided during the initial consultations between the spokesmen for the parties and the mediator (described earlier in this chapter). Typically, there will be individuals ultimately selected to serve on the finalized negotiating teams who were not involved in the earlier exploratory stages of contact. This final orientation requires somewhat more detailed attention to procedural matters, including:

   (a) explanation of the caucus/recess device to facilitate consensus development and decision making (see next section under the heading "Caucus and Recess");

   (b) projected schedule of separate and joint sessions, in keeping with participants' general preferences and limitations regarding acceptable days and hours to the majority of negotiation team members. In dealing with community conflict problems it can be expected that any number of prospective protest team candidates may have limited availability due to work-related obligations. Under such conditions, it may be necessary for the mediator and/or some influential local citizen(s) to prevail upon the employer to grant the employee in question the necessary flexibility to accommodate his/her participation. Respondent teams, on the other hand, are generally employed under conditions that allow more flexibility since it is often their employer who represents the respondent institution at the table;

   (c) elaboration of the mediator's role (e.g., chair functions in presiding over joint sessions, agenda development, caucus consultation, fact-finding, resource identification and enlistment, proposing alternatives to resolving agenda issues, assistance in preparation of a written agreement, etc.).

2. As an extension of the preliminary protest side discussion during initial party consultation with the mediator, the team should prepare a negotiation agenda setting forth in concise outline form the order of specific problems to be addressed. A copy of this agenda is given to the respondent team well in advance of the first joint session.

One of the most difficult but important determinations can be the decision as to the order of issues to be negotiated. There is no hard and fast rule as to whether it is better to deal first with the most intractable problems or to instead go initially with the relatively "soft" issues. There are persuasive arguments both ways. Much depends on circumstances and personalities involved as to which is the best strategy.

Clearly, it would be fruitless to spend many days in negotiation working from the softest to the most resistive positions, only to find that those saved for last were insurmountable. It would be equally futile if agreement to correct the relatively minor allegations made the respondent team feel as if they had already given too much, resulting in an inclination to resist accommodation on the more substantive grievances.

On the other hand, sometimes a relatively soft issue or two can be approached initially in order to "break the ice" and bring the parties to see that they can indeed agree on something! However, when a particularly stubborn issue is given early attention and can be successfully resolved, it can make the lesser matters to follow more manageable and even create a sense of momentum toward further accommodation.

Another crucial prenegotiation consideration relates to the timing of the initial joint sessions. It can be seriously detrimental if arranged prematurely. The mediator must be sure first that his/her own credibility has been established with both parties and that both are prepared with the necessary documentation to present their positions on each issue.

Under no circumstances should the negotiators be made to feel that substantive decisions (other than on procedure) will be made by the mediator. There should be an understanding that the decision-making role rests squarely with those who legitimately represent the disputants. It must be clear that the mediator, at best, can only offer options or refinements on information that can help expedite the decision process.

Further, it is highly desirable that negotiators be given the credit for successful strategies and solutions even when, in fact, the intermediary or some other external party may have been actually responsible for the progress or the original input.

ADVOCATE INTERVENER—A LEGITIMATE NEUTRAL ROLE?

To what extent and under what circumstances can the mediator afford to take on a responsibility for strengthening the position of a complainant group in preparation for negotiation with a more sophisticated and empowered respondent? Applying and justifying such assistance, as a means of enhancing successful mediation results and in a manner that would avoid damaging the mediator's impartiality, is a significant component of the model being described.

Whenever an aggrieved constituency is disorganized, lacking in resources or strong leadership, or is otherwise at a decided tactical disadvantage as against its opposing party, there may be justification for support and guidance from the intermediary, generally through the introduction of an "advocate intervener" role. If the complainant group, for example, needs and desires assistance in becoming better organized, or in formulating positions, or in interpreting legal implications, and so forth, its opportunity to become a viable party to the negotiation can be enhanced through the assistance of appropriate resources. It follows then, that if their objectives are not to be unduly frustrated through lack of support or "know-how," they are less likely to take their protest to the streets or to direct their dissent through channels that can only bring escalation of hostilities, rather than resolution of differences.

Some would say, with some justification, that simply to bring about negotiations between parties with clearly unequal resources or where one is without versatile leadership at its disposal is, in itself, an advocate position for the petitioners. The mere facilitation of such a process can be seen as a step toward creating a greater degree of equity between otherwise imbalanced adversaries. For such reasons, it was sometimes a real challenge to convince a more powerful respondent that it was in his/their best self-interest to communicate and negotiate with an unempowered or unprepared complainant. That bit of persuasion would often turn on the potentially negative (or even catastrophic) consequences that might be expected if the mediation option were to be rejected.

This supportive role of the intervener on behalf of a needful or unempowered party to mediation, although it may appear to compromise neutrality, can be applied with care and without deception. Yet, if it is to be successful, it falls to the mediator to persuade the opposing contender(s) that it is a matter of their own self-interest to endorse the procedure. At the core of such concurrence is recognition of the fact that a party severely disadvantaged by lack of sound information and advice from qualified resources is likely soon to face implacable frustration. The consequences of that scenario promise a failure of meaningful negotiation and forfeiture of a peaceful settlement. Without a genuine effort at minimizing disequilibrium, the weaker party is unlikely to accede to a process that is perceived to diminish options for greater success through confrontation or other more aggressive protest.

SITE SELECTION, TIMING, AND PHYSICAL ARRANGEMENTS

A neutral site at which to conduct mediation was normally selected during prenegotiation consultation with spokespersons for the parties. Churches, community agencies, government facilities, school buildings . . . any location with no obvious connection to contested issues was often the most appropriate option (although occasionally, both parties will agree on a site that does have such a connection but is nonetheless mutually acceptable).

Accessibility to the site and physical arrangements in the mediation room are most important. Environmental conditions (temperature, lighting and ventilation control, privacy, rest room and telephone access, etc.) should provide satisfactory comfort and convenience. A separate caucus room for confidential unilateral meetings, with table and chairs, is also highly desirable.

Seating arrangement is of special importance. A rectangular or U-shaped table configuration, with sufficient chair space on each side to accommodate participating team members without crowding, and with each team facing the other across the table, is ideal. If possible, the opposing teams, as they face one another, should be separated by a space of several table widths in order to allow both teams a degree of privacy when communicating with one another by passing notes or whispering, in situations not urgent enough to call for a caucus. The mediator, as moderator, is positioned so that he/she is approximately equidistant from each team seated to either side of the parallel table arrangement. It is a configuration that enables the mediator to have eye contact with each member of each team while sitting at an easy distance for effective dialogue with all participants.

A blackboard, flip chart, and/or other visual aids may be useful, as discussion leads sometimes to the need for graphic illustration or visual displays of information.

The timing of sessions can also be a significant consideration. Oftentimes one side will be represented by working people who do not enjoy much, if any, flexibility with regard to the days and hours during which they can be available to join in negotiation sessions. There have been instances when the mediator has approached the prospective negotiator's employer in an effort to accommodate participation. Depending on the nature of the respondent team, there also may be similar availability problems for them to resolve. In the end, if mediation is to proceed, team members must be selected on both sides who can offer reasonable assurance of being able to attend all, or at least most sessions. For those absences brought on by illness, family emergencies, or other unavoidable circumstances, team alternates (described earlier in this chapter) can replace the missing principal negotiator at the option of the team chairperson.

The matter of who should call meetings and ensure notice and attendance is determined in advance and in accordance with circumstances. In some cases, the mediator may offer to take on all or a portion of that responsibility, but normally it falls to the team chairpersons, coordinating with the mediator.

The question of the audio and/or video recording of negotiation sessions deserves comment. There are advantages and disadvantages to such arrangements. Both, of course, provide complete verbatim records of the proceedings, thus assuring accuracy and completeness in the recollection of points of discussion and reducing the probability of later disagreements over what was said by whom and the interpretation of key points. Both also offer useful training devices for later use by the mediator and/or the organization he/she represents.

On the downside of this question, however, it must be recognized that both these means of recording tend to inhibit a free flow of ideas, opinions, and commitments. This is especially true with regard to the use of video cameras, more pronounced yet if special lighting or other distracting "stage props" are required or there is otherwise a perceived "staged" effect. These conditions tend to make participants more self-conscious about the way in which they will come across on tape and therefore less candid and productive at the table.

Except under unusual circumstances, for these and other reasons it is more practical and more conducive to desirable results to simply rely upon a handwritten record. Such an account, rather than a verbatim transcript, can be limited to key actions, understandings, or agreements, as recorded by a paid or volunteer scribe (or by the mediator, if necessary and practical), and subject to review and approval by both sides.

MEDIA RELATIONS

We all know what happens when verbal information is passed second and third hand from the original source to the ultimate recipient for whom the message is intended. The content as originally stated can become almost unrecognizable by the time it reaches its destination. Each transmission from one individual to the next is subject to questionable interpretation, if not outright distortion, no matter the innocence of intention. The more people through whom the information passes, the more unreliable the substance is likely to become. It is difficult enough, even for a participant or an eyewitness to an event, to accurately and dispassionately describe what was directly observed, especially if the observer was emotionally involved. Therein lies the quicksand of negotiating through the media.

Even more troublesome from the standpoint of objectivity and unblemished perception is the relaying of events by someone with a vested interest in the outcome or in the reaction to that outcome. Much like a political candidate expressing positions on issues, or a transgressor caught in the act, the delivery is likely to have a "spin" favorable to the private motives of the spokesperson.

Beyond the hazards of prejudicial interpretation by a participant in the negotiation process responding to the media, there is also the ever-present specter of the reporter's possible subjectivity in recording the story. And, next-in-line news processors (headline and tab line writers, rewrite editors, news directors, broadcast personalities, publishers, etc.) may also be expected to further misdirect or misstate the information, unintentionally or otherwise. Journalists, no matter their competence or dedication to accuracy and impartiality, have been known to carry personal convictions and ideologies into their reportage. And as for determining emphasis and highlighting selected portions of an incomplete account, we're all familiar with the competitive dictates of the news business. There is the inevitable imperative to bring to readers, viewers, and listeners the provocative, the dramatic, and the explosive. There is the urgency to bring the story to readers, listeners, or viewers before rival media report the same information. All too often, these motivations come into play at the expense of factual accuracy.

All of this is to say that it behooves the mediator and the negotiators to understand and appreciate the foibles of news people. Diligence is often required in order to avoid having the mediation process fall prey to misbegotten publicity.

What precautions, then, are in order? What guidelines are useful that will protect the process from the harmful consequences of an undiscerning press?

Consider first that the likelihood of news reporters getting wind of a mediation process scheduled, or already in progress, varies widely with circumstances. In smaller and mid-sized communities especially, press and/or broadcast inquiry can be more readily anticipated, in part because informal communication is probably more active and because the smaller media may consider conflict resolution developments more worthy of priority attention.

Media interest in a negotiation initiative can also be expected, again particularly outside major urban centers, when the contesting parties have had previous publicity concerning their dispute and/or when the issues are seen to impact on some important aspect of community relations (e.g., school conditions, law enforcement, government services, neighborhood stability, etc.). Often it is a matter of whether leaders representing either or both disputing parties decide, prior to mediation arrangements, that it is in their best interest to inform news outlets of their grievances or positions regarding issues at hand. And certainly, if it was news before mediation was adopted as a resolution alternative, it is very likely to continue drawing public attention as the new forum is engaged.

Contacts with the media before, during, and after negotiations can spell the difference between success and failure. In some instances, however, it is of no particular consequence, usually because there have been no initiatives taken by the parties to generate publicity and there are otherwise no persistent reporters seeking out the story as mediation preparations get under way. However, when there is active media interest and the negotiation process is inadvertently thrust into public attention, it is essential that there be forethought and early mutual agreement between the parties and the mediator as to how the situation will be handled.

Generally, it is well for the mediator to be given responsibility for dealing with reporters but that arrangement should be exercised with the concurrence of both negotiating teams. The following guidelines in the CRS model were applied in the absence of counter-indications:

1. If practical, prepared statements should provide the major portion of information to be made public. Such releases should be reviewed and approved jointly by an appropriately designated team member from each side, along with the mediator. It may be advisable to enlist a mutually acceptable local media specialist to assist in preparation. Local educational institutions, or media outlets themselves, will sometimes provide such assistance.

2. Occasionally, news people will be "waiting at the doorstep" when the mediator arrives on the scene for the initial visit. At this point, particular caution and discretion must be exercised when making comments, although a "no comment" approach is not normally advisable because that may give the appearance of intrigue or "something to hide," sometimes motivating reporters to seek out less knowledgeable or less reliable sources of information. The best approach is probably to give emphasis to who the mediator is (his/her role, organizational connection, if any, etc.), how the mediator functions as an intermediary, and possibly a candid statement to the effect that until there is an opportunity to meet with the parties and complete exploratory preliminaries, there is no way to comment on the issues, the participants, or the prospects for resolution.

3. Questions from the media relating primarily to the background of the conflict, how mediation contacts were initiated, the nature of the process, the parties involved, the issues to be negotiated, should, if possible, be left entirely to the mediator. If there are to be statements given by anyone representing one party or the other, that person should be designated on each side, in advance, and all others should be constrained by their team chairperson from making any statements or otherwise responding to the media.

4. Once actual negotiations have begun, special precautions should be instituted to assure that there is no comment from anyone, including the mediator, as to the status of any given issue at any particular time. Nor should there be speculation in connection with the positions of the parties in any respect. The hazards of doing so are obvious enough. No one can afford to have portions of the negotiations appear to be taking place in the press. Inevitably, whatever is reported will be incomplete, if not inaccurate. The likelihood of misinterpretation is substantial and the resulting risk of deterioration in relationships between the negotiating parties considerable.

MEDIATION GUIDELINES

Joint Negotiations and Resolution Tools

> *Discourage litigation. Persuade your neighbors to compromise*
> *whenever you can. Point out to them how the nominal winner is often*
> *a real loser: In fees, expenses and waste of time . . .*
>
> — Abraham Lincoln

JOINT SESSION FORMAT VARIATIONS

Joint sessions are where the mediation process is most intensely tested. They may be well interspersed with separate unilateral meetings in which the mediator confers with the parties independently of one another. Indeed, some mediation cases are conducted entirely without joint sessions, with the mediator shuttling back and forth between the disputants. Such a format, however, diminishes some of the most significant benefits of face-to-face negotiation (such as more efficient use of time, establishment of direct, personal relationships, and "putting a face on the adversary," opportunity for give-and-take dialogue and for immediate in-depth clarification of statements and positions, etc.). In short, there is no substitute for unencumbered direct communication.

It is important to recognize that when the mediator serves in a conduit role (without joint sessions), consideration must be given to appearances that might suggest an advocacy bias. It is a very difficult task to carry the reasoning and rationale of one party to another without having the vital hat of neutrality become tilted, or even blown off. If the messenger is to "tell it like it is" in relaying positions and reactions between adversaries, it can be extremely difficult to avoid damaging the perception of impartiality.

Suspicion or distrust can also develop when one side or the other is unaware of what is being said and done between the mediator and the opposing party in their "secret" meetings. Conflict is the home of paranoia to begin with. Any activity that even remotely suggests the opportunity for conspiracy can quickly take on a life of its own.

Further complicating this scenario, we remember that the mediator tries to be as open as possible with the parties. Candor is a powerful antidote for misgivings. But there is also the uncompromising obligation to safeguard confidences and to avoid revealing, unwittingly or otherwise, strategies or other information shared with the mediator in a consultative capacity.

Some say that there should be a virtually complete basis for agreement before the first joint session is held, hammered out in separate meetings, with the mediator acting as a "floating intervenor." In some atypical cases, such an approach might be useful. But in the great majority of situations, direct face-to-face negotiation and interpersonal interaction provide the only realistic framework for resolution.

OTHER JOINT SESSION CONSIDERATIONS

Face-to-face dialogue between antagonists can challenge the mediator's moderating skills. Sometimes there is a participant at the table with a short fuse or a deep-seated hostility that comes to the surface. With patience and persistence, the mediator can often deflect the troublesome diversion. A brief recess to allow cooling off may be helpful. More often than not, the testy negotiator will censor his own behavior at the first signs of verbal or body language disapproval from his own team members. Even more influence can be exerted by the mediator who, as a neutral, may be seen by the disquieted team member as someone whose regard he does not wish to jeopardize, and will therefore moderate behavior when even subtle indications of disapproval are detected.

One party or the other, at times, is apt to assume a rigid or unreasonable posture largely because there is a misunderstanding or a misinterpretation of the opponent's viewpoint. Through artful questioning, rephrasing, separate consultation, and even a bit of cajoling, the mediator can narrow, define, and redefine issues and points of contention in ways that move the negotiations forward.

CAUCUS AND RECESS

The use of caucus[1] and/or recess[2] procedures can save or lose the day. Timing is often of the essence. It requires an alertness and a sensitivity on the part of the mediator to know when such a move is in order. Often a caucus is necessary when there are signs of disagreement within one negotiating team or the other. Sometimes, when a particularly substantive decision is about to be made, it is well to give the parties ample opportunity to "get themselves together." A caucus can be called by the spokesperson for either party or by the mediator. Depending upon the nature of matters to be discussed and the wishes of the caucusing team, the mediator may be invited to participate in part or all of the caucus session.

Use of the recess, other than for break periods, meals, or extended adjournment, and so forth, can also be applied judiciously. Especially when there is considerable emotional heat generated during negotiation, or when productive dialogue is inhibited for whatever reason, the recess can be used effectively to allow for tempers to cool or for order and reason to be restored. Sometimes, an extended recess can allow one party or the other to seek out key people with important information that might help clarify points of contention or uncertainty. They may be witnesses to past events bearing on deliberations, or they may be persons with specialized knowledge who might shed light on areas of disagreement.

---

[1] A private meeting of negotiators from the same team, usually of relatively short duration, bringing joint sessions to a halt in order to help facilitate confidential internal communication.
[2] A more extended temporary halt to a joint negotiation session that may last for hours, days, or even weeks, depending on reasons for the requested adjournment.

Caution must be exercised by the mediator to ensure that requests for caucus and/or recess are not being used merely as a delaying tactic or for other questionable purposes. It is the mediator, as chair of the joint sessions and in accordance with established prenegotiation procedural rules, who allows or disallows such requests that affect the meeting schedule. Recesses, especially those involving a relatively prolonged adjournment, may disrupt the flow of activity. Momentum is fickle. The party moving for recess may or may not be fully aware of such potentially troublesome consequences.

USE OF NONPARTICIPATING OBSERVERS

In the experience of some mediators functioning in community or other intergroup disputes, the option of having neutral local observers present during joint sessions has proven constructive in some instances. It is recommended that such persons be identified and selected through a process in which the parties make choices by mutual accord. Typically, these observers are known to be unaligned with any of the positions being negotiated. Ideally, they are well-regarded community figures, known for their integrity, objectivity, and interest in the peace and progress of the area. They may be teachers or other professionals, church or organization leaders, business people, or others with broad standing and reputation. As many as three, and probably not more than six or seven such observers, is considered optimal.

The method of their selection should be carefully determined. One procedure is to have each side submit a list of people who in their collective judgment best fit the purpose and who might be available and willing to devote the necessary time to the role. If there are names common to both lists, the best prospects are readily determined. If there is not a sufficient number agreeable to both sides, it may be possible to have at least one selected jointly and then have each team name one, two, or three, thereby providing a relatively balanced grouping.

Because it is often difficult for such individuals to commit the time required, it is well to have the names of at least twice the number needed, ranked in order of preference, thus providing possible alternates for those who may find it necessary to decline to participate. Before being asked to accept the assignment, they are given a briefing by the mediator as to the nature of their task.

There are some circumstances under which these observers are also in a position to offer information or advice privately to either or both parties during caucuses or recesses should such options be exercised. It is also permissible for one or both negotiating teams to have present, as nonparticipating observers, persons who have specialized knowledge that is expected to be drawn upon from time to time during the mediation sessions. Examples of such instances might include accountants, departmental supervisors, security personnel, community organization leaders, attorneys (if they are not designated active negotiating team members), or simply constituents of one party or the other. Clearly, such observers are not neutrals, and as such, need to be authorized through joint party approval.

The roles of the neutral observers (as opposed to resources invited by a negotiating team) are threefold:

First, their presence tends to bring a degree of stability to the negotiation setting. Both sides are aware they are being monitored by people of their own choosing and, presumably, people in whom they have trust and confidence. The resulting "leveling effect" can help reduce excessive rhetoric from team members and lessen the chances of arbitrary response from the institution or organization from which redress is being sought.

Second, selected participating observers can be used with considerable effectiveness during caucus sessions when broader community input may be seen as an important ingredient in decision making. They can be called upon to assist one side or the other to help interpret and evaluate issues and proposals for solution. They can also help with the development of an agreement instrument as well as take part in developing a mechanism for later enforcement of the agreement.

Finally, the observer may function as a liaison with community elements outside the mediation room who have a legitimate interest in the progress of negotiations or who have a stake in the outcome (e.g., representatives of local or other levels of government, and issue-related law enforcement agencies, community organizations, educational institutions, or reform advocates, etc.). Information coming from these observer sources is more likely to be free of bias then that originating from a spokesperson for either side of the dispute. Furthermore, their contribution in this connection can go far toward reducing the hazards of unfounded rumors and damaging speculation being spread by elements of the public that have no direct access to the process.

THE AGREEMENT— PREPARATION AND ENFORCEMENT

Vital to the successful conclusion of any mediation effort is the final agreement between the parties. Unless such an agreement is virtually assured of being implemented, there is little use in its creation. In this connection there are several noteworthy aspects to be considered:

- The agreement is reduced to writing as a primary requirement for practical results. It is signed by those authorized by their respective constituencies to do so. The mediator is also a signatory as a third party witness.
- If circumstances warrant, the mediator may be called upon to help develop and finalize the language of the written instrument, or others with particular capabilities in that regard may be enlisted, with concurrence of the parties. Sometimes a committee may be appointed, representing all appropriately interested principals, that can draft the document for later ratification or modification by the respective constituencies.
- The necessity of establishing an enforcement mechanism to assure that provisions of the agreement are implemented cannot be overstated. Such a mechanism can be created in a variety of ways. Whatever method is decided upon, it should arise out of mutual endorsement by the disputants. In some instances, a local human/community relations agency can assume responsibility for helping to settle any emerging disagreement over interpreting implementation provisions or progress toward performance. If the dispute was referred by a court of law, the judge may be willing to facilitate enforcement through a consent decree. Another alternative might be to turn to a professional private sector arbitrator or an arbitration panel. The parties themselves are free, of course, to turn to whatever source of such assistance that may be available and upon whom they can agree to utilize. Or they may simply decide to meet unilaterally in an attempt to reach their own decisions without any outside help.

The point here is the importance of such an enforcement mechanism provision being incorporated into the final written instrument of agreement. The provision should be as specific as possible in identifying the resource(s) to be called upon and the procedure under which such activity is to be carried out.

POSTMEDIATION FOLLOW-UP

In terms of postcommunity and/or institutional dispute settlement implementation, there are several considerations worthy of mention. First, it may be necessary for the mediator to provide the parties with some form of technical assistance, either through his/her own involvement or through making available appropriate consultants/specialists in helping to ensure effective execution of the agreement (as suggested in the previous section). Secondly, an evaluation of overall implementation effort and results can be a highly productive concomitant if performed within a reasonable time after signing of the agreement.

With regard to the possible use of technical assistance from someone other than the mediator, much depends upon the nature of the agreement (conditions to be remedied, costs involved and funding availability, time frames imposed, types of resources or expertise needed, etc.). When there are objectives to be achieved that extend beyond the capacity of the responding party to perform within its own means, outside support may be enthusiastically welcomed. Such assistance may be in connection with identifying and enlisting financial sources or expert guidance in a wide variety of relatively narrow areas. A few examples might include:

- Evaluation of human relations training being offered to public agency personnel responsible for dealing with sensitive cross-cultural issues;
- Survey of bilingual education curriculum, faculty, and facilities in connection with an agreement for additional funding to aid students with severe language handicaps;
- Analysis by a university resource center of current employment and labor market conditions in order to assess prospects for an innovative program to improve job opportunities for disadvantaged youth;
- Regional study of successful public secondary school programs to establish and utilize grievance mechanisms to deal equitably with student dissatisfaction;
- Assessment of public and private funds available to support a housing renewal proposal on an Indian reservation (under an agreement to relieve persistently substandard living conditions among Indians isolated from outside assistance programs).

Depending on circumstances, it may be appropriate for the mediator to return to the site of the conflict on the follow-up assignment, along with the specialist(s) engaged. Intimate knowledge of the participants and their leadership, and of the issues embodied in the agreement, can be a definite asset in working out technical assistance requirements.

The evaluation aspect of follow-up is essentially designed to reveal the extent to which the agreement has been successfully implemented. The mediator is the obvious resource of choice to perform this task, but again, the parties should be free to choose any other option available to them upon which they can mutually agree. Each provision of the agreement is thoroughly reviewed as to possible problems found to have delayed or prevented execution. Particular attention is given to the positive results achieved without noteworthy difficulty.

Interviews are conducted with key spokespersons from both negotiating teams and perhaps with observers and/or others involved in the mediation process, or others who have had opportunities for close observation of results. In any case, a reasonably balanced perspective is the goal. This exercise is one that should be helpful to both parties. To the disputants, it offers an objective evaluation of effort, consequences, and impact, and to the mediator a reflection of the effectiveness of the third-party intervention process, providing insights into possible need for procedural modifications.

Proper timing of the evaluation component is important. Generally, it should take place within six months to a year following signing of the agreement, although an even longer period may be necessary, especially in community conflict cases involving complex and/or emotionally charged grievances pertaining to the responsiveness of governmental agencies or other organizations having to contend with detached policy boards or cumbersome bureaucracies. In any event, the implementation time frame must be realistic in terms of anticipated administrative obstacles, yet be such as to avoid undue delay.

SUMMARY OF KEY ESSENTIALS

The primary essentials for successful community/institutional mediation can be summarized as follows:

1. A viable complainant nucleus representing a legitimate constituency, capable of forming a committed negotiating team under established mediation guidelines;
2. Reasonably well-defined issues over which the respondent party has the capacity and willingness to negotiate a settlement;
3. Consensus of the parties to reduce any agreement to a written, signed instrument, subject to whatever enforcement provisions are agreed upon in advance;
4. Recognition by the parties that although extended and intensive negotiation can be a slow, tiring and often frustrating experience, still little positive action is likely to occur without good faith intentions on both sides, facilitation of effective communication, and a controlled and tested process to help assure a productive outcome;
5. A pragmatic awareness by negotiators on both sides of the table that there is a give-and-take element required of them that will necessitate sound and thoughtful tactics and realistic expectations; recognition by all the parties of the limitations placed upon them by those they represent; a willingness to realistically estimate and understand the parameters within which they may be called upon to moderate positions, compromise objectives, or even capitulate on a given issue or proposed remedy in the service of larger objectives and higher priorities.

PRISON MEDIATION

Louisiana State Penitentiary at Angola

Peace cannot be kept by force;
It can only be achieved by understanding.

—Albert Einstein

A BOLD EXPERIMENT

Few institutions in our society invite change. The nation's penal systems are no exception. Corrections reform favoring more humane conditions or constitutional protections for those incarcerated has historically met with public resistance, if not hostility. Management professionals in this field, when inclined to consider new or innovative approaches to the custody and rehabilitation of convicts, typically find themselves without political support, largely because the electorate will punish office seekers for such a stand. State legislatures, when looking for budget economies or program retrenchment, have been notoriously inclined to look to corrections as a popular and suitable place to reduce or eliminate operating expenditures, especially those intended to relieve unduly harsh or overcrowded living conditions sometimes seen by administrators as contributing to rising tensions and chilling threats to a secure environment.

In the late 1960s and into the 1970s, federal court dockets had become seriously congested with claims from prisoners confined to state and local penal institutions. Most were seeking relief from alleged constitutional violations by their keepers. Cases typically centered on allegations of wrongful personal injury (or failure of the institution to protect inmates from such), illegal incarceration, mail censorship and other violations of privacy, denial of religious freedom, inadequate medical treatment, and inhumane disciplinary practices. The latter two complaints constituted the overwhelming majority of the litigious content.

The fabled jailhouse lawyer had become more than merely an irritant to corrections administrators. Inmates who sought to engage the legal system to overcome perceived injustices and to assert guaranteed constitutional protections had become a force to be reckoned with. It was in such a setting, early in 1972, that a few undaunted federal district judges were persuaded to turn to mediation as a possible alternative to the rising tide of inmate civil actions then pending on their dockets.

AN ALTERNATIVE TO LITIGATION IN PRISON PROBLEM SOLVING

It fell to the Honorable E. Gordon West, Chief Judge for the Middle District of Louisiana, to become the first among his peers to act as a catalyst for introducing mediation as an option to settle pending litigation before a federal court. After hearing a judicial conference presentation on the nature of the CRS-sponsored third party process to settle disputes, Judge West concluded that he had a suitable test. He had pending in his court more than a score of lawsuits brought by prisoners at the Louisiana State Penitentiary (LSP), typically referred to locally as Angola, the name of the community near which it is located. Each case had been filed under Sec 1983 of the U.S. Code seeking relief from, and in some instances damages for, alleged denial of civil rights, among other causes of action. The prospect of dealing with each of these filings through normal court proceedings would add immeasurably to an already heavily burdened docket.

After direct consultation with the mediator, then Southwest Regional Coordinator for the CRS Conflict Resolution Program, he made his decision. He would call upon Louisiana state corrections officials to discuss with CRS their willingness to have submitted to mediation some of the more critical issues contained in the lawsuit chosen by the judge for evaluation. As it happened, circumstances were such that an affirmative response was all but inevitable.

The prison at Angola, at the time of these developments, was an all-male adult detention facility, located about 60 miles northwest of the state capital of Baton Rouge, in a remote rural area. Standing on a site of more than 18,000 acres along the Mississippi River and its shoreline of fertile cultivation and plantation remnants, it was said to be one of the largest correctional facilities in the nation. It had a population in the early 1970s of approximately 3,500 inmates. A staff of some 300 corrections officers, primarily security guards, was drawn largely from nearby country towns and farm families. Some 70% of the prisoners were African American, but only a dozen or so of the paid staff were black.

Governor Edwin Edwards had been recently elected governor of Louisiana. Just weeks before mediation was proposed by Judge West, he had appointed a new director of corrections, Elayn Hunt. She formerly had been a criminal defense lawyer and, during previous administrations, an outspoken critic of the state's penal system. Without her determination to transform the Louisiana system from one reputed to be among the most archaic in the nation to one that might some day be seen as a model for other states to follow, it is unlikely that her corrections agency would ever willingly have come to the negotiating table to participate in such an unprecedented problem-solving format.

PREMEDIATION ARRANGEMENTS—FEDERAL COURT INITIATIVES

The first step in launching the third-party process was a meeting convened by Judge West at the suggestion of the mediator. Its purpose was to bring principal corrections officials together in order to explain to them the precise nature of the court's intention. It was highly desirable, in accordance with CRS entry criteria already established in other types of cases, to have the respondents *agree voluntarily* to the proposed alternative to litigation, rather than have it ordered by the court, although the judge had indicated that he was prepared to take the latter course were it to become necessary.

That meeting was held in chambers on June 9, 1972. Representing the state's interest were the director of the Louisiana Department of Corrections and her assistant, the warden of the penitentiary, and an assistant state attorney general. With Judge West, representing the intervenor resource, were three of us from the Community Relations Service: two administration of justice program officers, both from CRS headquarters in Washington, DC, and myself, the designated mediator.

This initial conference with the first of the two parties who would participate in negotiations (the other being convict representatives, yet to be identified) gave the state an opportunity to carefully examine the proposition in the presence of those most familiar with the procedure under consideration. They had a stream of questions. They were completely responsive and candid in answering questions posed by the judge and by CRS team members having to do with the availability of manuals and reports and on policies related to discipline/punishment procedures, programs for orientation, availability of educational opportunities for both staff and inmates, security guidelines, medical services and facilities, staff recruiting/training, and a host of other problem areas. Some improvements were shown to have already been implemented as a result of an earlier federal court order. They also acknowledged that measures to correct many other deficiencies had been neglected.

In the presence of and under the obvious influence of the new director of corrections, it was apparent that the warden and his attending staff were beginning to look upon truly meaningful reform and changes in prison culture as an inevitable wave of the future.

The in-chambers dialogue also resulted in establishing a rapport between the intermediaries and the respondents. It was necessary that they feel as comfortable as possible with the process and with the personalities with whom they would be dealing. That initial objective was achieved.

Among the key observations and tentative conclusions highlighted during the two-hour meeting were:

1. The mediation agenda would deal primarily with the two overriding grievances known to be at the core of the pending lawsuits: inadequate medical services and unnecessarily harsh or inhumane discipline.
2. Given agreement by the complainants, a neutral technical resource with appropriate prison administration background would be made available to both negotiating teams for consultation in helping to identify remedy options and to assess their practicality.[1]
3. Current conditions at the prison were described by officials as unstable if not explosive. A prison guard had been killed by a convict a few weeks earlier. Staff-inmate tensions were said to be understandably elevated.
4. In accordance with mediation guidelines discussed, it was agreed that there would be no attempt to resolve charges brought by individuals pertaining to their specific complaints. Rather, only those conditions seen to contribute to various allegations pending before the court would be placed on an agenda. It was agreed that should changes in these areas be agreed upon, it would likely render most inmate claims moot.
5. Extended discussion was given to the critical matter of how prisoners would be selected to serve on a negotiating team representing the interests of the entire

---

[1]James Freeman, one of two CRS program officers attending the meeting, had been designated to fulfill this role. The corrections representatives readily recognized that his credentials as a former prison administrator, his demeanor as a neutral and principled individual, and his insights into the dynamics of implementing change, would serve to contribute to the success of negotiations. It remained to be seen whether or not those selected to serve on the inmate negotiating team, anticipated to be predominantly black, would have a similarly favorable reaction to Mr. Freeman, himself an African American.

confined population. After painstaking consideration of a number of possible alternatives, it was decided that inmate representatives would be drawn from a group of plaintiffs whose cases were currently pending before Judge West. The judge agreed to solicit the claimants and their attorneys in that connection.

A word of caution was introduced with regard to this aspect of preparation. Some plaintiffs involved in pending litigation, it was pointed out, were seen to be chronic misfits in the prison population, some allegedly suffering from various psychiatric ailments. Some were said to be the outcasts of the institution, typically rejected by other convicts. A number of others were looked upon as devious and persistent opportunists who would go to any length to disrupt the system or to pursue drastic measures for frivolous purposes. A few were even known to have filed a lawsuit merely to get a trip to town to appear before the judge. On the other hand, there were said to be among the plaintiffs a number of highly motivated, intelligent individuals, considered by other prisoners to be leaders and spokesmen when confronting authorities in seeking relief from perceived abuses. Clearly, these were touted to be the more promising prospects for participation on the complainant mediation team.

6. Much attention was given to what state officials believed would be a serious impediment to reaching agreement on a range of issues—the gross inadequacy of available funding. Concern centered on acknowledged substandard features of the physical environment and on an array of services (medical, food, educational/vocational programs, staff training, recreation, etc.) that could not be significantly improved, they said, without a substantial infusion of dollars. It was an aspect of the overall problem of making improvements that was seen to be beyond their control and in the hands of a legislature that had been throughout modern history notoriously tight-fisted with budget allocations for the state's penal system development.

Within this rather gloomy historical outlook, however, there was a somewhat optimistic if cautious expectation. The corrections director was currently appearing before committees of state lawmakers who had various responsibilities for penal institutional oversight. She was pressing for substantial budget increases in staff salaries (to upgrade qualifications and professionalism) and a doubling of funds available for food service, medical care, and other key auxiliary functions, many at the core of pending litigation.

7. Notwithstanding the issue of monetary limitations and other anticipated restraints, the corrections director was forceful in her commitment to establish new avenues of communication between the incarcerated and their keepers. That, she said, would have no price tag, but could result in monumental rewards to the courts and to all concerned parties. Mediation, she declared, would offer a unique opportunity to do just that.
8. It was tentatively agreed that mediation would commence in early September, some three months hence, giving corrections officials time to "recover" from the state legislative session scheduled to adjourn in mid-July.

ON-SITE EXPOSURE TO CONDITIONS OF INCARCERATION

Ten days following the initial meeting with respondent state corrections officials in Judge West's chambers, the mediator and his two staff associates visited once again with the director of corrections, this time at the prison, joined by a new set of administrative staff members: the director of custodial services, the head of the LSP hospital, and a deputy warden. The exchange of views and information on this occasion further underscored the uncharacteristic candor of LSP officials.

Dialogue with our CRS team continued to reflect a genuine determination to seek out meaningful avenues of reform. Manuals and reports on discipline procedures, institutional programs, and facility development were readily made available. Policies with regard to security, convict behavior control and custodial practices, punishment criteria, staff recruiting and training, legislative activity, and a host of other areas of management responsibility were reviewed in considerable detail.

A tour of the 100-bed prison hospital unexpectedly revealed what James Freeman, our CRS corrections specialist, said appeared to be "a more than adequate" inventory of medical fixtures and equipment. Painfully clear, however, was the deficient level of professional staffing (one full-time physician, five medical technicians, and some 50 or more virtually untrained inmate personnel to serve a population of over 3,500). Housekeeping conditions appeared to be substandard but not intolerable. Hospital-related complaints were said to center on difficulties in obtaining diet foods, obstacles in getting permission to go to the hospital, and the lack of medications, especially after being transferred from one cell location to another.

The practices of the disciplinary board were looked upon as a critical prospective target for reform evaluation. Its key membership consisted of the education director and the associate wardens for treatment and for custody. One of the more apparent problems was that too often there was a tendency to delegate responsibility to lower and lower echelons of authority.

No one seemed to know just how many black correction officers were on staff. It was generally acknowledged to be fewer than ten among a total employment of some 350. None were in high-ranking or influential positions such as those dealing with classification duties like counseling, rehabilitation prognosis, evaluation of behavior, intake preparation, and so forth, Supplementing the paid corrections officers were about 200 armed inmate guards who worked within a "trustee guard system" that was both unknown to exist at any other state penal institution and a constant source of tension and antagonism.

An unannounced visit to one of the satellite units of the main complex, known as "The Red Hat" or "The Hole," confirmed one of the most vehemently expressed condemnations of the entire institution. It was a scene difficult to describe. It was the place where time was served for punishment in isolation from the main population and without access to recreational amenities, useful work programs, regular food service, and various privileges sometimes granted for good behavior—thirty-seven 5x8 foot cells, each unfit for human confinement, each holding two or three prisoners. A single concrete slab 18 inches wide served each prisoner as a bed with no mattress or linens. Inadequate ventilation (unimaginable in the heat of a Louisiana summer), and sanitation conditions unsuitable even for animals, let alone humans, highlighted the misery. Conditions were such as to deserve the reputation it had as a hell hole that inmates knew, if at all possible, was to be avoided at all costs.

In a further demonstration of the willingness of administrators to show us the worst of Angola's warts to whatever extent we chose, we were granted the opportunity to talk privately and at random with whatever number we wished of inmates in confinement at "The Red Hat." Rarely had outsiders, other than plaintiffs' attorneys, ever before been allowed to enter the remote location, let alone engage convicts in private conversation. Elayn Hunt's authorization for us to have totally free access to this heretofore largely clandestine part of the prison was but one more clear indication of her courage and willingness to risk serious repercussions in order to advance the cause of reform.

The bitterness of the men serving time at this maximum security unit was uniform. Pleas for relief from oppression poured from their lips. Some claimed to be seriously ill, and in several cases the truth of the claims were obvious. Many said they were sent to isolation for the most minor of infractions, in some cases simply at the whim of a guard extracting retribution for a personal dislike or grudge. Three sparse meals a day were described by inmates interviewed as being below subsistence level, main meals typically consisting of a few peas or beans, a spoonful of rice, a small piece of meat, and a single slice of bread. Showering was said to be allowed only once a week, even in the midst of oppressive summer heat. Although confinement to this unit was supposed to be limited to ten days, some were said to be returned to regular cells and then, after 24 hours, taken back to "the hole." Doubtlessly, some of the stories we heard were exaggerated, some perhaps fabricated. But the evidence of inhumane conditions and treatment, clearly apparent from our first-hand observation, could not be denied.

An impressive number of recent improvements and hopeful signs offset to some degree the grievous inequities. An earlier court order from Judge West in September 1971 under the findings of *Sinclair vs. Henderson* had provided the first significant reform measures introduced at Angola through legal action by inmates. It dealt largely with exercise for death row prisoners and publication of rules and regulations regarding the penalties that could be imposed for misconduct. A rapidly expanding work release program, also a result of the earlier mandate, was showing great promise as well.

The openness to untried remedies and innovation brought on by the new reform-minded corrections leadership, and the willingness of the governor to take political risks to bring about change, both contributed to the elevated prospects for the mediation experiment. We all recognized that the sprawling penal facility was still entrenched in retrogressive tradition, performing with inadequately trained and equipped personnel, and without sufficient funding to accomplish desired objectives. It was a "big bear," ponderous to move or change. Its reputation as one of the nation's most primitive institutions of its kind seemed well deserved.

With relatively minor exceptions, the prison's population was racially segregated, one of the few institutional settings where legally mandated integration had made only insignificant inroads. Only at intake processing were prisoners quartered on an integrated basis. Other than during recreation and work crew activity, virtually all incarceration time was spent segregated by race.

It was becoming clear to prison authorities that if mediation did nothing more than create a mechanism and precedent for some semblance of productive dialogue between the jailers and the jailed, it might just lead to better morale on both sides of the cell bars. They recognized too that in a yet more meaningful scenario, traditionally adversarial attitudes might give way to mutual cooperation in resolving complaints, thereby bringing about improvements—even to the point of avoiding the incidents of violent rebellion and serious injury or loss of life that had so characterized the past.

INMATE ORIENTATION BEHIND THE WALLS

Arrangements were made for the mediator to address an audience of some 50 or more inmates, many of whom were plaintiffs in various federal court filings. Others were known to have done legal research in the prison library. Some were in positions of leadership or influence in the various classified populations[2] around the complex. The purpose of the meeting was to explain the mediation proposal to a reasonable representation of com-

---

[2]Prison inmate classification is a system by which offenders are placed in work and housing assignments in accordance with their level of security risk and individual needs as determined by screening personnel. It is designed to assure optimal utilization of staff resources and effective inmate custody and safety.

plainants and to facilitate those in attendance taking the message for wider dissemination in the dining halls, recreation yards and work stations.

Because the speaker represented the U.S. Department of Justice, a law enforcement agency that may have been responsible for past prosecutions in which they, or friends or relatives, were convicted and put away, there were rather obvious signs of animosity. Early interruptions and skeptical questions made the early going somewhat foreboding, to say the least. At one point early in the presentation, an irate inmate toward the back of the hall began a charge toward the podium as if to attack me. Fortunately, he was collared by others in the audience before he could complete his mission! (It had been decided in planning for this occasion with corrections officials that it would be more effective to have no staff present because we were confident there would not be any disruptive or threatening behavior from those in attendance.)

In any event, as details of the mediation process were presented in a session that lasted almost two hours, there was clearly a lessening of tension and a gradual growing interest, and even enthusiasm, for the uniqueness of the experiment and the possibility of bringing about changes in policy and practice. That prison officials had already agreed to proceed, that the process was voluntary, and that participation was dependent on the willingness of the parties to continue, went a long way toward winning the inmates over. More importantly, the fact that any agreement reached would be captured in writing, signed by the negotiators, and would have the implicit sanction of the court, gave further impetus to a positive response. The assurance that an inmate attorney of their choice could serve them as a consultant-participant was the icing on the cake. I was careful in delivering my message not to overstate expectations. I made clear that there was no guarantee, or even assurance, that any agreement satisfactory to both sides would ultimately be reached.

The inmates were told that the ball was then in their court. It would be up to them to relay the information they had been given to as broad a segment of the prison population as possible.[3] In consultations with the CRS team, and with its approval, it was decided that team members and alternates would be selected from among the leaders of various inmate organizations and from those who had active filings before the federal court. By late September of 1972, that objective had been accomplished.

FINAL PREPARATIONS BEFORE GOING TO JOINT SESSIONS

On October 2, my staff corrections specialist and I met with the inmate negotiating team. Four of six team members were black. Dudley Spiller, a pro bono legal services attorney from Baton Rouge who was representing several LSP plaintiffs in pending law suits, had agreed to act as counsel and would have a place at the table beside the convict team.

Seated in a secure room with no guards or other prison personnel present, a full orientation was highlighted by:

- review of mediation procedures (role of the mediator, use of alternates, roles of observers and legal advisor, recess/caucus applications, etc.);
- discussion of the nature of the proceedings to be undertaken (court referral implications, voluntary basis of participation, withdrawal option, etc.);
- review and framing of issues (organization of material, priorities for order of presentation, corrective actions proposed, etc.);

---

[3]See addendum A, copy of a bulletin sent by the inmate team to the prison population announcing the mediation plan.

- discussion of adversary characteristics, strategy considerations, community relations problems, and difficulties relating to prison employees;
- sharing of letters received from inmates requesting interviews or other responses from the intermediaries and agreement by team members to assist in making appropriate contacts/explanations regarding these inquiries;
- coordination of timing for joint sessions so as to maximize attendance by those on the respondent team who would be traveling to the prison from considerable distances;
- final approval of three nonparticipating observers (the prison chaplain, a staff classification officer, and an inmate involved with providing legal aid) mutually agreed upon by both negotiating teams;
- election of a team chairman and vice chairman;
- extensive discussion of anticipated contacts with the media and agreement as to tentative plans for release of information, hazards of premature contact, and firm refusal by the mediator to allow media coverage during negotiation sessions (negating a proposal introduced and strongly supported by several team members).

Following this meeting, a prearranged conference with Director Hunt and several staff assistants dealt with the not insignificant matter of finalizing arrangements for a suitable location for the negotiation sessions. Several criteria regarding physical features had to be met, including a long and wide rectangular table and reasonably comfortable chairs to accommodate the two teams; nearby space for seating observers; an adjacent room in which negotiators could meet privately whenever a caucus was called; arrangements for clerical assistance to record substantive proceedings; reasonable temperature and ventilation control; convenient access to rest rooms; suitable refreshment break preparations, and so on.

The following morning the CRS representatives met for the first time with the finalized institutional negotiating team. Subject matter presented and discussed paralleled that of the meeting the day before with the inmates. However, additional and more detailed attention in this session was given to:

- the nature of the agreement instrument;
- problems anticipated regarding implementation of follow-up actions agreed upon;
- schedules for conducting joint sessions on a consecutive daily basis for an $11\frac{1}{2}$ hour period from 9:30 AM until 9:00 PM with one-hour lunch and dinner breaks for each of the next three days;
- urgency of continuing effort by senior management to communicate to all levels of prison employees the background and status of developments in the mediation process and the anticipated results.

FACE-TO-FACE NEGOTIATIONS—THE FIRST JOINT SESSION

On October 3, 1972, for the first time in the known annals of corrections administration, an experiment was about to be launched that would bring with it the potential for unprecedented innovation in the governance of penal institutions. It also held the prospect for a disastrous miscalculation, politically as well as in terms of institutional stability, that could bring about untold negative consequences, the nature of which no one could predict. But commitments had been made. The die had been cast. There was no turning back.

Representing the prison administration were five principal negotiators: the director of the state department of corrections, the LSP warden, a deputy warden, the associate warden for custody, and the chief of security. Three other senior staff members serving as alternates (seated behind the principals, but close enough for private communication or open commentary when called upon by the team chair) were the associate warden for treatment, the director of classification and the prison hospital administrator.

The complainant team's five members, along with three alternates, represented a reasonable cross-section of the prison population, drawn from the various population segments previously agreed upon. Legal Counsel Dudley Spiller took his place beside his clients.

Three nonparticipating observers, one selected by each team and a third by joint agreement of the parties, were an inmate representing the legal office, a prison classification officer and the institution's chaplain. The parties were in position. The trial balloon was ready to rise. It was time for the agenda to be brought to the table.

The mediator-chairman, calling this first joint session to order, presented a condensed outline of procedural preliminaries previously given separately to each team, followed by a review and discussion of the various perspectives on dealing with the media. By design, these early exchanges were intended to establish something of a comfort zone, encouraging dialogue mostly between team members and the chair, rather than having team members immediately positioning themselves over substantive issues. By and large, the rationale and recommendations set forth in the last section of Chapter 3 were ultimately agreed upon, although not without some notable dissent from several on the inmate team.

It was apparent that Director Hunt had prepared her colleagues well. The respondent team betrayed little of the anxiety or skepticism I had expected might surface early on, and the inmate team also showed little uneasiness, appearing to be settled in for a process of orderly discourse. In an afternoon and evening session that lasted 7½ hours (with an hour dinner break), the two sides engaged in wide-ranging and vigorous, but civil, give-and-take, ultimately reaching agreement on seven separate issues. Most of these matters, being of relatively minor importance, were placed early on the agenda to instill a feeling of consensus before moving on to more difficult problems likely to bring on heated debate or possible impasse. These initial accords were:

1. Established dormitory shower hours;
2. Creation of a joint inmate/administration committee to prepare and submit certain revisions to the existing prison rules and regulations and to make subsequent recommendations at a future joint mediation session;
3. An amendment to prison rule regarding "failure to obey orders";
4. An amendment to rule on "waste of food";
5. Action deferred until next session on a proposed amendment to rule on "haircuts and mustaches";
6. Withdrawal by the prisoner team of a proposal to amend the rule on inter-dorm visitation;
7. Amendments to penitentiary directive regarding "inmate correspondence."

SECOND JOINT SESSION

The second negotiation session was held on the following day, October 4. It was a marathon docket called to order at 9:30 in the morning and adjourning at 9 o'clock that night. All parties had agreed to the grueling schedule in spite of the fact that some participants on both sides of the table (administrators, attorneys, observers, alternates, etc.) had to juggle outside commitments in order to assure availability at Angola. Increasing the number of hours at the table on a single day was seen to be more practical than trying to meet for shorter periods over an extended number of days. It took the entire session to deal with seven more issues, resulting in the following:

1. Agreement on an amendment to regulations governing hair styles and beard growth;
2. An impasse on a proposal to modify conditions under which exercise would be made available to inmates confined to lockdown;
3. Agreement on a proposal to change the way credit for time served is earned after a disciplinary sentence is imposed;
4. Agreement to alter the maximum detention time imposed after confinement to isolation for a violation has been ordered;
5. Agreement to establish a grievance process to assure top prison management reasonable opportunity for feedback from inmates as problems arise;
6. Agreement on amendments to a penitentiary directive regarding indefinite sentences; entitlement to written reasons for denial of release;
7. Agreement to close down the isolation control cells known as "the red hat."[4] This point in the negotiations was especially critical. It marked the first time in which the institutional team sought to caucus before responding to a major inmate proposal. Their deliberations lasted almost 30 minutes. It was apparent that Corrections Director Hunt had chosen this moment to exert her influence on her administrative associates, resulting in one of the most far-reaching reforms to be achieved throughout the mediation process.

THE THIRD ROUND

A third successive and final day of negotiation on October 5, from 10:00 a.m. until 9:00 p.m., seemed to benefit from the momentum of the day before. Contrary to expectations, all fourteen remaining issues were settled without significant dissent. It is noteworthy that half of these were related to medical services. Agreement was reached on each of the following agenda articles:[5]

1. Freedom to hold and express religious and political beliefs and to possess related printed materials;
2. Conditions of involuntary transfer to lockdown;
3. Cellblock visiting privileges;
4. Cellblock television privileges;
5. Access to foods packaged in glass containers;
6. Determinations of inmate need for medical treatment;
7. Propriety of prison physician's orders;
8. Availability of first aid;
9. Preventative medical and dental examinations;

---

[4]This unit of 37 cells, in an isolated section of the prison acreage, was the most dehumanizing and primitive lockup in the institution. It was used for punishment confinement for periods of up to 10 days. Its contemptuous designation by inmates as "the red hat," overstated or not, stemmed from its reputation as a place where convicts were severely beaten on the head, causing their headgear to turn red from blood. The closing of this unit as a result of the mediated agreement was considered a major achievement which, standing alone, would have been sufficient justification for the entire negotiation effort.

[5]See addendum B, copy of final agreement.

10. Conditions under which sick call would be made on the cellblocks;
11. Availability of emergency services;
12. Medical technician training;
13. Establishment of an inmate grievance committee;
14. Provision for suspension by management of certain rules and regulations during emergency conditions.

THE FINAL CHAPTER—AN ACCOMMODATION BEHIND PRISON WALLS

The true test of any mediated agreement lies in the extent to which issues resolved actually impact on conditions that brought about the conflict in the first place. Of equal importance are the effects on the subsequent relationships between the contesting parties. Without improved communication and lessening of distrust, there is little likelihood of a sustained capacity for problem solving and stability. Without the good faith implementation efforts of the respondents in executing changes agreed upon, it is likely that resolutions on paper will mean little.

In late January of 1974, some 16 months after mediation ended, the Louisiana State Advisory Committee of the U.S. Commission on Civil Rights (USCCR) held a 2½-day hearing in Baton Rouge as the focus of what was to be known as the *Louisiana Prison Study.* It was billed as part of a national assessment of policies, practices and conditions in adult penal institutions. Testimony about the mediation experience was taken from the director of corrections and a number of her key administrators at Angola, along with five LSP inmate witnesses[6] and various community representatives with related interests (including some of the state's more vigorous prison reform advocates).

The chairman of the prisoner team, Leotha Brown, offered some of the most pertinent testimony, corroborated by others appearing before the panel. Highlights of his remarks centered on the then current status of mediation agreement implementation, including more than a dozen processes, relaxation of correspondence restrictions and discontinuation of mail censorship, control of major issues fully applied, and three pending. He emphasized some of the more significant reforms including: elimination of ambiguities in prison rules, establishment of an ongoing grievance over abusive practices by jailers of prisoners confined to lockdown, closing of the "red hat" isolation cells (except for emergencies where no alternative is available), extension of rights of inmates held in isolation, and markedly improved condition of physical plant facilities.

The witness went on to elaborate on significant improvement in the manner of treatment of inmates by security personnel and other staff since the conclusion of mediation (although admittedly not a perception necessarily shared by everyone in the confined population who would be influenced by individual experiences).

Further inmate testimony before the commission, however, was not entirely favorable. One witness, Douglas "Swede" Dennis, an observer/advisor to the convict team (then serving his 17th year of incarceration), was unhesitating in his criticism of institutional follow-up. The grievance process, he said, was a "beautiful concept on paper," elections were conducted honestly, and representation was well conceived, coming from all areas of the prison complex. But, he contended, the grievance committee structure in its original form lasted only about six months and had been gradually eroding ever since. The process would not survive, he said, unless staff changed their attitudes toward inmates and began viewing them less like irresponsible children and more like adults. Security personnel, he went on,

---

[6]The five Angola inmate witnesses (and those from two other state adult penal institutions) were selected by the USCCR staff without recommendation or influence by any state authority.

were too strongly committed to controlling behavior beyond reasonable limits. Particularly exasperating, he continued, was the fact that officials wanted the grievance committee to be passive in its participation, encouraged to simply inform the administration of problems but having no voice in problem solving.

Nonetheless, this same witness went on to describe the new discipline procedures generated during mediation as having been organized into what he considered to be among the best such systems in the nation.[7]

Senior staff attitudes regarding the mediation agreement might be characterized by an off-the-record comment made to me during the hearings. Richard Crane, recently appointed legal counsel to the department of corrections, said ". . . the mediation agreement is like our 'constitution.' We refer to it constantly." Crane's testimony alluded to the fact that a copy of the agreement (again referred to as "our constitution") had been distributed to every inmate. He also announced that of more than 4,000 disciplinary hearings conducted under the new system, only 65 had been appealed to the director. That, he stated, was ample proof of the program's effectiveness.

When Director Hunt delivered her remarks, she answered a question put to her by a panelist: "Can mediation be extended to other institutions in the Louisiana system?" Her reply: "Yes, I am so inclined," although she went on to qualify her answer by pointing out that time constraints on her and her principal administrators (many of whom would necessarily be participants in any future mediation) were such as to make any future mediation a questionable prospect.

Warden Murray Henderson's USCCR testimony led him to explanations of why he thought some of the inmates expressed dissatisfaction with implementation progress. The three issues referenced by those complaining witnesses as being unfulfilled had become a cause for his concern. He pointed out, for example, that the added pay-telephone installations had been stymied because the phone company was unwilling to respond to an order for equipment they considered unlikely to generate sufficient revenue. The agreement regarding standby use of the "red hat" control unit for emergency quarters, another point of postmediation contention, was said to have been rescinded.

The facility would be converted to an electric shop. The third matter of alleged neglect had to do with the inmate handbook that had been agreed upon in negotiations. The warden asked for patience, pointing out that the research and preparation for publishing had taken considerably longer than had been anticipated, that other higher priorities had slowed progress and that the final product would be available in the near future.

Reporting on minority recruiting results, Warden Henderson noted that there had been virtually no black employees at the prison six years earlier and that now there were more than 80 African-American corrections officers, including a counselor and three lieutenants in the security force.

As for allegations of continuing problems with the grievance process, he acknowledged that there had been differences between staff and inmates regarding interpretation of various provisions in that section of the agreement, but that those contentions had been largely overcome with the application of the recently installed "substitute counsel" program.

Ms. Hunt died at a relatively early age in February of 1976. Her commitment to building a model corrections system was carried forward by her able assistant, C. Paul Phelps, who replaced her later that year. By 1980, many substantial changes had been made. The armed trustee guard abomination had been eliminated during Hunt's tenure, and the number of security officers nearly quadrupled. Four new camps had been constructed, reliev-

---

[7]Counsel substitutes (inmate legal advisors) had been created to represent prisoners charged with violations. Rights established included those facilitating the interviewing and calling of witnesses, allowing cross examination (including opposing corrections officers), and opportunity for appeal of discipline procedures to reach as high as the director of corrections.

ing severe overcrowding, and significant renovations were completed in existing housing facilities (http://angolamuseum.org/story.htm).

In January 1994, Angola was awarded its first accreditation from the American Correctional Association (ACA) and has since maintained that status. (ACA accreditation is a recognized credential for identifying an institution as stable, safe, and constitutional.) In the years that followed, LSP continued to build on its path to elevated achievement and progressive leadership remained at the helm. In 1995 an LSP museum was opened in Baton Rouge to document and preserve Angola's history and its remarkable transition from one of the most primitive prisons in the country to a model of exemplary correctional policy and practice. In 2002 Angola's correctional officers' training academy became the eighth in the nation to be accredited.

In 2005 LSP had an inmate population of over 5,000, operating with a budget of some $94 million. At this writing, Angola is said to be the only maximum security institution of its kind in the United States to offer on-site associate and baccalaureate degree programs to its inmates.

Convicts also operate the only FCC-licensed ratio station located in a maximum security prison. Several inmate-produced documentaries and other film projects have won prestigious awards, including an Oscar nomination. The extraordinary reforms and adaptations of the last three decades have been truly monumental. It is fair to say that had it not been for Elayn Hunt and her vision of achieving excellence at a time when obstacles seemed almost insurmountable, it is unlikely that the Louisiana State Penitentiary would have risen from the depths of ancient standards to the heights of its ultimate accomplishment. Her recognition of the mediation process as precisely the right device for instituting change is powerful witness to the creative possibilities that can materialize in a process of good faith negotiation under effective neutral third-party guidance.

The only tragedy was that she did not live to see her vision come to full fruition.

JEFFERSON PARISH JAIL, LOUISIANA
AND SELECTED PRISON CASES

Together we must learn to compose the differences,
not with arms, but with intellect and decent purpose.

—Dwight D. Eisenhower

ANOTHER PERSPECTIVE

I have chosen to include this additional chapter on court-referred prison mediation, this time from a somewhat different frame of reference than that of the previous chapter. Rather than focus on *the process itself* and how it played out in other corrections settings, this segment will give greater emphasis to *external* perceptions, primarily those of the federal judges from whom the earliest referrals originated, from others who found themselves to be participants in the process, and yet others who simply sought to familiarize themselves with the nature of the experiment of settling convict grievances through third-party-arranged negotiation.

It was not merely coincidental that the second penal custody case to be referred to our agency should also come from the state of Louisiana.[1] Several factors influenced that outcome. Perhaps most prevailing was the fact that the state's single maximum security prison at Angola had already demonstrated prospects for the productive use of mediation in a correctional environment. It had shown, too, that the political risks could well be of little consequence. Louisiana Governor Edwin Edwards had gambled by acquiescing and apparently had lost no public favor. Local elected officials could find some comfort in offering endorsement, or at least refraining from opposition, should another warden of a state facility or a parish[2] sheriff be confronted with a litigious inmate population and

---

[1] Inmate allegations, Jefferson Parish Jail, Louisiana, referred by Judge Jack M. Gordon, United States District Court, Eastern District of Louisiana.
[2] A political subdivision in the state of Louisiana corresponding to a county in other states.

requested by the court to make a decision regarding "voluntary negotiation" as an alternative to litigation.

There were influences other than judicial persuasion that tended to further open doors to correctional mediation. The 1970s was a time of growing unrest among those incarcerated in the nation's jails and prisons. With a disproportionate number of African-American inmates (and increasing Hispanic imbalances in some parts of the country), the momentum of federal civil rights legislation enacted almost a decade earlier had not bypassed prisoners seeking relief from perceived abuses by their keepers. Tying their grievances to constitutional guarantees and/or newly created antidiscrimination legal requirements, the federal courts were becoming clogged with petitions for redress that were beyond their capacity to address in a timely manner. Interracial tensions and the incidence of violent conflict between racial-ethnic factions in the prison population, and between convicts and security personnel, were commonplace. Thoughtful corrections administrators were coming to recognize that there was something to be said for improving prisoner-staff relationships if a desired level of nonviolence was to be successfully achieved. Innovative ways to communicate and to understand inherently antagonistic roles and perspectives were beginning to make inroads into the legendary and seemingly inevitable acrimony so characteristic of the nation's corrections systems. Those first few administrative officials who were ready to allow inmates a virtual degree of power-sharing by negotiating complaints face-to-face across a table from them were probably looked upon by many of their peers as having lost their senses.

But the culture involving responsibility for institutional incarceration dies hard. Counterbalancing a willingness by some professionals to explore new avenues for change, an overwhelming number of such officials resisted and rejected any outsiders whom they saw as unwelcome intruders in a business about which they knew more than anyone else (a posture certainly not entirely without merit—after all, it was *their* profession). When Jefferson Parish Sheriff Alwynn Cronvich, whose charges in his parish jail were busy filing law suits, was first introduced by the court to the notion of negotiating issues with inmates, he was not surprisingly said to have been incensed. Such a prospect, it might be anticipated, would seem to him to be an incredibly naive and impractical invention. And this sheriff was no hardened traditionalist. He had already established himself as a progressive among his professional colleagues. In the decade or so before the time of Judge Gordon's proposal to try mediation, he had instituted numerous ambitious and desirable programs to raise qualifications of deputies and to provide them with upgraded training. He had established a cadet program, a crime lab, and a neighborhood watch program. He was not a man without instincts for improving and modernizing law enforcement practices in his bailiwick, a suburban bedroom community wrapped around New Orleans with nearly a half million inhabitants.

Were it not for Sheriff Cronvich's having consulted with Warden Murray Henderson, an active participant in the recently concluded Louisiana State Penitentiary (LSP) case, he might well have asserted his right to decline the court's proposed alternative to legal contests. So it came to pass that those inmates confined to the Jefferson Parish jail during this time of heightened awareness of offender rights litigation were among those who brought allegations of abuse and denial of rights against their jailers' policies and practices.

As already indicated, because the nature of procedures, issues, and roles in this and other later corrections mediation cases were not sufficiently different from those in the Louisiana State Penitentiary narrative, there is no need to dwell further on such description. Rather, we turn here to how this intriguing novelty of dealing with confinement in the criminal justice system was viewed from a distance—by the courts, by political observers, by the media, and by other prospective parties seeking to evaluate mediation as a conflict management tool in their own institutional settings.

A MIXED RETROSPECTIVE

Early in 1972 in New Orleans, a group of 5th Circuit judges met with the author, then regional mediator for the Community Relations Service (CRS) based in Dallas. Through arrangements made by our Dallas office with Fifth Circuit Chief Judge John R. Brown, they had agreed to an exploratory roundtable discussion of potentials for court-referred mediation. The idea of an extrajudicial alternative to certain of their pending cases seemed to some of them, at least, worth examination. Several of the justices could not veil their skepticism. Some pressed for assurances against running afoul of their inherent responsibilities (of which I could offer little confirmation, having had no previous related experience).

It wasn't long before the dialogue turned to growing concerns over the monumental caseload on the dockets of so many of the federal courts brought on by petitions from inmates in jails and prisons around the country. It was a subject that gave impetus to a more positive outlook among those assembled. It seemed to be a possible port in a storm they were eager to circumvent. In the end, it was two of the eight or ten judges assembled that day who took the plunge by engaging CRS to partner in the mediation experiment.

The first jurist on the federal bench to raise the lid of uncertainty and peer inside the proposal package was Judge E. Gordon West of the Middle District of Louisiana in Baton Rouge. Like many of his colleagues, he was wrestling with daunting legal and administrative overload challenges emanating particularly from convicts at the Louisiana State Penitentiary (LSP) in nearby Angola. The story of that prototype probe into the mediation process was the subject of the preceding chapter. But what of the outcome, at least from Judge West's perspective? How did he see the consequences of his decision to follow his instincts rather than bow to customary practice?

The answer to those questions is perhaps best illustrated in a memorandum prepared by Dorothy Beasley, an assistant attorney general for the state of Georgia, who had contacted several judges for assessments of their experience with mediation referral to CRS. It was in the year following the end of the Angola case (late 1973) that she contacted Louisiana Judges West and Gordon. Their responses to her inquiry were to be shared with a federal district judge in Georgia, Anthony Alaimo, who had apparently made initial contact with the state attorney general's office seeking information about procedures, implementation orders, and so forth for possible adaptation on similar cases pending in his court.

Judge West, in his response, provided the Georgia official with a detailed developmental account of his decision to try mediation at LSP, how the process related to pending case status, and how he perceived the effectiveness of the experiment. Key points shared with Ms. Beasley included:

- The referral of mediation to state corrections officials was handled informally. There was no order staying any of the cases pending results of mediation. He simply held them in abeyance. Some cases were withdrawn by the plaintiffs as a result of the negotiated written agreement whereas others that dealt with issues not resolved at the table remained active (some pending cases included personal individual incidents of alleged wrongdoing for which relief was sought and which were not permitted a place on the mediation agenda).
- Neither the judge nor anyone representing the court took part in any of the mediation proceedings.
- The process prescribed by CRS to select negotiating teams representing the institution and the inmates was described in some detail without any findings of legal incompatibility. Attention was also given to the nature and compre-

hensiveness of the mediator's separate orientation meetings with representatives of both parties, preparing them for engaging in joint sessions. The judge agreed to send to Ms. Beasley a copy of the final mediated agreement.

- In the weeks and months following the conclusion of mediation, the court received complaints from some prisoners that prison authorities were not fully abiding by the terms of the agreement. At the time of this Georgia inquiry, Judge West was awaiting the arrival of a new magistrate whom he intended to assign to hold hearings on those matters determined to be worthy of evaluation. Certain unresolved issues regarding medical care and disciplinary measures in one of the pending petitions were said to have been referred by the court to the Civil Rights Division of the Prison Mediation Commentary U.S. Department of Justice for intervention in that one case.

- The judge pointed out that the mediation process was intended to render the pending law suits moot and that he was disappointed with the extent to which administrators had apparently failed to implement reforms agreed upon. They had been accused by plaintiffs of neglect and willful lack of good faith. After having his expectations soar as the mediation proceedings went forward, the aftermath implementation problems, he said, presented an unanticipated letdown. It was on this critical element of Judge West's assessment that discussion led to a possible strategy that could overcome such a troubling outcome. It was proposed in his exchange with the Georgia official that a mediator, or several mediators, independent of the department of corrections, be made available by the state on a continuing basis to monitor implementation of mediated agreements. When necessary, they could reconvene the parties to settle differences or at least to clarify lingering problems in connection with performance deficiencies. Such intermediaries, it was suggested, could be drawn from universities or other resources with appropriate expertise. The idea struck Judge West as quite possibly being the necessary ingredient to resurrect his earlier faith in the practicality of the mediation option in dealing with one of his knottiest classes of cases.

- One question of judicial concern expressed by Judge West went to the matter of whether or not a mediated agreement can be binding on inmates who come into the system after the document is ratified. It was a question yet to be definitively answered, but about which he had little confidence in its having the legal legs upon which to stand.

- Clearly, Judge West's early enthusiasm for the potential of mediation as an alternative to litigation was sorely tested by what he saw in the execution stage as a distressing conundrum. It is well to recognize, however, that conditions at Angola did in fact make quite remarkable progress in the years following mediation, but not until some time after Ms. Beasley's inquiry. To many observers it was to be expected that the implementation of some provisions of the agreement would not be accomplished overnight. Later testimony from LSP administrators before the U.S. Commission on Civil Rights would lend credence to that assertion. When examined in its entirety, what appeared on the surface to be a relatively simple objective was shown often to require considerably more time than could have been anticipated.

The ultimate reforms that led to national recognition for major changes and improvements in facilities and operational practices at Angola have already been described on the final pages of Chapter 5. The extent to which those very significant developments could be attributed to the stimulation brought on by the mediation experience can be only a matter of conjecture.

A SECOND OPINION FROM LOUISIANA: CHAMPION
OF COURT-REFERRED MEDIATION: THE JEFFERSON PARISH JAIL CASE

In contrast to the state penitentiary case, the second federal judge in Louisiana to embrace mediation in an attempt to resolve pending inmate litigation (referenced earlier in this chapter), found the experience to be worthy of high marks, to say the least. Judge Jack M. Gordon, sitting on his district court bench in New Orleans, had followed the earlier Angola proceedings with great interest. He had been one of the Fifth Circuit justices who attended my orientation session in New Orleans well over a year earlier. After consultations with Judge West, who apparently encouraged him to proceed, Judge Gordon decided to pursue a parallel course of action with regard to filings pending in his court from offenders being held at the Jefferson Parish jail located in New Orleans' largest suburb.

It was the same Georgia state attorney who had contacted Judge West on behalf of a federal court judge in her jurisdiction who was coupling her inquiry with Judge Gordon's mediation experience, just concluded a few months earlier. A record of her telephone contacts with Judge Gordon reflects the court's opinions and conclusions.[3]

The referral to mediation, as in the LSP instance, was described by the judge as informal and without any order being entered. He had called in the parties to the pending lead suit and orally "persuaded" them to engage in mediation. The following were response highlights of the inquiry exchange:

- Only one significant issue of those on the mediation agenda had not been resolved (concerning mail privileges), and that was later scheduled for trial. Otherwise, the entire scope of first amendment rights were laid to rest. It was the judge's observation that the mail privilege issue too, would have been dealt with successfully had it not been for the fact that the plaintiffs' attorneys seemed to see that part of the complaint package as an opportunity to establish legal precedent.
- The judge expressed unreserved commendation for the process and the way in which it was conducted. He characterized the procedure and the results as being nothing less than "remarkable." Bringing disputants closer together to find common ground instead of driving them further apart in an adversarial legal action, he indicated, was a superior concept. He was especially impressed with the marked changes in the posture of the sheriff who chaired the respondent team and whose attitude toward the inmate team was gradually transformed during mediation from undisguised repudiation and hostility to genuine respect and sensitivity.
- The plaintiffs were said to be represented by energetic and determined reform-minded attorneys. Known for his personal commitment to judicial restraint, Judge Gordon was mindful of the fact that neither judges nor attorneys nor other lay people know much about the subcultures and complexities of running a jail or prison. But he also suspected that conditions at the Jefferson Parish jail might well fail to meet constitutional standards, and he was committed to an equitable determination and to whatever changes might be justified.
- The inquiring Georgia official was interested in details of how, when, and where joint sessions were held and how the mediation team participants were

---

[3]Memorandum dated September 14, 1973, Interoffice correspondence from Dorothy Beasley to file, Department of Law, State of Georgia.

selected and introduced to the process. Judge Gordon described such particulars, pointing out that circumstances in a local jail can be quite distinct from a state-run prison. In the case of the Jefferson Parish jail, just as might be expected in similar county or municipal confinement facilities, there was not even suitable space to accommodate acceptable physical arrangements for mediation. The sheriff had to be willing to allow the inmate team members to leave the jail and go to the nearby courthouse, the most convenient and readily accessible alternative site, where the sessions would have to be held.

- Reaching accord required six half-day meetings. At the request of the parties (and much to the surprise of the mediator, given the court's initially stated intention to remain detached), the judge agreed to attend one of the later sessions at which there was a stalemate over the question of mail privileges. Even though there was no final resolution to this one impasse, the judge observed that the inmates seemed quite disposed to accepting changes proposed by the respondent team but, as previously noted, apparently were dissuaded by their attorney-advisors. Beyond reaching any accord in this segment, however, there were said to be noteworthy signs of greater understanding and sensitivity between the principals that seemed to be enhanced during this thwarted exercise and in spite of its futility. The judge's first-hand observations of the interaction between the teams led him to conclude that beyond any installed reforms, he could see alterations in traditional role images and attitudes that could only lead to an improved climate in jail operations. He felt, in his words, that relationships between the principals "were a thousand percent improved and a thousand percent better than would have resulted had he imposed his own order." His summary of further observations included:

- One very significant aspect of the use of mediation for parties in a local jurisdiction is the fact that offenders are generally being held for much shorter periods of time than they would be when confined to a state facility. Many such inmates are simply awaiting transfer to a penitentiary to serve a longer sentence than a jail is intended to provide. Therefore, there is likely to be less continuity and less sustained effect on the part of those confined as a result of participation in, or witnessing of, the mediation experience. But as for the impact upon jail leadership and personnel, whether in administrative, security, or other functions, there can be important and lasting changes in policy, practice, and relationship modification, their tenure being generally stable and their career interests being influenced by new developments in their assigned responsibilities.

- The court was particularly taken with the way in which CRS used resource professionals to consult with the parties and to provide neutral expertise during deliberations. In the present case in Jefferson Parish (as in the Angola proceedings), a former warden of a federal penal institution and a CRS staff corrections specialist, James Freeman by name (who was also African-American, as were all but one of the inmate team members), participated in the team orientations. He had won the confidence of all concerned before they came to the table to begin negotiations. His contributions to the success of the outcome were considerable.

- Emphasis was given to the fact that there is a tendency among opposing parties in litigation to adopt extreme positions with the expectation that they may influence a judge or jury to award them what could be seen as a favorable verdict. Although such a strategy may characterize early positions in mediation as well, such inclinations are expected to be much less likely in mediation where there is no arbiter to try to influence.

- The judge made it clear to me and to the parties that they should not feel constrained to deal only with the issues set forth in the pretrial order. He wanted the agenda to be open-ended to allow any previously unidentified problems that might surface during mediation to qualify for attention. Any issues enumerated in the pending law suits that were resolved in a mediated signed agreement were to be eliminated by a pretrial order declaring such matters to be moot.
- In his concluding remarks to Ms. Beasley, Judge Gordon said he would welcome any further inquiry directly from Judge Alaimo and that his enthusiasm for the mediation process was such as to see it as a viable court-referral option in many types of community disputes. He said further that he wouldn't hesitate to champion the cause of mediation and the use of the Community Relations Service in that role and that he couldn't understand why such a meritorious concept hadn't resulted in far greater demand from the judiciary for such assistance.

In a separate documented response to an inquiry almost a year later from a CRS legal staff member in the New York regional office, Judge Gordon touched on several observations not reflected in the earlier inquiry from the Georgia Law Department. Among them:

- It was nothing short of amazing, he said, to see the chemistry at work during negotiations. Each side could be seen trying to outdo the other in finding workable accommodations to agenda issues. As the process progressed, both sides became more open to compromise, "to lessen their demands and to work out equitable solutions..." He was particularly struck with the fact that in most civil rights confrontations one of the great problems is the lack of meaningful contact and communication between leaders of opposing parties.
- It was pointed out that that it would be a mistake for a judge to approach the concept of mediation with the notion that it would resolve all inmate-initiated pending cases and significantly lessen the case load. Rather, he would say mediation should be referred by a court in the hope that there would be improved relationships between the parties, that there would be agreement to work together voluntarily to repair differences, and that there would be a recognition of the fact that resolution of issues in contention according to the strict letter of the law can be a less satisfactory option for settlement. His experience in the Jefferson Parish case suggested to him that inmates can achieve greater benefits through mediation than they could though litigation. He underscored the right of plaintiffs to return to legal remedy when mediation proves wanting.
- Questioned about the terminology used in his opinion referring to the mediated agreement as "binding," he said he had not intended to use that term in a strictly legal sense because it could not be held binding on future generations of prisoners; but he would consider it binding on the sheriff who signed it. As a practical matter, however, he thought it to be binding on everyone because, in the final analysis, he has found that both prisoners and officials want peace. In support of that assessment he pointed out that since the conclusion of mediation in the Jefferson Parish case, he had not heard of any problems at the jail and he had received no further filings in his court.

Upon conclusion of the Jefferson Parish Jail mediation and the subsequent trial to settle the single unresolved issue of regulations governing inmate mail privileges, Judge Gordon issued an opinion that was seen to be unprecedented in the annals of federal court proceedings. A substantial portion of the document was devoted to the mediation effort and the manner in which it was carried out.[4] In a post-trial follow-up letter to the mediator, the judge stated that he chose to incorporate such information as a way to pass along the successful experience to others.

THE GEORGIA STATE PENITENTIARY AT REIDSVILLE

This third example of CRS prison mediation illustrates certain aspects of this class of cases that were not found in the two previously discussed actions in Louisiana. Again, there is minimal attention given to process details except where they reflect elements that have not been touched upon in earlier cases.

In this instance, the only documentation of these proceedings available for review was a series of cassette tape recordings. After considering its usefulness as a training tool and as a reliable verbatim account for possible future reference, the parties had agreed in advance to allow such recording by either or both the mediator and the respondent team. Only two in a series of five multiple sessions recorded have been available to the author, those having been the first and second of the five sessions. So even though there was less than half the total time recorded accessible for reporting here, there was sufficient content to make the inclusion of certain aspects of this case worthwhile.

The Reidsville facility, one of fifteen in the Georgia penal system, is located in the southeastern part of the state, some sixty miles west of Savannah. It housed maximum security convicts including many transferred from other locations because of serious violations of security regulations or other behavioral problems that required confinement in a more controlled environment.

Unlike so many of his colleagues who were attempting to deal expeditiously with inmate petitions on crowded dockets, Federal District Court Judge Anthony Alaimo did not initiate the mediation request. Rather, he was responding to a contact from Dr. Allen Ault, the Georgia Commissioner of Corrections. Dr. Ault was concerned about unrest at the penitentiary after a serious incident, and wished to investigate mediation, having learned about the Louisiana cases. It was after that contact that the judge requested the state attorney general's office to seek detailed information about those court-referred experiences (already described in this chapter). Having received such information, and having concluded that mediation was worth investigating, he contacted CRS for further exploration and ultimately to take the preliminary steps necessary to set the stage for mediation.

TEAM ORIENTATION

In the usual process progression, orientation meetings were held first with the institutional representatives including the commissioner of corrections and members of his senior Reidsville staff and state legal counsel. There followed meetings with selected inmates, among those with legal briefs pending in the federal court, along with several of their pro bono legal assistance attorneys from Atlanta. Joining me at the table as a CRS corrections consultant was Bert Griggs, superintendent at the Chino Institute for Men in California, a penitentiary recognized for successful reform innovations. During the course of these

---

[4]For a full reproduction of the court's opinion, see Addendum C: Frazier v. Donelon, 381 F.Supp 911 (1974), action instituted pursuant to 42 U.S.C./1983 and 28 U.S.C. 1343. The court appended to this opinion the final mediated settlement agreement between the jail authorities and the inmates.

meetings there were several developments and observations that were not common to earlier descriptions of this phase of premediation preparation and are therefore cited here:

- It was agreed that case discovery activity would be held in abeyance until mediation was concluded, whether or not it was successful. It was also made clear that engaging in mediation in no way affected the right of inmates to return to court in connection with whatever issues might remain unresolved.
- Because many of the expected participants (attorneys, state officials, observers, resource specialists, etc.) would have to be commuting from Atlanta (over 200 road miles) or other distant locations, and because many of them had potentially conflicting priorities, commitments and responsibilities, I was obliged to give the strongest possible emphasis to the fact that the time required to participate in negotiations would be substantially longer than they were likely to envision and that they should not commit to mediation unless they were willing and able, without reservation, to make the necessary and extensive time available at Reidsville.
- It was decided during preliminaries that the mediation agenda would be divided into two phases. The first phase would consider those issues that exclusively impacted only black inmates. The second phase would deal with problems that largely affected the entire population without any particular regard to questions of race. That seemingly rational provision proved to be more complex than originally anticipated. For example, one assertion had to do with discriminatory job assignments—that the more undesirable jobs were given to blacks. At first thought to be suitable for phase I, it was quickly recognized that changing job assignment patterns would undoubtedly affect nonminority inmates equally. There was also a question raised as to whether phase II deliberations might require a change in the composition of the inmate mediation team.
- Both sides agreed that it would be of utmost importance to assure that the entire prison population, as well as employees, be kept as fully informed as possible of the nature of the proceedings and the progress of negotiations. This would be accomplished through periodic meetings and through written communication arranged by institutional personnel, subject to review and coordination by the inmate team.
- The question of which inmates would serve on the complainant team raised important issues. Many of the pending court petitions were filed by plaintiffs all living in a single dormitory. That fact was seen to be problematic in that those individuals were clearly unrepresentative of the general population, especially significant because some of the core allegations had to do with conditions said to exist in cell blocks and dormitories well beyond those occupied by the complainant inmates. It had further implications in that various wings in which prisoners were confined were also differentiated with regard to the level of security imposed. Recognizing these imbalances as valid impediments to a satisfactory process, it was decided to reduce the number of plaintiffs of record on the team and to have as many as five alternates (a total of ten on the team, plus counsel) to help assure a more inclusive representation.

The Reidsville case provided a distinct illustration of one of the mediator's more earnest admonitions to the parties when arranging for joint sessions. The ideal circumstances of the site to be utilized have been referenced elsewhere on these pages. Mediators are quite accustomed to usually good-natured teasing about our concerns for the shape of the table or the positioning of negotiators as they prepare for engagement. But the fact is that the physical environment in which proceedings are held can have very considerable ramifications, well illustrated in this instance.

The Georgia penitentiary visitors' room was a cavernous space in which we would spend many long hours in dialogue and consultation. Although it left much to be desired in the way of comfort amenities, it had been determined to be the most practical place in the institution to meet elemental requirements for accommodating as many as 30 or 40 seated participants and observers. It did provide a suitable area for caucus privacy, convenient access to rest rooms and telephones (no cell phones in those days!), practical security arrangements, reasonable temperature control, and so forth. Part of the reason for the poor audio quality of the tapes upon which the substance of this narrative was drawn was an exceptionally noisy air conditioner. Clanging steel doors, amplified ringing of telephones, and the flushing of nearby toilets sometimes interfered with participants hearing and understanding one another just from one end of the table to the other. Clearly, it was a marginal site for mediation, but one to which we all had to adapt.

Dr. Ault suggested that it was his intention to appoint subcommittees from his management team during recess periods away from the table. Doing so would enable him to examine first-hand evidence in connection with inmate claims of observable problems of substandard facilities/conditions or routine practices. His intention found no objection, as it would obviously help management deal with issues on the table with greater effectiveness. It was also agreed that prison specialists/supervisors in anticipated problem areas such as food service, medical care, security, and so forth could be called to the table to provide direct "testimony" regarding activities and conditions with which they were the most familiar.

During the initial administrative team orientation phase I was asked to describe a "typical" mediation session. My answer: "There is no such thing as typical." At times, I suggested, those at the table would be alternately bored, angry, excited and hopeful, or dismayed, discouraged, and ready to throw in the towel. Beyond that, it was hard to say.

The inmates were cautioned by the mediator during orientation to couple their allegations with suggestions for resolution, even if they felt they didn't have sufficient knowledge about the causes of the problem or of what corrective measures would be appropriate or practical. Given equally strong emphasis to the respondent team during their orientations was the fact that *the perceptions* of problems among members of the prisoner team may bring on even more intransigence than the actual existence of a wrongful condition or action. In other words, if it *appears* as a problem, it matters little as to whether it is a valid charge. It must be received by respondents with the same consideration that would be expected if the allegations were supported by sound evidence. As such, it was pointed out that moderating or eliminating faulty perceptions may be as difficult but as important as taking corrective measures to fix a confirmed problem.

The question was raised as to whether or not a written, signed mediation agreement, in the absence of a consent decree from the court, would be held to be an enforceable contract between the parties. No one present could speak confidently to that issue. To our collective best knowledge, there had been no legal test in that regard.

Always a matter of great concern, especially among institutional respondents, is the matter of dealing with the media when they get wind of newsworthy developments, as they almost inevitably do. In this Georgia case, and typically in most other like situations, there was a tug of reasoning in opposite directions as to the best way to respond to journalistic probing. On the one hand, when giving frequent and extended access to the media, there is always the risk of reporting inaccuracies or misleading information resulting sometimes in unnecessary damage to public perceptions. There is also the hazard of creating false negative reactions between the opposing negotiating teams when a statement from one side or the other creates irritation or worse.

As a matter of standard practice, the mediator generally sets the guidelines for media relations, establishing that he/she be the only source authorized to respond to such contacts. Commissioner Ault was especially sensitive to the need to avoid any appearance of secrecy. He shared with CRS the desire to spread the word about the use of mediation as an alternative to legal action. The key understanding was that the mediator, in responding to news people, would avoid any public references to the identity of issues on the agenda, the status of proceedings or the positions of the parties. Rather, emphasis would be given to the nature of the process of mediation, who the parties were, and at appropriate times when the parties were ready, to announce any significant updated developments suitable for public dissemination. It was also understood that once mediation was concluded, the parties would be free to express whatever views they felt were appropriate.

Attention was drawn during orientation sessions to the question of handling an impasse situation. I underscored two options: (a) Set the issue aside for a time, returning to it at a later point in proceedings in the hope that positions might moderate; (b) Accept the reality of being unable to reach accord and recognize that among ten major agenda items and a score of subissues, one or two deadlocks need not impair overall achievement.

A question was raised as to whether or not it would be necessary or desirable and practical for any agreement to be ratified by the entire inmate population before being adopted for implementation. The subject had not arisen in previous prison cases. It was decided to set the matter aside for possible later consideration. It did not arise again.

AT THE TABLE PRELUDE

The first series of joint sessions was held on January 16-17, 1974. The mediator introduced all participants and acknowledged several guest observers. Commissioner Allen Ault chaired the respondent team with Warden Joe Hopper as vice chair. They were joined by three more primary team members (the deputy warden, the assistant warden for security, and the deputy commissioner for inmate administration from Atlanta), and by two attorneys from the State Department of Law, also from Atlanta. There were no designated alternates on the management side.

Because Dr. Ault was interested in exposing to mediation key officials from outside his domain (at least partly in anticipation of developing later corollary relationships that might be useful in possible future conflict resolution activity in the Georgia prison system), he invited a number of observers to attend the sessions if they so desired, as their schedules permitted. The action was taken with the consent of spokesmen for the inmate team. Among them were two faculty members from the University of Georgia in Athens, both with the Corrections Division of the Institute of Government. Also attending some sessions were a parole board review officer, the chairman of the state institutions committee of the Georgia legislature, and the chairmen of the state senate and house penal affairs committees.

The inmate team was chaired and vice-chaired by James Watson and Arthur Guthrie, respectively, both African Americans. Available records for this account do not indicate which members of the inmate team of five principals and four alternates were black, but if memory serves, only one of the nine was Caucasian. Joining this side of the table were three attorneys, all from the Legal Aid office in Atlanta and all connected to plaintiff representation in the pending cases before Judge Alaimo—Sanford Bishop (lead), Henrietta Turnquist, and Nolan Caulfield.

Preliminary matters discussed included: (a) Exchanges and collection of information and materials between one or another of the team leaders and Judge Alaimo, and/or between the two team chairmen, was seen to have led to duplication and confusion; it was agreed to channel any off-session written communication through the mediator; (b) Key procedural guidelines were revisited, including rules limiting participation during table dialogue to the five designated team principals and their counsel, but allowing alternates to engage in private caucus discussion; (c) The mediator reemphasized that time would be a most precious commodity and that it would take cooperation from everyone to avoid wasteful diversions, especially departures from the agenda. Caution was also strongly advised in calling for excessive or unnecessary caucus breaks. Given the fact that a significant number of team members on both sides had to commute to the prison from considerable distances, it was pointed out that economy of time utilization was of particular importance; (d) Attention was drawn to the agenda issue calling for desegregation of all functional areas of the prison (cell blocks/dormitories, dining halls, recreation facilities, medical clinic, etc.). It was made known that an option was available through CRS resources to consult with representatives of the state prison in Jefferson City, Missouri, where successful desegregation had been recently implemented; (e) I appealed to all at the table for patience in dealing with issues and probable irritation likely to surface in clashes of personality and/or contravening positions; (f) Dr. Ault stated that any agreement resulting from mediation would be submitted to the Board of Corrections for endorsement and, if approved, would become departmental policy. Both sides, it was acknowledged, wanted an enforceable agreement, with or without a forthcoming court consent decree; (g) Dissatisfaction expressed by inmate counsel centered on the mediator's confidential contacts known to have been made with Judge Alaimo. Explanation of the substance of those visits as being concerned only with *procedural* matters was sufficient to relieve apprehensions, along with assurances that matters of agenda progress and party positioning would be shared with the court only as a result of joint consideration and with approval by both parties.

CORE AGENDA ISSUES

In constructing the agenda during consultations with representatives from both negotiating teams, it had been decided that the first issue to be deliberated would be the alleged disparities in living conditions between cell blocks and dormitories occupied by black prisoners as contrasted to those housing nonminorities.

A management spokesman began by presenting word pictures of the five four-story buildings in which all the population was found while confined to quarters, identifying in which wings and which floors each racial group resided. After a description of the physical layout, complainant team counsel proceeded to deliver a detailed enumeration of alleged inequities. Emphasis was given to faulty commodes, lack of hot water, wet/damp floors (under bunks were said to be the only place occupants could store personal belongings, subject to the risk of being damaged by excessive moisture), inoperable sinks and showers, and poor lighting, heating, and ventilation. These grievances were presented without suggesting an unequal *number* of such inequities, but rather claiming a significant disparity in the *condition* of such.

Responding to this set of complaints, Dr. Ault and various spokesmen for the institutional team explained in some detail past and current efforts to obtain funds from the departmental budget office for a long list of repair and replacement needs to improve such conditions throughout the institution. A contract was said to have already be let for new lighting equipment. The administration's history of frustration and discouragement in obtaining necessary funding for renovations (for structures built in 1936) was articulated with convincing evidence of vigorous and persistent effort.

Countering that position was the inmate claim of *disproportionate deterioration* of physical properties based on *the racial composition of occupants*, a condition separate and apart, they said, from available overall funding to improve infrastructure. After extensive discussion, respondents agreed to perform a careful inspection of the various quarters in question to determine the extent to which the inequity allegations were valid. It was suggested that the black inmates had no way of knowing what conditions existed in the white-only sections and that they were drawing assumptions without the ability to confirm their conclusions from actual observation (parried by the opposition with contrary argumentation). The issue was tabled until an inspection could be done and examined again at a later session. The funding availability obstacle, it was recognized, would still likely limit the extent of corrective measures that might be taken.

The next agenda topic opened was considered by most to underlie any other reform initiatives, albeit among the most daunting to be confronted—prison-wide desegregation. The Georgia state corrections system had been under court-ordered desegregation for some period of time. Implementation had been delayed because of anticipated disruption and prospects for serious tensions, possibly resulting in violence with a breakdown of security control. Buoyed by successful like action in penitentiaries elsewhere in the country, Dr. Ault announced his determination to move ahead in carrying out the lawfully mandated requirement. He proposed to meet with inmates and staff at various levels of operation and to prepare a plan that could be executed with the least disruption or threat to safety. A target date was put forward for implementation by March 1, allowing some six weeks for consultations, research, and plan development. A specific date was said to be inadvisable, given the variables likely to be encountered.

Unexpectedly, inmate team spokesmen, after caucusing, took issue with the timing of the proposal. They submitted that four weeks, rather than six, would be ample time to accomplish the task and vigorously defended that contention. At this point there ensued one of the lengthiest debates of the entire process. Dr. Ault, with firmness but showing no irritation, suggested that if inmate counsels' objective was to win concessions instead of trying to find the most promising and peaceful path to their mutually agreed upon goal of eliminating segregation, it would be difficult to reach satisfactory resolution. He went on to elaborate further on the litany of steps he foresaw being required to finalize a desegregation plan. He recounted some of the specific activity that good planning would require—researching the experiences of other state prisons that had been successfully desegregated, consulting with inmates and employees about their ideas for a peaceful transition, anticipating problems and establishing goal-setting, pressing for legislative support for adequate funding to accomplish renovations, and so forth. Not surprisingly, side issues began to emerge adding complexity to what was originally a rather simple matter—the determination of a date for performance of a major operational transition that both sides agreed was vital to any meaningful reform.

One of the related concerns bearing on the desegregation challenge was the condition of severe overcrowding. Desegregation, by allowing more flexibility in housing assignment, would tend to provide some relief. It followed that a program to increase parole release would likewise offer some degree of remedy. But because parole policy and decisions were outside the authority of prison administrators (in the hands of a totally independent state parole board), the institutional team could make little commitment beyond promising an effort to persuade the parole board of the need to possibly liberalize standards and procedures that would result in higher numbers of qualified parolees being released.

A point had been reached when patience was wearing thin, particularly for Dr. Ault and his associates. Legal bickering among attorneys on both sides and nit-picking over relatively inconsequential differences on wording and such, were becoming a serious impediment to timely progress. Further irritation was beginning to show also because the inmate attorneys had been, since the beginning of negotiations, the principal negotiators and spokespersons for their clients, rather than having adopted a more passive and intended role as legal advisors. To exacerbate matters, when the joint session on February 27 was convened, the inmate team appeared with what was then a fourth attorney (a law professor from Rutgers University in New Jersey) to be seated at the table. This was the meeting at which the GSP team would lay on the table its plan for facility desegregation. It would later lead to a proposal to limit participation on either team to a single attorney-advisor.

The session began with a report by Dr. Ault on visits he made, along with his deputy and me, to the Louisiana State Penitentiary at Angola and to Jefferson City, Missouri, where inmate populations had been successfully integrated. A tentative plan outline was presented said to have been based on more than 600 pages of investigation notes, including results of visits with both staff and inmates at the two out-of-state institutions. It was pointed out that any desegregation plan would necessarily apply to the entire state penal system facilities at some 15 scattered sites involving well over 3,000 prisoners. It was acknowledged that this initial plan would be lacking in many details of implementation, and was characterized as a concept offering to be later developed into a full-fledged program document.

Not surprisingly, inmate counsels voiced many concerns with what they implied was too little and too late. First, they expressed dissent over any delay that would be occasioned by the need to desegregate the entire system at the same time. It was said that mediation had been pursued in an effort to deal with conditions at Reidsville without regard to other system facilities, and that corrective measures should not be encumbered by any wider considerations that would dilute progress at the principal target institution.

Another point of contention revolved around the question of whether to initiate desegregation in phases (dorms, cell blocks, dining halls) as favored by the management team or to do it all at one time throughout the entire complex, as favored by the inmate spokesmen. A new camera security system was said to have been approved under a federal grant but had not yet been endorsed with state matching funds. If and when installed, it was expected that such equipment would help the understaffed guard force to deal more effectively with threats to inmate safety and to improve overall security conditions.

The administration team was particularly intent on establishing a series of 5-member inmate committees, one from each dormitory or cell block (four elected by secret ballot and one appointed by the warden) that would play a significant part in deciding on the best courses to bring about desegregation. The warden would have veto power to disqualify any one elected inmate he deemed unsuitable for the assignment, after which a second election would be held for that slot, the results of which the warden would have no option to overrule. Such committee members would be given appropriate identification badges and given free access to various parts of the prison in working out plan details for housing together compatible members of the population.

The second day in this series of deliberations was devoted to:

- Minority staff recruiting, in which one of every two vacancies would be filled by a black candidate (given qualified availability) until parity with the racial composition of the prison population was reached (41% black).
- A proposal by the institutional team set forth that: (a) inmate elections drawing upon each housing unit to form a composite committee be held within the next two weeks, after which those elected would be given appropriate orientation as to their responsibilities; (b) a new mediation team be formed from the newly elected representatives, to consist of five principals and five alter-

nates with provision for appropriate racial proportions; (c) both mediation teams to be assisted by no more than one attorney-advisor and that such counsel *not be seated at the table*, but directly behind his/her client negotiators; (d) upon agreement by the new mediation teams of desegregation plan essentials, attorneys for both sides meet in Atlanta to construct acceptable language for a finalized document; (e) a special edition of the prison newspaper that would feature current information on the nature of the desegregation plan and how it was to be implemented.

- It was further proposed that Judge Alaimo be requested to appoint a special master, to be joined by one representative from each mediation team, to deal with whatever residual issues that might arise (e.g., ongoing responsibility for maintaining desegregation, any necessary later continuation of the mediation process, etc.).

The following agreements were reached by the conclusion of these two sessions:

- A new set of rules and regulations regarding disciplinary procedures would be submitted to the board of corrections on March 11 to include: (a) the right of an inmate to face his accuser, (b) the right to counsel when appearing before a hearing panel, (c) within prescribed limits, the right to call witnesses and to cross-examine, (d) clearer definitions regarding penalties for specified infractions, (e) consideration was to be given to providing a written copy of the charges against an accused inmate scheduled to appear at a disciplinary hearing.
- A summary of any and all disciplinary action reports would be made available to any legitimate inquiry.
- Prisoners will not be subjected to involuntary transfers for punitive reasons.
- Details of the precise roles inmates would play with regard to the desegregation plan preparation and implementation would be determined in joint consultations soon after the newly elected team was chosen and organized. A resource expert on desegregation would be made available for guidance to either or both parties as circumstances require.
- Management would issue orders making clear that the security of inmates participating in mediation and/or desegregation will be protected and that any harassment or interference would not be tolerated.
- An "inmate substitute counsel" program proposal (inmates representing other inmates at disciplinary hearings) would be given careful and objective consideration by management in determining whether such a system would provide for more equity. Other such programs known to exist elsewhere in the country were to be examined and evaluated.

Two-day sessions continued into March and April. Negotiations became more contentious. Plaintiff attorneys (rather than the inmate team representatives) were showing signs of increased impatience and an erosion of confidence in mediation successfully reaching their objectives. Those objectives, though not stated in so many words, seemed to suggest a preference for having many of the issues on the table adjudicated in the courtroom rather than "voluntarily" across the table. There was growing discomfort among these reform-minded advocates that remedies needed to become legally sanctioned and would not meet that test in a written, signed agreement, even if reduced to a mandating court order. Their intention, it seemed, was to "make law" rather than simply to reach agreement.

Judge Alaimo, too, felt that the mediation process was taking longer than he had anticipated. It had been almost six months since the parties began their experiment in finding common ground. He was ready to bring them back to his courtroom for trial. The prison system was successfully desegregated and other issues were eventually laid to rest. The trial ended some ten years later.[5]

---

[5]Revealed in the author's telephone contact with Judge Alaimo on 10/21/2005, some 20 years after the case had concluded.

SCHOOL DESEGREGATION

Little Rock, Arkansas

*I fail to see how we Americans will be able to communicate effectively with . . . peoples
of other cultures when generally we don't even know how to communicate with the
neighbors next door, much less our neighbors on the other side of the tracks.*

—M. Scott Peck, M.D.
The Different Drum/Community Making and Peace (1987)

SHADES OF AN HISTORIC PAST—EQUAL EDUCATIONAL CHAOS

The saga of student desegregation at Little Rock's Central High School in 1957-58 will likely stand in the annals of the nation's civil rights legacy as a turning point that changed the course of history. *Brown v Board of Education of Topeka, Kansas* had made racially integrated public education the law of the land some three years before Arkansas Governor Orval Faubus, in early September of 1957, ordered the state's national guard to turn away nine black students attempting to enroll at Central High. Not until President Eisenhower a few weeks later, at the request of the mayor of Little Rock, sent a commanding presence of federal troops and federalized national guardsmen to the scene were the black students safely escorted into the school building. The eyes of the world were focused on a symbolic episode in America's struggle to provide its promise of equal opportunity for all.

It was out of that genesis, more than 25 years later, that the desegregation issue again came to haunt the public schools of Little Rock.

AN ATYPICAL SCENARIO

This case was included in the selections for this writing to illustrate broad applications of mediation in part because of the uniqueness of its elements. One of its more interesting and complicating distinctions centered on the nature of the parties. A typical instance of dis-

puting parties engaging in mediation of school desegregation issues would find two parties—a minority-based plaintiff group with limited resources, and often with little political clout, confronting a more powerful or influential institutional respondent accused of
discriminatory practices of one kind or another. In this circumstance, we find not two but
three principal parties with conflicting interests, each of relatively equal authority and
community standing. None of the three represented a racial or ethnic constituency. Yet the
contested issues were at the very heart of the civil rights agenda of the day.

Another notable feature of this situation was the level of media interest and coverage.
Seldom a day passed when the mediator was in town or when party representatives were
meeting on their own in connection with these proceedings, that one or more reporters
weren't camped at entrance or exit doorways before and/or after closed meetings. A court
order had been issued setting aside provisions of the state freedom of information act and
thereby barring public and media access to meetings between the parties.[1] Not surprisingly, there were many early strong and trenchant objections by many journalists regarding
what they considered to be violations of the state freedom of information statute.[2]

The two highly competitive daily newspapers were especially vigorous in their persistence. This condition was both an asset and a liability in its effect on an ultimately successful outcome. It was helpful in that the quality of reportage was generally commendable.
The public was kept well informed on an issue that was at a peak of emotionally laden concerns over prospects for long-distance busing and the perceived inevitability of resulting
disruption in the educational process. It was helpful , too, from the mediator's perspective
at least, in that the intense coverage tended to moderate antagonisms between representatives of the three parties, keeping interaction within more civil bounds.

A third unusual aspect to this case concerned the fact that the court added a previously untested dimension to the mediation process by calling for a fact-finding report to be
provided prior to the onset of negotiations and to be used as a device for forming a common denominator regarding pertinent information and perceptions by the parties and by
selected citizen observers.

CORNERS OF CONTENTION AMONG EDUCATIONAL HIERARCHIES

The urban Little Rock School District had filed suit in federal court to require two adjacent school systems (North Little Rock and Pulaski County districts) to consolidate into
a single county-wide entity in order to eliminate segregation throughout the metropolitan
area to a degree that would fully satisfy legal mandates. The action resided with Judge
Henry Woods, U.S. District Court in the Eastern District of Arkansas. Having learned of
the civil rights–related mediation experience of the Community Relations Service (CRS) of
the U.S. Department of Justice, Judge Woods decided to call upon our resources in an
attempt to provide an alternative to litigation. In his order dated May 6, 1983, he formally
requested such assistance.[3]

The court chose to have the mediator at the outset perform a fact-finding mission,
prior to the parties engaging in any negotiation, in what he described as "help he needed
with the background of the case." The move was looked upon as an attempt to distill and

---

[1]Representation on each district's team was limited to no more than one elected school board member, thereby
avoiding conflict with a key provision of the freedom of information act.
[2]Addendum D: Press clippings reflecting on media reaction to various aspects of the closed meeting ruling with
respect to mediation proceedings.
[3]Addendum E: *Little Rock School District v. Pulaski County Special School District #1*, Order No. LR-C-82-866,
dated 5/6/1983.

organize pertinent information, most of it already in the public domain, so that the court and the parties could be dealing with a commonly understood and accepted set of facts and influences.

The information gathering task was begun with a request to each of the three school district superintendents for basic current year materials such as: (a) personnel rosters, (b) any existing court orders or desegregation plans under which each district was operating, (c) maps showing attendance zones and school locations, (d) grade configurations, property age and racial composition for individual schools, (e) faculty and staff profiles by race, (f) detailed school bus transportation arrangements, patterns and costs, (g) operating budgets and sources of revenue, and (h) descriptions of elected governing boards with regard to positions and officers, history of racial composition, and method of electing board members (at-large, single-member, other).

Public perception and understanding of the court's initiatives at this early juncture was perhaps best reflected in a newspaper editorial published in one of the two Little Rock daily newspapers[4] and by a later detailed analysis on the pages of the second journal.[5]

The 33-page fact-finding report was completed at the end of August and submitted to Judge Woods and to the parties (after affording them opportunity for prerelease review, suggested corrections, and refinements). In my correspondence accompanying distribution of the report, it was pointed out to the recipients, among other matters, that: (a) the report could be used as a reference source during the mediation process; (b) the report was intended not only to bring together pertinent comparative and statistical data in a single document, but also to set forth related perceptions, from the parties as well as from interested citizens, reflecting a wide range of diverse opinion likely to generate disagreement; (c) the reliability of the mediator's condensations of 23 lengthy interviews would have to be taken in the context of interpretation, ideally accomplished with maximum concern for accuracy, balance and objective reporting.

In recognition of the need to keep the public as well informed as possible and to project an image of relative transparency as progressive stages of development were reached, Judge Woods decided to make public the mediator's report. Detailed news accounts and editorials followed, a sample of which is exhibited.[6]

Preparations for mediation team selection and orientation, and establishing a projected schedule of joint sessions, were accomplished without delay. A critical determination before final plans could be completed centered on the matter of a suitable site for conducting negotiations. For the sake of a neutral setting, facilities associated with any of the three school districts were ruled out. Hillary Rodham Clinton, then Arkansas first lady, senior partner in a prominent Little Rock law firm, and chair of the State Educational Standards Committee, had been one of the 23 individuals I interviewed in preparation of the fact-finding report previously described. It was she to whom I turned for suggestions about a site unidentified with any of the three school districts that would be conducive to comfortable, convenient, and private meetings. Graciously, she got on the phone and promptly made arrangements for us to use a conference room in the rather imposing new corporate lodge of one of Little Rock's prominent companies. Proceedings were set to begin on September 28.

Two of many news and editorial press clippings during the first week of negotiations reflect on those activities.[7]

---

[4] Addendum F: *Arkansas Gazette* editorial dated 5/14/1983.
[5] Addendum G: *Arkansas Democrat* analysis feature dated 6/26/1983.
[6] Addendum H: *Arkansas Democrat* news report dated 9/8/1983.
[7] Addendum I: Press clippings from Little Rock daily newspapers dated 9/29/1983.

The opening series of three meetings of the parties covered fourteen distinct topics:

1. media relations,
2. opening position statements,
3. plaintiff discovery proceedings,
4. elaboration on plaintiff's position on consolidation options,
5. clarifications of defendant positions regarding their denial of liability for resolving the urban district's segregation problems,
6. clarifications concerning plaintiff's terminology and rationale,
7. perceptions of causes of problems,
8. reactions to recommendations made in March 1983 by the Eighth Circuit Court of Appeals in connection with transferring and exchanging students among adjoining school districts,
9. white flight considerations,
10. remedy strategies,
11. attracting private school students to public education,
12. demographic presentation of racial distribution maps,
13. proposition to modify Little Rock School District boundary lines,
14. resource consultation with school officials from other areas that have undergone parallel desegregation challenges.[8]

By mid-October the negotiating teams had been convened six times, each for periods of from 2 1/2 to 7 hours. Several consolidation proposals had drawn interest but none produced unanimity. Three proposals on the table, some drawing on elements extracted from information delivered by the consultants, were ultimately rejected. Content ran the gamut from total county-wide consolidation to simple interdistrict transfers of students. At one point, two of the three districts were willing to accept in principal a solution based primarily on boundary adjustments to achieve roughly the same racial composition in all three districts but the third team was unwilling to pursue such a course. The mediation process had reached a point of near impasse.

Before throwing in the towel, I proposed to try one more consultation with outside resources. The parties agreed. This time we would call upon Dr. Gordon Foster, Director of the University of Miami Desegregation Center, who had served as an expert witness on desegregation issues in more than 30 cases at both the federal and state levels. A second choice to bring external expertise into the mix was Dr. Christine Rossell, Associate Professor of Political Science at Boston University. She was co-author of two books on school desegregation and white flight and had published some 25 articles on the subject. The parties were brought together again for the second round of expert consultation on November 10, still willing to participate in a search for further options that might find appropriate application and mutual acceptance.

On the following day, in something of an act of desperation, I donned a hat with which I was notably unfamiliar and took an initiative that was normally outside my purview and even outside my own role description outlined during team orientations. Given that the parties were still without significant movement toward accord and that a long shot was in order, I put before the three teams one final proposal of my own creation. Its elements were based on new formulations gleaned from the weeks of meetings and consultations, generated in the hope that my new configuration might satisfy the naysayers.

---

[8]Arrangements were made for CRS to provide two such consultants: Dr. Joseph Johnson, Superintendent, Red Clay Consolidated School District in Wilmington, Delaware and Dr. Susan Uchitelle, Executive Director, Voluntary Interdistrict Coordinating Council, St. Louis, Missouri.

It was not to be. After three rounds of consummate investigation and probing dialogue, remedies were exhausted. It was time to close shop.[9] The delay of the original trial date to January 3, 1984, was approaching. The question of whether the court felt that mediation was worth the effort, even in its abortive attempt, was clearly stated in correspondence from the judge to CRS dated on the day the trial was set to begin. In his generous appraisal of the mediation effort he said that our agency had ". . . gone over and beyond the call of duty in attempting to settle this intricate and controversial matter. Although the parties did not reach an agreement, I am convinced that through his efforts the issues have been sharpened and the trial time will be greatly reduced." He went on to say that all the parties to the litigation had advised him that they too were most impressed with the manner in which the mediation process was executed.

A "DRACONIAN SOLUTION"

The case went to trial as scheduled. The court found that the two defendant school districts had indeed "engaged in unconstitutional and racially discriminatory acts resulting in substantial interdistrict segregation." Complete county-wide consolidation was ordered in accordance with the plaintiff district's original petition, the most repugnant alternative to the defendants among all the remedies considered during mediation.

Four full months into the proceedings, on April 30, Judge Woods held a hearing at which all parties had the opportunity to present whatever testimony they wished concerning remedial aspects of his order. In the introduction to his final memorandum opinion dated 11/19/84 (a year almost to the day since the termination of mediation) the judge noted that the defendant districts had ignored the opportunity to make modifications or submit other satisfactory options. "Rather than offering alternative plans or constructive criticism of the (plaintiff district's) plan," he wrote, "the defendant districts chose to attack the consolidation concept at every juncture and destroy the LRSD plan. Much of their effort seemingly was aimed at relitigating the liability portion of this case rather than assisting in the formulation of a workable solution to the interdistrict violations which were found to have occurred . . . it was hoped that, without prejudicing their right to appeal, the defendant districts would take a more constructive approach to the remedial portion of this case . . ."

In response to defendant complaints that they had been denied satisfactory opportunity at the April hearing to offer substitute remedies, the court held a second hearing on July 30 at which time the intervenors, including the Little Rock Classroom Teachers Association, also were invited to participate. On this occasion, the two defendant districts each presented their own designs for meeting the court's mandate. Both were found wanting. The Pulaski County plan retained three autonomous school districts, relying on specialty or magnet schools to attract voluntary transfers from one district to another. The North Little Rock district's offering also involved keeping its own autonomy but with various district boundary adjustments that were seen to rely heavily on voluntary transfer motivations by patron families. Another variation was presented by one of the intervenor parties containing no significant features that would ultimately cure constitutional violations. Both were rejected by Judge Woods. In the end, the only plan the court could approve was that sponsored by the Little Rock plaintiff district for "a countywide interdistrict remedy . . . to correct . . . the violation found to exist and that this is the only manner of placing the victims of this discrimination in the position they would have occupied absent the discrimination. . . ."

---

[9]Addendum J: *Arkansas Democrat* news report dated 11/12/1983.

At the conclusion of the trial, Judge Woods sent me a copy of his final order. That was several months after my retirement from federal service and after having established a family publishing business. In my acknowledgment for that courtesy, I responded in part with an observation that I believe underscores an enduring maxim concerning mediation as an alternative to litigation. In short, it is an irony that one or both parties to mediation, especially in civil rights matters, often fail to recognize that a legal remedy is likely to be far more onerous to them and more difficult to implement than would likely have been true in a voluntary, good faith negotiated settlement.[10]

---

[10]Addendum K: Concluding correspondence from mediator to Judge Woods dated 11/24/1984.

POLICE ABUSE ALLEGATIONS

Port Arthur, Texas

If you succumb to the temptation of using violence in the struggle,
unborn generations will be the recipients of a long and desolate night
of bitterness, and your chief legacy to the future will be
an endless reign of meaningless chaos.

—Martin Luther King, Jr.

ALL AMERICA CITY

A 22-year-old black man, Clifford Coleman, being held in the local jail on charges of dis-orderly conduct and use of abusive language, was shot to death by a white police officer in Port Arthur, Texas, on December 29, 1974. The incident occurred after the detainee had been stopped for questioning regarding a recent series of armed robberies. He was known to police as a result of several earlier misdemeanor arrests. The fatality occurred during an attempt by the victim to escape custody while being booked at the police station. He had told witnesses before the shooting that he feared being beaten by officers if he were to be confined in jail.

An investigation by the district attorney's office found Coleman had assaulted officers during a scuffle before fleeing the scene and being shot in the back a few blocks from the police station. Typical of such situations, details of the actual course of events leading to the fatality were framed in contrasting perceptions between black community leaders and city officials. Rumor, suspicion, and distrust built on past discontent over images of inequitable representation in local government, limited educational and economic opportunity, and alleged incidents of abusive police authority, quickly fed widespread protest. Prominent black professionals, including the school board president and a port commissioner, joined the public outcry.

The Port Arthur city attorney, quoting the Texas Penal Code, announced that "a peace officer is justified in using any force, including deadly force, that he believes to be imme-diately necessary to prevent the escape of a person from a jail, prison, or other institution for the detention of persons charged or convicted of a crime." A county grand jury exon-erated the officers involved in the shooting, and tensions in the black community mounted. A protest committee was formed, the Concerned Citizens of Port Arthur Association (CCPAA), for the purpose of confronting city officials with charges of police misconduct—the unjustified use of deadly force in connection with the escape as well as a series of grievances alleging various racially biased discriminatory practices by local law enforcement personnel.

This south Texas coastal city, some 90 miles east of Houston, had then a population of over 57,000, about 40% of that number African American. Leaders of the black community had convened a series of mass meetings, one that drew well over 2,000 anguished protesters. Some 300 demonstrators showed up at city council chambers at a time when a ceremony had been scheduled to celebrate the city's designation by the National League of Municipalities as an "All America City." Demands that the police chief be fired had been rejected by the city manager, and his counterproposals went nowhere. The NAACP was riding the crest of discontent with renewed energy in mobilizing community activism.

More serious consequences followed. Two large lumber yards were destroyed by fire in suspected arsons. Other arsons had been attempted. Vandalism was a growing problem.

Responding to its mandate to attempt intervention when racial unrest threatened community stability, the Community Relations Service (CRS) sent a conciliator, Gustavo Gaynett, to Port Arthur to assess what steps might be taken to lessen tensions and to establish reasoned communication in addressing the issues at hand. In his consultations with the contending parties it was decided that conditions were favorable to invite mediation. Black leadership agreed to refrain from organizing further protests while the mediation option was being examined and, if found mutually acceptable by opposing parties, implemented.

Before the mediator's arrival on the scene, a significant white community backlash had surfaced against the proposal to have the city negotiating with a "select, self-appointed" group of blacks who they said had no legitimate grounds for influencing public policy or coercing police reform. A stream of counter-protest hate mail had been generated, with white extremists threatening violence. Some businesses were touting their concern over perceived catering to minority complaints and biased reporting by warnings of their withdrawal of advertising from the Port Arthur daily newspaper if they didn't desist "from contributing to unrest."

Adding to the woes of city officials was a continuing major strike by employees of one of Port Arthur's large oil refineries. The presence of strike breakers had resulted in several incidents of disorder. Tensions resulting from developments in that sector of the civic landscape had been contributing substantially to community disquiet. Attention to that crisis was drawing heavily on police and other municipal resources. Mediators with the Federal Mediation and Conciliation Service (FMCS), in their labor-management intervention roles, were already getting notable media scrutiny prior to the introduction of a parallel process proposed to be undertaken to resolve totally dissimilar issues centering on complaints of discriminatory practices.

Despite their own immersion in labor unrest, Texaco, Gulf, and other petroleum companies with major installations in the area made no secret of their support for the city's commitment to a search for racial peace. They were employers of large numbers of minority workers, giving them a vested interest in the betterment of race relations beyond any altruistic motivation. George Dibrell, the city manager, was faced with a critical timing strategy. Several of the six city council members would be up for reelection some two months hence. He was convinced that he could best win acceptance of change after voters cast their ballots in the April 1 elections. Even though almost half the population was black, the proportion of white registration was considerably higher. Given a choice, elected officials would be unlikely to risk defeat at the polls by alienating the major constituency even if their personal instincts favored a conciliatory approach to racial discord.

In mid-January of 1975 I made my first visits to the troubled city, meeting separately with African American leadership and city officials. These initial contacts were devoted largely to routine matters of describing the general elements of the mediation process, detailed explanations of procedural rules and guidelines, anticipated time commitments, media relations, negotiating team selection criteria, review of allegations and agenda parameters, and so forth (as similarly set forth in other mediation settings described in earlier chapters). Fortunately for conflict resolution prospects, this was a time when movement toward higher police professionalism was well under way in many cities across the country. Just months before the onset of mediation in Port Arthur, the Texas Criminal Justice Council had published a manual of standard operating procedures. Many police departments were studying the document, and some were well on their way to applying new model rules of conduct. The use of deadly force, a crucial element in the updated policy recommendations and incorporated in the Texas Penal Code, prohibited lethal response unless necessary to protect the officer's life or the life a third party. Other guidelines spoke to the degree of force necessary in making an arrest, use of warning shots, and other restrictions regarding the use of weapons.

Port Arthur's then current procedural manual prohibited the use of firearms in connection with misdemeanor offenses, but did allow an officer to use "any force, including deadly force" to stop an escape from a jail or other penal institution. The new provisions of the Texas Penal Code raised a question that called for an answer before mediation could settle core differences in opposing positions. That question was whether or not the state code *mandated* police behavior in strict accordance with its particulars or whether it simply *suggested* guidelines, open to interpretation and/or modification by individual law enforcement agencies.

Prior to the first joint session, I had made exploratory contacts to identify possible law enforcement consultants and to obtain useful reference materials for distribution to the parties, as appropriate. The research staff of the International Association of Chiefs of Police was especially helpful in providing sample written firearms policies, training excerpts, and other research documentation.

BEYOND VIOLENCE—TO THE TABLE

The first joint sessions were held on January 29. Both parties had agreed upon a four issue agenda: (a) firearms policy and the use of deadly force; (b) minority representation among sworn officers; (c) arrest and detention procedures; (d) police relations with the minority community.

Following introductions and announcements, a number of the usual preliminaries delivered by the mediator including consideration of resource options, dealing with the media, dialogue and trust issues across the table, agenda flexibility, reemphasis of selected procedural matters, the use of tentative or interim agreements, and so forth, quickly brought heated debate. A foremost concern by the complainant CCPAA organization centered on the question of who would be chosen to serve on the city team at the mediation table. Among their principal negotiators named were the chief of police, the chairman of the Port Arthur Civil Service Commission, and the personnel director, along with the city attorney and city manager, who chaired the team. No elected officials were to participate. Negotiators had been selected on the basis of their professional knowledge and expertise regarding matters of law enforcement rather than their political standing. The CCPAA felt that the top of the political power hierarchy should carry the first line responsibility of facing citizen discontent. Part of the black team's unease was the fact that staff negotiators would have no authority to make decisions at the table and that council members getting second-hand reports would have insufficient understanding to take any informed ratification action. The matter was taken under advisement.

Moving back to the agenda call, Police Chief James Newsom and City Manager George Dibrell sought to turn attention to a more subdued discussion. In an effort to provide background fundamentals, a comprehensive management survey of the police department conducted in 1968 by the International Association of Chiefs of Police (IACP) was presented and copies distributed. Rather than try to examine and discuss the document at the time of its introduction, it was agreed to postpone any further consideration of its content until CCPAA team members could read and digest it.

An early irritant to the protest team was the presence of one of the city team alternates, a uniformed senior police officer wearing an exposed side arm. It fell to me as the mediator to later meet privately with the respondent team to resolve the matter before the next joint session.

Another ancillary issue consumed almost half the allotted time for the first meeting. George Wikoff, the city attorney, raised the question of the legality of any policy or regulation made by a local jurisdiction with regard to establishing a firearms policy that in any manner would depart from the specific language of the current Texas Penal Code. His position, simply stated, was that *the law is the policy*.[1] It appeared that he was unimpressed with the fact that Dallas, San Antonio, Beaumont, and other Texas police departments had already adopted recommendations in this connection to limit police discretionary leeway. Recent notable research done by the IACP and the Texas Criminal Justice Council had already promulgated guidelines in support of such reforms.

It was agreed that city representatives and the mediator would consult with the district attorney and other appropriate legal authorities to determine whether such questions of statutory validity posed any impediment to revision. It was further agreed that such inquiry would be completed, if possible, before the teams were scheduled to reconvene in about two weeks. With these preliminary matters finally set aside, there was a welcome ease in antagonism along with movement toward healthy, productive, and even cordial exchanges. There would be no further consideration of specific agenda issues until the teams were called together for the next series of meetings.

Before leaving town for a two-week recess, the mediator scheduled meetings with several principals and key community contacts. The first of these were with City Manager George Dibrell. We discussed several developments including: (a) a confidential memorandum from a sizeable group of local business representatives regarding a meeting they had with *Port Arthur News* publisher Jack Scott on the ways in which the newspaper had been delivering news and editorials regarding the shooting incident and expressing their displeasure at the editorial positions taken that were seen by them to lack objectivity and to feed discord among blacks in the community; (b) his reaction to the CCPAA request to have elected city council members represent the city at the mediation table; and (c) discussion of arrangements and prognosis for my meeting with police command staff scheduled for later in the day.

Next of the morning appointments was a courtesy call on the executive editor and the publisher of the newspaper. My primary objective was to suggest and encourage more attention to the mediation process and to the nature and role of our agency. Both men were more than receptive to putting greater emphasis in their releases on the educational aspects of the unfamiliar and unprecedented proceedings about to unfold.

A late morning consultation in Beaumont (the county seat) with the Jefferson County Criminal District Attorney, Tom Hanna, and his first assistant, was cordial and productive.

---

[1]Addendum L: See related press clippings (1/29-30/1975).

Copies of the Texas Criminal Justice Council Manual on Police Discretion and of the 1974 Texas Penal Code were provided. Discussion of key elements of these documents centered on the legal conflict questions raised by the Port Arthur city attorney. The DA's comments in that regard, as far as the state code was concerned, indicated that a local jurisdiction would not be in violation even if it chose to disarm its entire police department! He said the code provided only those limits *beyond which discretion could not go*, but placing no restrictions on *lowering* those parameters to a point where deadly force justification might require even greater restraints. Hanna stated that he and/or his staff would be available for any interpretive or other questions that might arise as mediation progressed.

An afternoon meeting back in Port Arthur with the police chief, the three division commanders, and four principal supervisors centered on: (a) review of the mediation process and the CRS role; (b) "rapping" on firearms policy, police-community relations and related subjects; (c) CRS resource recommendations, (d) acknowledged need for greatly improved communication between police and the community at large and most especially the minority segment. Following the 2 1/2-hour meeting, Chief Newsom took me on a tour of their modern operational facilities and jail and illustrated the scene of the prisoner confrontation and escape that led to the rebellious response and accusations of police abuse.

It was on this day of adjournment of the first coming together of the parties that Mayor Bernis Sadler made public his intention to create a 50-member biracial committee to deal with interracial problems and local crime conditions.[2]

The two-weeks break before resuming the second series of mediation sessions was in part programmed in order to give me an opportunity to further explore the statutory ramifications that seemed so crucial in facilitating continued negotiations. Those contacts included the legal section of the Dallas Police Department, the Texas Criminal Justice Council, the state Attorney General's office, the Governor's General Counsel and other legal staff, the International Association of Chiefs of Police, and the Port Arthur Civil Service Commission. Each of these resources was wholly responsive and helpful, several offering to be available for on-site consultation if and as needed.

Press reports of the day dealt further with the issue of participation in mediation by elected officials and with action taken by the Port Arthur NAACP chapter (not directly involved with mediation) calling for a federal civil rights investigation to overturn the grand jury findings that exonerated the officers involved in the Coleman shooting.[3]

As the weight of evidence mounted, from highly creditable sources, that city attorney Wikoff's position was inconsistent with theirs, his stance narrowed to these essentials: (a) Only a ruling from the state attorney general could suffice as an answer to his question of legal legitimacy; (b) His motives in serving as legal counsel to the city's negotiation team were not to be construed as obstructionist or dilatory; that the state's Criminal Justice Department project would be strengthened if these questions of legal sufficiency could be settled promptly, before other police departments adopt such policies without assurances of support in law; and (c) His focus question was restated with new phrasing: "Does a city have the power or authority to prohibit that which the state sanctions or allows?" An insightful editorial in the *Port Arthur News* offered commentary on current negotiations regarding weapons policy.[4]

---

[2]By a most unlikely coincidence, the *Port Arthur News*, on the very day of this first joint session, carried a front page story bearing directly on the subject of "... legal requirements and restraints of Texas law with sound principals of police practices...." Extensively referencing conclusions and recommendations from some of the most prominent state and national law enforcement authorities, the article provided the mediator with ideal information affirming the legality of proposed revisions and enabling him to join with the parties, before their adjournment, in effectively laying the matter to rest.

[3]See addendum M, related press clippings 1/31, 2/1/1975.

[4]Addendum N: See related press clipping dated 2/9/1975.

City team chairman Dibrell reported to me during the recess period that neither the mayor nor any of the other five city councilmen were inclined to take part in mediation, nor even to attend any sessions as observers. Their position was said to be based on their conviction, among other things, that it would be inappropriate to dilute or withdraw their delegated authority to staff professionals whose judgments and recommendations they would have to depend upon in large measure for ratification action.

SECOND JOINT SESSION

Arrangements were made for two consultants to join the mediator at the table—Jefferson County District Attorney Tom Hanna and Gordon Johnson, Program Coordinator for the Texas Criminal Justice Division (CJD) in the governor's office. After introductions of these guests and summary explanations of their roles related to law enforcement legalities, the agenda was quickly moved to the crucial issue at hand—deadly force use of firearms policy parameters under Texas law, particularly with regard to the authority of a municipal jurisdiction to limit or prohibit that which the state allows, and the liability of an officer found guilty of a violation. A wide-ranging discussion with substantial participation by the two resource people led to these observations/conclusions:

- The district attorney acknowledged that the question raised of legal authority was unknown, not having been tested. He said that differences between the penal code provisions and locally promulgated regulations on discretionary practices would likely lead to serious difficulties and complications. He questioned the wisdom of adopting local regulations that would likely be struck down by the courts as inconsistent with the penal code.
- The CJD spokesman described the background of the current project of his agency (to limit the use of deadly force) in which a nine-member panel of prosecutors, defense attorneys and judges was to be appointed to examine thoroughly the issue raised by the Port Arthur legal counsel, with an eye toward finding answers to the questions at hand.
- A draft proposal prepared by the Port Arthur city attorney was brought to the table for a sentence-by-sentence review. Vigorous exchanges followed between the parties and with considerable input from the consultants, leading to these developments:
  1. The language in the draft, taken almost verbatim from the current penal code, was seen to be cumbersome "legalese." Even the district attorney was hard pressed at some points to explain in lay terms what was meant. How then, the question was asked, could such language be appropriate for a local police department's operating policy to be understood by line officers, many with no more than a high school education?
  2. It was suggested that such a policy should contain provision for utilization in police training.
  3. It was readily recognized on both sides of the table that there needed to be a section on definition of terms, because much of the wording could be easily misunderstood or confusing (especially with regard to the precise meaning of such phrases as "abusive treatment," "reasonable belief," "deadly force," "sufficient provocation," etc.).

I spent most of the evening at dinner with the city manager. He shared with me a number of new areas of information. He pointed out that there had been only two citizen fatalities by police use of deadly force in 20 years. One was said to have been in connection with the robbery of a black-owned business. He discussed candidly political cross-currents and prevailing attitudes among city councilmen and business people toward racial issues. He said he was already convinced that the mediation process was an extraordinarily useful tool for urban problem solving. He indicated his intention to have me address a state-regional group of city managers (of which he was then president) at some near-future meeting.

The next day I spent the morning hours studying the city's draft proposal, the firearms policies of the Dallas and San Antonio police departments, a highly relevant research paper on "discretionary justice," and excerpts from the American Bar Association's study on "Standards for Criminal Justice—The Urban Police Function." A later visit with the city manager centered on a review of the aforementioned literature I had earlier reviewed, along with his sharing further developments regarding political alignments, current oil industry strike positions, and city finance issues and problems.

An early afternoon meeting with the CCPAA chairman, Rev. Ransom Howard, and his vice-chairman, A.Z. McElroy, provided an opportunity to discuss anticipated positions for the joint sessions scheduled for later in the day. They indicated that their team would probably go along with adopting the city's proposal, given the three modifications proposed the day before. They stressed their intention to avoid moving to the second agenda issue, police-community relations, until the first order of business was settled.

THE THIRD ROUND

The city's draft proposal for a firearms policy was once again on the table for discussion. CCPAA team members grew increasingly critical. Chairman Howard, having spoken with an unnamed official with the San Antonio PD, proceeded calmly but firmly to recite his views on the deficiencies seen in the city's proposal. He deplored the "lack of humanity" in the language of the document, the lack of citizen input in its development, and the dubious nature of city objections to the legal vulnerabilities of any policy that would restrict certain use of force practices allowed by law.

One complainant team member, who had been virtually silent during earlier sessions, emerged as the angry, bitter voice of what was said to be a consensus position. He charged various city team members with deliberate delaying tactics. He characterized the city's proposal as a mere recitation of the state penal code and totally without meaningful controls over unnecessary use of deadly force. He challenged his opponents to "draw up an acceptable instrument together with us, here and now." The dialogue grew progressively more contentious, with spokesmen on both sides occasionally losing control of their feelings, leading to my insistence that further such deterioration in rational communication would lead to a premature adjournment and possibly serious damage to the entire procedure, which had been beginning to make notable progress.

In response, the CCPAA chairman called a caucus. Tempers cooled and a strategy emerged. A new position was laid out. Without any outward show of anger, Vice-Chairman McElroy calmly tore up their copy of the draft policy proposal in the faces of the respondents and said simply that they wanted only two things: (a) full participation by the CCPAA team in designing and recommending a firearms policy to the city council, and (b) that there be no further delays in dealing with the issue.

At that point, I suggested that a joint committee be appointed to work through details and then return to the table for consideration by the full delegations. After some debate, the suggestion was declined. Instead, dialogue was begun then and there to develop an entirely new document with all team members and alternates on both sides participating.

For the two hours remaining before scheduled adjournment, wording was hammered out for the initial introductory section using the San Antonio policy as a basic guide.

It soon became apparent to all concerned that to continue with such a large number of people engaged in developing a proposal was too slow and impractical. At the conclusion of this session, both sides agreed to have a smaller number of participants assigned to "work sessions" in order to come up with a mutually acceptable instrument. It was further agreed that the first such meeting would be held the following day with the final results reported to the mediator in Dallas by telephone as soon as the task was completed, so that the next mediation sessions could be convened.

As might have been anticipated, the subcommittee assigned to put together a new proposal took far more time than anyone had expected. Much research and many weeks of meetings were required before the use of deadly force conundrum was in shape to take back to the mediation table, enabling final consensus and recommendation to the city council. It had taken more than three months to find the end of the tunnel on the first of the four agenda issues. Those who participated in the deliberations, however, showed obvious satisfaction, not only with the resolution reached, but with the values associated with a new path of communication resulting in vastly improved mutual respect and understanding between historically antagonistic community elements.

When mediation resumed after disposing of the firearms policy polemics, attention turned to the question of minority recruiting. Port Arthur Civil Service Director Dave Brinson had prepared a report, distributed to the negotiating teams, outlining the city's initiatives in recent times to recruit, hire, and promote blacks in the police department. My agency offered the services of any of several consulting resources to assist in this area of concern. Two engaged were Dr. James Witt, Director of the Criminal Justice Center at Marquette University in Milwaukee, Wisconsin, and Eugene Robinson, a technician-specialist on Witt's staff. Their operation was reputed to be a respected authority in the field of minority utilization in criminal justice systems. He proposed to have staff from his office conduct a survey (at no cost to the city or to the Community Relations Service) to determine recruiting potentials and obstacles to successful results and to develop new techniques for attracting minority peace officer candidates. The police department at this point in time had six African-American and one Hispanic among a total of 84 commissioned officers, an infinitesimal representation in relation to the ethnic composition of the city's population.

The Port Arthur city council debated and approved the proposed survey, but not without "opening a new can of worms." The mayor publicly disavowed the survey proposal, tying it to sharp criticism of the CCPAA and its leadership. His stand on the survey question was in contrast to the favorable expressions of support from the remaining six council members (one of whom was black). It marked one of the rare occasions when the mayor had virtually no concurrence from any of his colleagues. Fortunately, his stance was not serious enough to threaten the progress of mediation, although there was heated reaction from some complainant team members.

It was agreed to hold the recruiting issue in abeyance until the survey could be completed and satisfactory agreement reached on remedial action. In the interim, negotiations would move on to the third agenda topic—police-community relations (PCR).

ON TO THE NEXT ISSUE

The first seven of fourteen questions posed on matters of police relations with the minority community (and to some extent, with the community at large) were discussed in detail with Police Chief Newsom providing most of the response. Particular attention was given to:

1. A $69,000 grant under the federal Law Enforcement Assistance Agency to establish a PCR program upon which favorable action was expected within weeks;
2. Personnel selections to fill four anticipated vacancies for three sworn positions (a black sergeant in charge of the operation and two white officers) and a secretary in the PCR function to be formed; strong negative reaction from the CCPPA team for lack of consultation with black community leadership in formulating the program and setting recruitment/hiring standards for staffing the new unit;
3. Recent consultation with a PCR specialist from the International Association of Police Chiefs who spent several days in Port Arthur providing guidance in structuring the new program;
4. Arrangements made to send three newly designated PCR officers to a training program conducted by the Texas Department of Public Safety, scheduled to begin in a few weeks;
5. Forcefully stated support from the city manager for seeking minority community input on program and personnel matters before determinations are made; his decision to delay all city actions until the mediation consultants were heard;
6. Recognized need for a citizen grievance mechanism as an indispensable element of an effective PCR program;
7. Examples given by CCPAA team members of specific incidents and conditions that formed the rationale for the questions set forth in the PCR issue.

Following the foregoing exchanges and after adjournment, two members of the city team, both civil service board officials, took me aside for an impromptu "letting it all hang out" catharsis. They expressed feelings that had been gathering steam since mediation began.

Although they acknowledged the effectiveness of the process in some respects, they were especially resentful and disturbed over the fact that all they could hear was a constant harangue over police misconduct, but no attention to the nature of abuse suffered by police and the responsibilities of black community leaders to help fight the high crime problem in their own community. They cited a number of frightful crimes committed by blacks and their perceptions of unreasonable and ill-informed protest reactions when arrests are made of known felons who are a menace to the entire city. They agreed that an effective PCR program might be the only hopeful way to bring about improved understanding. They also thought that carefully structured group confrontation meetings between police and minority activists might produce worthwhile results.

The Marquette University team arrived that evening. I briefed them once again, in greater detail than previously, on background and current developments. I was optimistic that their visit would have important and constructive results in support of mediation objectives.

Their survey activity began early the next morning when they met with city officials to outline their procedural format. Access to personnel records and appropriate staff was fully facilitated. Extended discussion centered on minority recruiting and utilization problems experienced in the past, staff structure, culture and personalities, and the nature of historical relationships among influential racial groupings with local government authorities. The mayor underscored his recent initiatives in forming a triracial-ethnic committee to seek intergroup harmony and the need for resource assistance in bringing it to fruition.

Dialogue continued on the remaining seven of fourteen agenda questions posed under the police-community relations topic. Particular emphasis centered on:

1. Reasons why crimes are typically unreported in the black community and why there is little cooperation with the police department (widespread perceptions of police as oppressors, lack of confidentiality of source identity, fear of reprisals by those reported, lack of practical procedures to encourage and facilitate reporting law breakers, etc.);
2. Projected PCR unit roles;
3. Media problems tending to damage positive perceptions;
4. Need for greater educational effort to produce more dialogue and to foster greater understanding between police and minority poor.

At dinner, a review with Dr. Witt of his activity that day at the police department examining records and interviewing personnel, was highlighted by:

1. His praise for the department's personnel records system;
2. Results of the community survey from his team associate, Gene Robinson, indicating optimism for a successful minority recruiting campaign;
3. Optimum level of cooperation received from all police and other city officials;
4. Projections for completion of survey and submission of written report to the chief of police within two weeks;
5. Anticipation of continuing and intensive on-site technical assistance in helping to implement forthcoming recommendations.

Before departing Port Arthur the next day, I arranged a meeting with Sgt. Cedric Clayton, the black officer tentatively designated to be supervisor of the PCR unit, and the Marquette resource team. It was an opportunity for in-depth sharing of ideas and a review of survey findings. The sergeant stated that he and many other officers on the force were convinced that the introduction of mediation had clearly prevented further deterioration in race relations and averted what was almost certain to be continued violence. Other discussion was directed to the prognosis for PCR programming, varying attitudes in the community toward mediation, factionalism in both the black and white communities, and the status of black leadership and organizational viability.

After a break of several days, the ninth and tenth joint sessions were scheduled for an anticipated wrap-up of the PCR issue. This series would be devoted largely to consultations with two officials of the National Association of Police-Community Relations Officers (NAPCRO)[5] and, given the absence of other priorities arising, would be followed by initial attention to the final agenda article, "Arrest and Detention Procedures."

Selected press reports of early May 1975 provide detailed coverage of developments during this period of activity.[6]

Port Arthur City Manager Dibrell by this time had become a staunch advocate of the mediation process. His grasp of its potential for resolving serious problems of citizen discontent with governmental services had become a subject about which he was now inclined to share with counterparts across the state. As then regional President of the Texas City Management Association, he was in a good position to bring the subject to the attention of colleagues. He did so in mid-May, before mediation in his city had concluded, so confident was he that the results would be of significant interest and value to other municipal administrators. In response to his request, I addressed that gathering with a full

---

[5]Robert Barton, St. Louis Police Department, and Major Leroy Swift, Kansas City Police Department.
[6]Addendum O: See related press clippings dated 5/5-15/1975.

accounting of the issues being negotiated, also covering the role of my agency in dealing with community conflict situations.

THE FINAL ROUNDS

Joint sessions were reconvened on May 21. The first meeting was devoted to a wide variety of issues, including the hiring of a special police legal advisor to review, revise, and codify departmental regulations, policies, and training guidelines. Chief Newsom provided a step-by-step explanation of the arrest process from the point of contact with an offender through to the point of booking and custody. He also discussed use of the video monitoring system and newly established security measures intended to help avoid the possibility of another escape incident such as led to the Coleman fatality.

City team chairman Dibrell described updated details of the Marquette University technical assistance regarding minority recruiting and plans for them to return shortly to begin directing the implementation of a recruiting campaign.

One touch-and-go segment of these deliberations found Chief Newsom expressing strong reservations about incorporating any arrest or detention procedures into written policy for fear of "handcuffing" the police in performance of duties. With persistent prodding from the complainant team, as well as more subtle persuasion from the city manager and the mediator, he reluctantly agreed to work with the city attorney in trying to formulate a statement "that he could live with."

The most serious disagreement throughout the dialogue centered on the difference between agreeing to a *guideline,* which is essentially considered preferable but optional for adherence by officers, and the nature of a *regulation* that is mandatory, a violation of which would likely result in disciplinary action. The matter was finally set aside to await the results of the policy language for later presentation.

It was agreed that I would seek to find several well-conceived sample policy statements from other Texas police departments for possible adaptation. Such was obtained and forwarded, coming from the cities of Dallas and Killeen (more nearly in the population range of Port Arthur).

By month's end a comprehensive 50-page report from the Marquette Center was in the hands of the parties. It covered a broad range of evaluative observations regarding present departmental structure and past recruiting efforts. Then followed a series of recommendations for initiating an all-out campaign to identify and attract black prospects to wear the badge. Marquette specialist Gene Robinson would be on hand to launch the new program during the first week in June.

The ambitious mission was not without troubling impediments. Robinson had encountered problems with several of the black officers he had been attempting to enlist in the planning and execution of the project. Some were reluctant to accept his role and direction as the architect of the plan. Some simply lacked the commitment or priority to achieve stated objectives. But notwithstanding these early signs of naysaying, the Marquette consultant was confident that one or two of these minority officers upon whom he was depending for active participation would, in fact, take on the necessary leadership and had the capacity to contribute significantly.

The twelfth joint session focused on completion of remnants of the first agenda issue—firearms policy and the use of deadly force. Chief Newsom and City Attorney Wikoff were at odds through much of the discussion as to the most appropriate wording. In the end, consensus was reached and recorded for inclusion in the ultimate policy statement to become an attachment to the mediation agreement.

Next on the table for settlement was a proposed document to be utilized by the police department in connection with "stop and frisk" practices. Surprisingly, the city attorney presented a statement that, with minor modifications, was an almost complete adoption of the recommended rules set forth in the model procedures of the Texas Criminal Justice Council's manual on police discretionary conduct (originally introduced by CRS to guide agenda discussion). With only limited dialogue and a few clarifications, the matter found ready agreement by both sides.

As the session progressed to its final stages, civil service selection procedures again became a focal point of attention, having been discussed and tabled in earlier phases of negotiation. The problem of having to choose applicants with the highest scores was at the core of contention. Eight entry vacancies at the time had been looked upon as a hopeful opportunity to apply aggressive affirmative action initiatives in recruiting minority candidates. The civil service selection requirement was an obvious obstruction.

Heated exchanges erupted. A cloud of uncertainty and second thoughts about the wisdom and practicality of instituting a major minority recruiting program without being able to rely on actual placements threatened a serious impasse. The argument centered mostly on the authority of the Port Arthur Civil Service Commission to take the steps necessary to bring about better racial balance without violating governing state law.

Much of this dialogue turned on opposing views among the three civil service officials present. One of the three expressed confidence that they could come up with creative solutions. In later private conversation with CCPAA team members he said he thought he could muster a majority of the commission to support whatever interpretation of the regulations might be necessary. A major concern of the two opposing commissioners was their fear that the city would be placing itself in a position of precarious vulnerability to litigation. They contended that white applicants who scored higher than a minority candidate, and were nonetheless bypassed, would, under existing law, have a strong cause of action.

The Marquette consultant offered several possible options. One involved an arrangement with local businesses in which minority applicants who passed entry requirements, but did not score high enough for selection, would be temporarily placed in "holding positions" until an appropriate placement in the police department could be made. An alternate proposal involved creating suitable nonsworn positions within the police department, with likely availability of federal funding, in which a similar "holding" device could be employed. A third possibility suggested that an "advanced hiring" procedure could be used by taking the projected turnover rate over the next three years and applying those extra positions to the current budget allotment, in effect borrowing against future manpower budgets and thereby multiplying the immediate number of available vacancies. Such a move, it was said, would presumably create opportunities for a larger number of minority placements by making it feasible to reach lower scoring candidates.

In a visit with the city manager the day following these sessions, I was briefed on a series of intentions the team chairman had in mind. He had formulated a summary of new policy declarations that he felt would provide the momentum to move the negotiation process toward ultimate resolution of all agenda issues. He said he would first present his proposal to the police command staff and then take it to the city council for tentative approval. If accepted by the mediation principals, with whatever modifications might be further incorporated, he said he would take the entire package to the Jefferson County District Attorney for final assessment in its passing legal muster.

After circulating several preliminary drafts of a final agreement, I agreed to prepare a final version that included a provision for a CRS commitment to have the mediator return to Port Arthur in the event of any disagreement between the parties as to good faith implementation by the respondents. The completed document was mailed within days to the two team chairmen, followed by yet additional modifications requiring circuitous coordination of written and telephonic communication between my office in Dallas and the party contacts in Port Arthur.

On Monday, July 28, with the last revisions earlier inserted and jointly endorsed by both sides, the determinative document was presented to the city council. The occasion drew widespread media attention well beyond Port Arthur and the county seat of Beaumont. Comprehensive news and editorial coverage in both print and broadcast outlets, in Houston and other major cities in the region, went a long way toward overcoming the limited public awareness of the emerging concept of conflict resolution through mediation.[7]

Both parties to the process had made compromises in reaching final agreement. Virtually all participants acknowledged they had not produced a perfect agreement; however, there was unanimity of confidence that it would result in a substantially more effective police department.

To my knowledge, the Port Arthur case was the first in which substantive changes in police policies and practices were developed jointly by city and citizen committees using the mediation process. The experience was further distinguished in the extent to which outside resources were utilized. Consultants were brought to the mediation table from all across the country as the parties increasingly recognized that some of the issues required professional or technical assistance in helping them reach sound conclusions. Members of both participating teams demonstrated a high level of willingness and capacity to debate sensitive issues with minimal rancor and with open-mindedness. The teams were consistent in devoting themselves to the task at hand. Seldom were more than two members of either team absent from a negotiating session (of a total of nine on each side of the table), even though those in the black group often had to miss work to be in attendance and city team representatives frequently had to rearrange sometimes urgent priorities in order to maintain continuity in their involvement.

MEASURING SUCCESS

The long-term impact of a mediated agreement is the ultimate criterion upon which success can be measured. Written words about the intentions of the parties ring hollow without satisfactory implementation of lasting change. The final covenant in this case spelled out in explicit language what police behavioral guidelines and policy imperatives were to be put in place.

For months following the termination of negotiations, the city council engaged for further ongoing assistance some of the resource agencies CRS had provided to help develop and implement the community relations and minority recruiting elements of the agreement.[8] Recommendations had been made by the Marquette consultants that the city increase its police manpower by at least 30 more sworn officers, increase salaries for entry recruits (and successively up the ranks), and improve minority recruiting potential by providing tutoring for black applicants to help assure optimal entry qualifications and test score results.

Early efforts were not encouraging. Although nineteen minority candidates were on hand to take the first examinations, none passed all of the required tests and background checks to qualify. Recruiters lamented the fact that they faced considerable resistance from

---

[7]Addendum P: See related *Houston Post* article dated 8/2/1975.
[8]Marquette University Criminal Justice Center and the National Association of Police-Community Relations Officers.

contacts they were making with those who seemed to represent the most promising applicants. When a PCR unit was later operational within the department, modest success was finally achieved with the hiring of a highly qualified black recruit.

More than a year after mediation had concluded, City Manager Dibrell was invited by the editors of a prominent law enforcement journal to submit a feature article on his experience with mediation in dealing with civil rights and civil unrest issues. It is one of the few documented public accounts to be found of an in-depth perspective from a party principal having participated in a complex and successful mediation proceeding. At that point in time the implementation phase of the agreement had progressed to only a limited extent. Many of the provisions were expected to take several years to be implemented in their entirety. But Dibrell was completely confident that the course had been set and that the results were already worthy of high praise. A reprint of that writing is found in the addenda section.[9]

Four years later, the chairmen of the two mediation teams, Dibrell and the Rev. Ransom Howard, were invited to participate in a nationwide conference on police use of deadly force and related issues, held in Silver Spring, Maryland. They appeared together on a panel to examine and discuss four cases of negotiated settlements of police-community disputes drawn from cities from around the country. Their retrospection on the impact of mediation after the passing years is reflected in a local press account following their return home.[10]

At this writing more than three decades after the mediation experiment in Port Arthur was concluded, there are striking changes in the racial/ethic makeup of elected municipal representation and police department composition. The number of minority uniformed police officers and civilian personnel has increased dramatically since the mid-1970s. A majority of the governing city council is African American. The mayor is Hispanic. A former chief of police was black.

Port Arthur, like many other southern and southwestern cities of similar size and and temperament, has become a community of proportionate representation and a place where barriers to equal opportunity have been significantly moderated. No claim is made that it has reached a state of ideal interracial equanimity, but there is no denying that the meaning and privileges of citizenship have been transformed in this small corner of a democratic society.

---

[9]Addendum Q: Postmortem Article.
[10]Addendum R: *Port Arthur News* article dated 12/13/1979.

POLICE-MINORITY COMMUNITY RELATIONS

From Hostile Confrontation to Meaningful Dialogue —The State of Texas

The Time has come for this nation to fulfill its promise . . . .
We face a moral crisis as a country and as a people.
It cannot be met by repressive police action. It cannot be left
to increased demonstrations the streets . . . it is a time to act . . .
Those who do nothing are inviting shame as well as violence.
Those who act boldly are recognizing right as well as reality,

—John Fitzgerald Kennedy (June 1963)

TURMOIL IN TEXAS AND THE NATION

In many urban centers of the Lone Star State, and to some extent in smaller communities, from the early 1960s and throughout the 1970s, African American and Hispanic dissidents focused much of their protest energies on police-community relations. It was an intensely emotional issue. Throughout much of the nation, civil unrest was often sparked by a police-inflicted fatality or sometimes no more that a routine traffic stop or arrest in which police were seen to have been unnecessarily abusive to a minority subject being detained. Following passage in 1964 of the most momentous federal civil rights legislation since reconstruction, it was a time that produced dedicated nonviolent dissent along with widespread lawlessness.

Barely a year after the watershed Congressional action to ban discrimination based on race, creed, color, or national origin, America watched a six-day orgy of large-scale violence in a section of Los Angeles that was almost entirely populated by blacks. The Watts riots of 1965 resulted in more than 30 deaths, over 1,000 injured, and an estimated 100 million dollars in damage or destruction to 600 buildings, most occupied by white-owned businesses. It all started when a white policeman pulled over a black motorist who had been seen driving somewhat erratically. Family member passengers in the car, it was reported, after an angry exchange of words, apparently resisted the officer's directives. A crowd had gathered. A bottle was thrown at the police cruiser. The alleged violators were arrested and they departed the scene.

The entire neighborhood, a section characterized by high unemployment, poverty, substandard housing, drug dealing, and so forth, erupted in flames, looting, and random attacks on any pale-skinned interloper who happened by. It was only the first in a series of major disturbances that swept the country over the next three years—in New York City, Detroit, Newark, Cleveland, Chicago, San Francisco, Baltimore, and Washington, DC, to say nothing of numerous less notable riotous events elsewhere. No American city, it seemed, was immune to interracial/ethnic strife. "Burn baby, burn" was the mantra of those who could see no limits to their militancy. Protest marches, arsons of black churches, and murders of civil rights activists were among the consequences of equally unrestrained retribution.

In the midst of the chaos arose organized militancy. In the black protest movement, mainstream organizations that had held center stage since the mobilization against racial discrimination, were being challenged for influence and leadership by more strident voices. The National Association for the Advancement of Colored People (NAACP), the Southern Christian Leadership Conference (SCLC), and the Urban League, among others, were being painted with the brush of ineffective moderation. Challenging their place in the civil rights hierarchy was the emerging younger, less patient, and more aggressive generation calling for the "black power" formula of provocative action replacing what, at best, these new revolutionaries saw as meek and servile pleading. The Black Panthers and the Student Nonviolent Coordinating Committee (SNCC), the latter thought by some to be misnamed in view of its bellicose image resulting from the hard core rhetoric of its leadership, was awakening a dormant rejection of the pace of progress toward "equality for all."[1]

In the Hispanic population, particularly in Texas, there was a parallel groundswell of young, combative, reform-minded resisters who had grown impatient with what they saw as an agonizing crawl toward the goal of equal treatment for all. Traditional, well-established civil rights organizations such as the League of United Latin American Citizens (LULAC) and the American GI Forum were being criticized, much as were their counterparts in the black community, as being too inclined to buying into the "gringo" values and cultural character of the more affluent and influential Anglo power structure.

The late 1960s and early 1970s found "Chicano power" competing with "black power" for public attention and in raising anxieties among white civic and business interests in metropolitan areas throughout the land. Among the most active groups to seize the militancy initiative in the barrios of the southwest were the Brown Berets, co-founded by Carlos Montes. Like the Black Panthers of that day, they became something of a symbol of pride in Latino culture, ethnicity, and historical heritage. More than that, they represented a cause for unrestrained resistance to what was seen to be a chain of injustices with which Hispanics had to contend throughout their history of American citizenship.

Perceptions of abusive police behavior and recounted experiences of poor working class families and Mexican American youth being profiled for unjustified or illegal treatment by law enforcement authorities was an early priority issue for assault.

---

[1]Stokely Carmichael became chairman of SNCC in 1966 and later the "honorary prime minister" of the Black Panther Party. He articulated a view of civil rights strategy that called for African Americans to form and lead their own organizations and to reject the values of integration into a white society. His raised hand and clenched fist came to symbolize the concept of black power and led to a spreading mood of black pride and separatist philosophy in opposition to the nonviolence ideology of Martin Luther King, Jr. and others. "Achieving social justice," he would say in his writings and speeches, "by integrating black people into the mainstream institutions of the society from which they had been excluded, is based on the assumption that there is nothing of value in the black community . . . (and that) the goals of integrationists are middle-class goals, articulated primarily by a small group of Negroes with middle-class aspirations or status . . . based on complete acceptance of the fact that in order to have a decent house or education, black people must move into a white neighborhood or send their children to a white school, reinforcing among both black and white the idea that 'white' is automatically superior and 'black' is by definition inferior." Therefore it could be concluded, he would go on to say, that integration is "a subterfuge for the maintenance of white supremacy."

Adding to the foment of the Chicano self-determination movement and to the unease of Anglo equilibrium, the Raza Unida Party in Crystal City, the Zavala County seat in rural south Texas, caught the nervous attention of the political establishment of the Lower Rio Grande region with the new brown assertiveness. Another foot soldier in the battle for Latino recognition and power-sharing, Jose Angel Gutierrez, was brazenly organizing a political juggernaut that would accomplish the impossible. He succeeded in carrying out a voter registration campaign that would replace Anglos in most significant public offices in the county—contested seats for city council, school board, judgeships and other key governmental posts. The sacred cows of politically tainted South Texas were unceremoniously bludgeoned with a new reality that would eventually change forever the entire complexion of local and statewide governmental elections and representation.[2]

Not to be overlooked in the rising tide of racial/ethnic identity and proclamations of justice denied was the advent of the rebellious Native American reformers under the banner of the American Indian Movement (AIM). Established power structures had yet another threatening color of power to face—red power.

AIM will probably always be most remembered by those who engaged them at the Pine Ridge Reservation, South Dakota, in 1975, as among the most ferocious gun-toting renegades ever to oppose the overwhelming resources of the United States government in armed confrontation.[3] Some historians may depict them in more empathetic images as heroic warriors determined to overcome untold hardship and years of unjust treatment by the white society within which many Native Americans felt themselves imprisoned. Not the least of their principal grievances centered on what was perceived to be a system of justice that ignored countless beatings and fatalities, many victims being Indian activists, virtually all such incidents gone uninvestigated. The all too familiar cry of police brutality and prejudicial arrest and detention standards, as applied to Indians, was an ongoing cause célébre.

Some would say that AIM mellowed as the years passed, but it has survived. Its most concentrated activity at the dawn of the twenty-first century, along with some of its spin-off organizations, was still in the place of its origins—the south side of Minneapolis. Its agenda has turned largely to an emphasis on health care, drug abuse prevention, job training and educational motivation.

For purposes of this presentation, it is noteworthy that again, one of the underscored grievances of a minority citizenry is directed toward allegations of abusive law enforcement and biased judicial practice.

Needless to say, the wave of minority inroads in politics, employment, education and citizen status brought notable counteractive elements to the surface. The Ku Klux Klan and white citizen councils, among other detractors, drew their share of adherents to oppose the incessant trends toward providing equal opportunity and anti-discriminatory protections. But in the final analysis their intent to deprive and to intimidate had relatively little impact. Too many Americans had come to embrace the new age of diversity and equitable citizenship.

---

[2]The story of CRS conciliation involvement in a 1969-70 Crystal City dispute is the subject of Chapter 10.

[3]The siege at Wounded Knee was the culmination of years of increasing friction between Sioux Nation dissidents and the U.S. Bureau of Indian Affairs (BIA). Populace resentment ranged from perceived denial of basic human rights to restrictions against innocuous but traditional practices regarding religion, ceremonial dress and hair styles. Separate incidents of the torture and killing of two elderly native men by white thugs, with no subsequent charges being filed, raised the level of rage beyond containment. The protracted 71-day firefight that brought the federal relationship with Native Americans to it lowest ebb in modern times found well-armed agents of the Federal Bureau of Investigation, along with BIA police, in a weaponry showdown with AIM militants determined to prevail. CRS played a major third party role in helping to keep the standoff from deteriorating into a repeat of the full blown massacre at the first Wounded Knee conflagration in 1890, at the same site that took 150 Indian lives along with 25 fatalities among U.S. soldiers.

A TIME FOR INNOVATION

By the mid-seventies, most police departments in major U.S. cities had operating internal affairs divisions set up to deal with citizen complaints. Some had earned the confidence of minority constituents and the community at large. Others were seen as lacking in the integrity necessary to assure vigorous and fair investigations of alleged police malfeasance.

In May of 1977, Houston, Texas' largest city, was without such a mechanism. The Harris County Trial Lawyers Association, along with several state legislators and minority organizations, were calling for a citizen's review board that would provide for lay people to sit in judgment of sworn officers accused of wrongdoing. The rationale for such effort was based on the assumption that a civilian review board would prevent the perceived abuses of the police investigating themselves, assuring impartial disposition of cases and thereby avoiding what was seen as inevitable cover-ups to protect brother officers

On the other side of the coin, police administrators, usually with strong political support, not surprisingly stood firmly in opposition to having any but accredited law enforcement professionals performing such an important and sensitive function. That position prevailed in most jurisdictions and ultimately was shown to be the only practical approach to achieving satisfactory results, although internal affairs findings were often targets of vigorous criticism from skeptical detractors.

After sending delegations to other Texas police agencies to investigate policies and operations, Houston Chief B.G. Bond brought his agency on board with the establishment of his department's first watchdog unit to deal with citizen complaint processing.

It wasn't long before some of the state's more concerned law enforcement leaders were ready to take proactive initiatives in trying to improve relationships with those who saw them as something less than the peace officers that title inferred. Many saw their internal affairs programs as only a beginning on the road to polishing their image with recalcitrant groups in their communities.

Recognizing the need for a catalytic ally to create an environment conducive to new approaches to police-community relations, CRS headquarters approved my proposal for our office to provide a third-party facilitator/coordinator in devising and executing an innovative plan. Having made the recommendation, the implementation task was promptly placed in my hands with virtually no parameters within which I would be obliged to operate.

Because of the sometimes shrill voices and growing unrest coming from the Spanish-speaking barrios, and increasing support from their advocates in the political, legal, and legislative enclaves of Texas, I decided that the focus of any new CRS remedial program would be in that direction. After months of informal telephonic and written exchanges with contacts among both police agencies and Mexican-American organizations, two centers of interest emerged. From the civil rights activists, and moderates as well, the consensus issue of greatest import in police-community relations was almost universally agreed to be the use of deadly force by police officers in the stop, arrest, and custody process when dealing with Chicano[4] subjects.

The second key area that needed to be addressed, a concern especially among those in law enforcement, was the fact that there had been virtually no meaningful communication between leadership elements of one camp and the other.

Given these two advisories, neither of which were any surprise to us, but importantly, originating with the parties themselves, we were able to plan our next steps. By September of 1978 it was time to bring together representative spokespersons from both

---

[4]An ethnic pride term in wide use in that day, less common today.

sides of the divide to see whether useful dialogue could be established, at least in a preliminary format. We would invite five police chiefs (from Corpus Christi, Dallas, Austin, San
Antonio, and Brownsville) and top leaders from the Mexican-American Legal Defense
Fund, the League of Latin-American Citizens, the American GI Forum, Image de Tejas,
and the Brown Berets, to convene at the CRS regional office in Dallas. Also invited were
a member of the Mexican-American Caucus in the Texas House of Representatives, a
member of the Texas Commission on Law Enforcement Standards & Education, and a
representative of the Texas Advisory Commission on Intergovernmental Relations (as an
observer).

The agenda was devoted primarily to the two matters previously identified. It was
agreed in advance that there would be no debating questions of fact regarding any specific incident in which a police officer or group of officers had been accused of wrongdoing.
Such incidents could be referenced, but only for purposes of illustration.

From my third-party perch as chair of the session, after introductions and procedural
preliminaries, I laid out my own perceptions of how I saw the two sides lining up on the
principal topics. Commenting on the protest viewpoint, I underscored the simple fact that
police were seen to be more readily inclined to use deadly force when the subject they were
confronting was a minority group member. Incident after incident in which the police, in
effect, became judge, jury, and executioner, were offered as the source of the grievance.
That perception, I pointed out, was further aggravated by the fact that fatalities too often
arise out of relatively insignificant events such as traffic violations, using foul language, or
public intoxication. Even in more serious offenses, the rationale went, the bottom line in
an officer making a deadly-force decision should be limited to those times when the life of
the officer or any other person was being threatened.

Turning to an interpretation of the application of force issue as seen through the eyes
of police authorities, the dilemma was said to center on the fact that the general public had
no reasonable understanding of the frequent challenges officers face in relating to citizens
under circumstances that, by their nature, give rise to defensiveness, anxiety, or fear, sometimes requiring split-second life-or-death decisions. Inevitably, serious errors in judgment
will occur, sometimes leading to the tragedy of taking an innocent life. Questions of civil
or criminal liability, the counter position argued, must be determined by the courts rather
than an uninformed segment of the community relying on media reports, rumors, and
unsubstantiated information.

The police assessment was further described in terms of the ever-present problem of
insufficient funding to attract and recruit the best possible applicants or to provide the best
available training to maximize ideal performance.

The foregoing presentation of two points of view was introduced not as any complete
or universal reflection of party positions, but simply as a useful point of departure in stimulating dialogue and addressing core issues. I suggested that a primary objective of our
meeting would be to determine whether a larger meeting, perhaps a statewide conference
attended by a substantial and balanced number of appropriate representatives from both
camps would be beneficial.

Lively exchanges brought not only some important exposure to opposing views but
also impacted significantly on attitudes as to the perspicacity of previously unknowable
adversaries, accustomed to communicating only by shouting matches or trading barbs in
the media. The meeting culminated in unanimous agreement to form a steering committee
charged with developing further coordinated efforts to improve communication and
understanding. An eight-member committee was named a short time later that included
police chiefs from Dallas, Austin, Corpus Christi, and Lubbock (the latter in his position
as vice president of the Texas Association of Chiefs of Police), and the sheriff of Scurry
County in rural west Texas (in his role as president of the Texas Sheriffs' Association).

Representing Hispanic leadership were the associate counsel of the Mexican-American Legal Defense & Education Fund, the executive director of LULAC, and the chairman of the Texas House of Representatives Mexican-American Caucus.

Reference material distributed in advance by my office to all participants in the Dallas meeting included an article published by the International Association of Chiefs of Police titled "Aspects of a Policy to Limit the Use of Firearms." It brought attention to the fact that professional leadership in law enforcement around the country was seriously addressing the issue and that it was recognized as a vital and legitimate subject for examination and reform. A second enclosure in the same mailing was a Dallas newspaper editorial giving an account from a reasonably detached source of an incident reflecting a typical scenario in which the problems at hand were vividly illustrated. The meeting drew widespread media notice. A press report and later editorials are exhibited.[5]

Within a month, the newly formed committee had its first meeting in Austin. Its primary objective was to plan one or more in-state regional meetings to extend participation in sharing ideas and perspectives and to deepen examination of the issues. The first conference was tentatively projected to be held in San Antonio with law enforcement agencies drawn from south of a line connecting Houston/Galveston, San Antonio, and Del Rio. Details of actions taken are summarized in two of many published accounts.[6]

Weeks of preparation were launched. After extended discussions about whether to invite minority representation other than Mexican-American, it was decided that there were significant enough differences in the nature of issues that doing so would compromise effective programming. Further, it was agreed that combining racial/ethnic participation would require a much larger attendance, again detracting from optimal productivity. A total target attendance was set at 200 registrants, approximately half representing each of the two convening groups.

Before finalizing plans, a survey was conducted to determine whether prospective law enforcement conferees within the pilot area would be likely to attend. Sponsorship and possible funding opportunities were explored. Workshop control techniques and responsibilities were given careful attention, designed to avoid unproductive rhetoric, off-subject digressions, excessive time monopolizing, accusatory/blaming statements, and so forth. Arrangements for providing advanced briefings/training for those chairing sessions were put in place. Workshop and plenary session topics and formats were agreed upon. Rules for media coverage were formulated, placing primary responsibility on members of the steering committee and me, as conference coordinator. Applicable research and commentary literature for distribution to conferees were discussed and identified.

In mid-November, Austin Police Chief Frank Dyson (then designated to co-chair the steering committee, along with Ruben Bonilla, Jr., State Director of LULAC) sent the proposed survey letter to south Texas law enforcement agency administrators asking them to indicate whether they would likely attend a conference as described.[7] About one-third of those mailed were returned. All but two favored the conference and indicated they would attend. Of the 86 respondents, 72 were police chiefs, 12 were sheriffs and 2 were city marshals.

The trial balloon had been floated. There was ample interest to proceed. Subcommittees on site arrangements, program planning, funding, registration, media relations, and other responsibilities were appointed and went to work. The Texas Police Association came through with funding for the historic meeting, supplemented by additional support from the Hogg Foundation for Mental Health. The conference coverage

---

[5]Addendum S1-2 *Dallas Morning News* article, 9/23/1978; editorials, *Dallas Morning News*, 9/26/1978 and *Corpus Christi Caller*, 9/28/1978

[6]Addendum T: *San Antonio Express-News*, 10/21/1978; *The Daily Texan*, 10/23/1978.

[7]See addendum U: Conference proposal letter dated 11/13/1978.

area was expanded beyond San Antonio on the north to Austin and beyond Houston eastward to Beaumont/Port Arthur and Orange. Each law enforcement agency would be limited to a single representative, the chief executive officer, with exceptions granted only on pre-approval by one of the two conference chairmen. Parallel requirements were applied to community organizations. The total registration limit of 200 would be accepted on a first-come/first-served basis.

TWO PERSPECTIVES—ONE RESOLVE

After almost five months of planning and ongoing subcommittee meetings, the doors opened at the El Tropicana Hotel in San Antonio on March 23, 1979 to an unprecedented day-and-a-half forum dubbed *A Symposium on Contemporary Issues in Texas Police-Community Relations*. The import of the event was demonstrated by the program participation of Texas Attorney General Mark White, Legal Counsel Glen Murphy of the International Association of Chiefs of Police, Gilbert Pompa, Director of the U.S. Justice Department's Community Relations Service, Donald McEvoy, Program Director of the National Conference of Christians and Jews, and representatives of pilot police programs in Memphis and San Francisco. The full program is exhibited.[8] More than vital intergroup communication, some said, it was an experience in communion.

Press coverage spread throughout the state and beyond. Typical news accounts appearing in Dallas and Houston newspapers, and an editorial from Corpus Christi, are seen in the addenda section.[9]

Buoyed by the success of the San Antonio meeting, the steering committee wasted little time gathering steam for another symposium, this time to be a convocation of registrants from a band of towns and cities in north-central and west Texas. The impetus had been given extra energy when recently appointed Houston Police Chief Harry Caldwell (who served on the symposium steering committee), a few weeks after the San Antonio meeting concluded and had been given preliminary follow-up committee evaluation, wrote to CRS Director Gilbert Pompa extolling the impact of the initial experiment and urging a continuation of similar effort to reach other parts of the state. He said, in part:

". . . I am of the opinion that it was the greatest coup ever counted by the Community Relations Service. . . . The overwhelming consensus is that the San Antonio meeting was a tremendous success in that it allowed for the first time face-to-face meetings between groups who needed very badly to establish personal communications. . . . I would petition you to encourage CRS staff members in Texas to proceed immediately with the North Texas meeting without waiting for the transcript of any of the San Antonio proceedings and without any undue delay."

By early August 1979, *Symposium II* on Texas Law Enforcement and Community Relations, to be held in Fort Worth, was in final preparation stages. Dallas Police Chief Glen D. King replaced Chief Frank Dyson from Austin to co-chair the expanded 12-member steering committee as a representative from the new collection of law enforcement agencies. Replacements also included police chiefs from Abilene, Wichita Falls, Amarillo and Plainview, and the sheriff of Deaf Smith County in the west Texas panhandle. Also new to the committee were Jose Cano, State Director of the American GI Forum, Dr. John Matthews, Coordinator of Law Enforcement & Police Science at the Texas Criminal Justice Center, and Richard Sambrano, State President of Image de Tejas.

---

[8]See Addendum V: San Antonio conference program dated 3/23-24/1979.
[9]See Addendum W1-2-3: *Dallas Times Herald* dated 3/24/1979; *Houston Chronicle* dated 3/24/1979; *Corpus Christi Caller* dated 3/28/1979.

The Texas Police Association was again the principal source of funding and an active sponsor, supplemented by additional support from the Hogg Foundation for Mental Health. The agenda featured procedural rules, a format, and program content similar to the San Antonio meeting (selection and training, media relations, complaint processing/internal investigation, and use/control of excessive force). A set of presentation guidelines for use by speakers and panelists was developed as an outgrowth of recognized needs demonstrated in San Antonio, resulting in improved content discipline.

The intended registration limit of 200 was unavoidably oversubscribed. Word of the high praise in all quarters for the San Antonio meeting had created more interest in attending than could be accommodated. In a postconference letter of appreciation to program speakers, panelists, and moderators, I wrote, in part:

". . . I wish all of you could have heard just a portion of the praise for the program that came our way. Seldom is there a collection of people brought together for such a purpose that results in virtually universal respect and approval. . . . There is an irresistible temptation to compare this second conference with the San Antonio prototype of last March. The very least that could be said is that they were more different from one another than we might have anticipated.

"The Saturday luncheon walkout certainly added a touch of nostalgia. Most of us remember well the days when there could be no meeting on racial-ethnic related issues without the almost sure expectation of overt protest directed against one or another of the principal participants. It was somewhat ironic in this case, since Assistant Attorney General Drew Days, the target of the dissidents' displeasure, was himself a civil rights activist in the sixties and could easily have been 'wearing their hat' on this occasion, had the clock been turned back a decade or two. It was also interesting to note that the protesters chose to attack the head of the one federal office that has been more active than any recent predecessor in pursuing remedies for the very allegations of abuse about which they are concerned.

"Some have observed that there were noticeable differences in the temperament of the conferees as a whole. In San Antonio, I suppose, there was a certain excitement connected with a first experimental effort. There was possibly a greater exhilaration when the delegates found they could communicate with one another with surprising openness and candor. Others have suggested that since the participants in San Antonio were basically from south Texas, where Hispanic culture and influence may be perceived by many Anglos with greater familiarity and harmony, there was a certain cross-cultural relationship already in place before the meeting was convened.

"In any event, the Fort Worth symposium, though perhaps different in tone, was distinctive in its own right. A business-like professionalism was noted that tended to raise the level of engagement. The mix of law enforcement representation, this time including a number of non-local jurisdictions (including state and federal agency registrants), undoubtedly also played a part in the nature of participation and the outcome of dialogue. All said and done, the consensus was that the Fort Worth affair was highly successful and contributed significantly to prospects for better Texas police-community relationships in the future. . . ."

In the last analysis, the long-term consequences of the exhaustive effort that went into the two events would be measured by any long-term impact at the local level, especially where conflict and animosities characterized police-community interaction. Translation of the spirit and content of the experiment into grass roots action to address issues and create new solutions to old problems would be the test of substance.

Many follow-up activities were initiated in communities that had participated and in some other places where the idea had caught hold through publicity or inadvertent communication. Task forces and other groupings were established in many areas to create ongoing communication and joint problem-solving opportunities between law enforcement agencies and local minority organizations.

A follow-up feature article in the *Houston Chronicle*, less than three months after the Fort Worth meeting and about ten months following the San Antonio assembly, offered a view of precisely that line of inquiry and presented some specific illustrations of significant changes that had already been brought about, notwithstanding that many observers were cautious about overdrawn optimism.[10]

My assignment to the CRS Texas police-community relations project did not end with the wrap-up of the conferences. Part of my ongoing responsibility was to initiate appropriate activity to help ensure that the issues confronted would continue to get the attention needed to overcome impediments and to sustain progress. In the summer of 1980 a sequel effort was launched to form a statewide task group on citizen complaint processing that would provide a vehicle for continued exploration, refinement, and implementation of recommendations generated at the symposia. Fourteen law enforcement executives (almost half of whom were not previously involved) were joined by four key minority-community-organization spokesmen in a series of meetings that began in November.

Viewpoints were collected and recorded on a wide range of topics under the general heading of complaint processing. The agenda was described as an attempt to identify those elements of *any* complaint process that are at the foundation of sound management, effective implementation, and healthy relationships with various publics in the community. It was postulated that complaint processing, perhaps more than any other facet of police administration, tends to evoke perceptions in minority communities, and elsewhere, that question professional integrity and cast doubt on "the ability of the police to police themselves." It was accepted as axiomatic that when there is suspicion or conviction that police activity is shrouded in secrecy, that officials are unresponsive to criticism or allegations of misconduct, and that there is no willingness to acknowledge shortcomings or mistakes, that the ultimate result can only damage credibility and erode healthy police-community relations.

The group would ask themselves what can and should be done, at the very least, to ensure that the public has opportunity to examine and understand fully procedures to assess the guilt or innocence of a peace officer accused of wrongdoing? What would be the best way to evaluate an existing complaint system? Dozens more areas of inquiry were posed, to be dissected, prioritized, and incorporated into policy protocols. Procedural matters focused on the intake process, use by offenders of counsel or other advisers, the rights of the accuser and the accused, dealing with frivolous complaints, the role of internal affairs offices, and a long list of other issues. Public outreach considerations dealt with making written departmental complaint procedures available to the public (including Spanish translations), establishing complaint intake stations in the community, and inviting some degree of civilian participation in policy development and rule making.

Recognizing that it was impractical, if not impossible, to suggest a universal model or standard for complaint processing,[11] the group published a document intended as a guide for police agencies that could be adapted to individual circumstances. Beyond that, it was offered as a stimulant to at-risk factions in a community to work together toward more open and frequent interaction and cooperation.

The final product was a 15-page document, printed with funds provided by an anonymous corporate donor, titled *Texas Law Enforcement Agencies and Citizen Complaints— A Guide to Process, Procedure and Practice for Public Safety Agencies and Community Organizations*. Problem categories addressed (beyond those already noted) for which remedies were proposed included:

---

[10]See addendum X: *Houston Chronicle* dated 1/28/1980.

[11]Impractical because police policies and practices are greatly influenced or controlled by the nature/size/structure/culture of the agency, court decisions, civil service regulations, local and state ordinances, community attitudes, collective bargaining contracts, and other factors.

- A widespread image in disadvantaged communities of law enforcement officers as a close-knit fraternity insulated from those they are sworn to protect, often seen as prone to willful abuse of citizens without cause and a system of cover-up by whatever means necessary;
- Fear of filing complaints before an authority expected to reject, ignore, insult, or worse—to punish for making accusations of wrongful conduct;
- Polarization that occurs as a result of stereotyping when police are judged by the least worthy among them and minority activists are equally misjudged by the relatively few who attract attention through illegal or otherwise abhorrent behavior;
- An appearance of secrecy sometimes created by enforcement agencies as a result of the professed need for confidentiality of records and the barring of media from information that might expose hidden facts;
- An often lack of bilingual personnel to deal with interrogation and evidence-gathering when subjects have little or no competency in English;
- A confusing array of jurisdictions in understanding options for registering complaints other than the offending department (local, state, federal authorities).

Five primary elements of an internal affairs program were presented in some detail: (a) intake procedures, (b) case processing and disposition, (c) disciplinary measures, (d) access to records and investigative information, and (e) public education.

Concluding commentary stated, in part:

"We encourage community leaders to take local initiatives that will avoid festering problems and growing disenchantment. If there is doubt about the way in which departmental policy prescribes the use of handcuffs, stop and frisk procedures, use of firearms, affirmative action or other subject of community concern, *find out about it!* Make an appointment to sit down with the chief executive or other appropriate authority for a full review of the issue. . . . There is a potential in virtually every community, large or small, to improve police-community relationships. There are opportunities for racial and ethnic organizations, as well as for those in the community at large, to improve the climate for partnership and mutual confidence. This pamphlet . . . is meant to provide a framework within which public safety agencies and community interest groups can review and evaluate local conditions with an eye toward sharing concerns and developing mutually beneficial initiatives.

"Often, there are real desires for cooperative effort but no handles for specific and constructive program development. What is needed, sometimes, is a cross-fertilization tool. This document is meant to provide that tool."

Results of applying new mechanisms and fresh ideas to the problems under review were sure to be uneven, but as the years passed there were remarkable transformations taking place. Unprecedented numbers of minority recruits were successfully drawn to the badge. During the early 1980s initiatives by Texas police departments were underway to form partnerships with local human relations agencies, church coalitions, governmental bodies, and directly with minority/civil rights groups, to carry out follow-up objectives.[12] The next decade saw the appointment of black and Hispanic officers to top command positions in many police agencies. Now, more than three decades later, it is commonplace to see men and women of color at the top of the organization chart.

Still, in the first decade of a new century, peace and harmony between some citizens and those in the uniform of peace officers are not universal. Old enmities linger, but not

---

[12]See addendum Y1-2-3: Letters dated 4/15, 6/28, and 9/21/1982 referencing examples of postconference initiatives.

nearly as often nor as intensely. As in all occupational groupings, there are the miscreants under the color of law who poison the well. And there are reformers who are insatiable in their quest for a flawless society.

But make no mistake. A new day did dawn on the civil rights horizon and the future seems to offer the hope of fulfillment to those who dream, as did Martin Luther King, Jr., of "sitting at the table of brotherhood" and of finding common ground for understanding, tolerance, and acceptance among all humankind.

STUDENT BOYCOTT OF PUBLIC SCHOOLS
IN CRYSTAL CITY, TEXAS

Healthy discontent is the prelude to progress.

—Mohandas Gandhi

Restless dissidence among students has been a hallmark of the educational experience from time immemorial. The infectious shoulder-to-shoulder common cause of youth has been known to shake power brokers and arouse public support for change. In some instances it is the embodiment of our national heritage as a training ground for the democratic tenets of an open society. In contrast, at times it becomes a vehicle for the chronic malcontent in search of a cause. It is manifested mostly on the campuses of higher learning but can also be seen often at the secondary school level. Such was the case in Crystal City, Texas,[1] in late 1969.

A RIO GRANDE VALLEY CULTURAL CAULDRON

Crystal City in the 1960s was a microcosm of the underclass discontent that led to the historic reforms of that decade in America. The ingredients were ripe for ethnic revolt. There was determined and aggressive Latino leadership, widespread poverty, an overwhelming minority population, and a dominating Anglo minority with a tight hold on virtually all positions of governmental and economic influence. The politicization of Chicanos was under way.

---

[1]Crystal City, seat of Zavala County, is located deep in the Rio Grande Valley of Texas, just over 100 miles southwest of San Antonio and about a one-hour drive from the Mexican border. Its population in 1970 was about 8,000, more than 90% Mexican American. It has long laid claim to the title of "Spinach Capital of the World." A statue of cartoon character Popeye, that yesteryear mighty consumer of spinach, stands symbolically across from the city hall.

After several years of motivating and organizing activism, a passionate firebrand rebel, Jose Angel Gutierrez,[2] led the movement for dramatic political change. A voter registration campaign in late 1969 sought to gain control of key city and county elected offices. Newspapers throughout south Texas and beyond were reporting on "the Crystal City Revolts." The bold and unprecedented uprising became something of a platform from which was launched LaRaza Unida Party,[3] later destined to evolve into a statewide political force with considerable impact on the level of Hispanic participation in the governmental life of the Lone Star State. The commitment of La Raza was to organize "brown power," raising ethnic consciousness, rescuing cultural heritage, and "ending oppression to the Chicano Mexican people."

A student boycott of public school classes began on December 9, 1969. Better than half the total enrollment (almost 90% Spanish-surnamed) stayed home. A list of more than twenty grievances announcing reasons for the protest included:

- Discriminatory methods of electing student representatives and choosing recipients for honors or recognition;
- Failure to establish effective bilingual and bicultural programs;
- Retention of faculty and/or administrators who demonstrate prejudicial behavior toward Mexican-American students;
- Oversized classes resulting in a poor learning environment;
- Unwillingness to train teacher aides from among parents available for such service;
- Failure to provide a school environment that would motivate higher achievement and create positive attitudes toward education;
- Requirement for students to perform janitorial duties;
- Suppression of opportunities for free expression and disallowing student selection of speakers;
- No consideration given to declaring September 16th (Diez y Seis, a Mexican holiday celebrating "the cry for independence" in 1810) a school holiday and/or an occasion for special observances;
- Insistence on unfair and unnecessary dress codes;
- Absence of Mexican-American counselors;
- Anticipated unwillingness to grant amnesty for students who participated in the school walkout;
- Application of double standards in applying discipline and in enforcing regulations;
- Failure to investigate an Anglo school board member for illegally serving on both the school board and the county commission;
- Reduction in the school drop-out rate (often referred to by Chicanos as the "push-out" rate, estimated at over 70% in the Crystal City district) through eliminating inequitable practices;
- Maintenance of a double standard in connection with administration of examinations in language proficiency;

---

[2]Graduating from Crystal City High School in 1962, now-Professor Gutierrez later earned several graduate degrees including an MA from St. Mary's University in San Antonio, a PhD from the University of Texas/Austin, and a law degree from the University of Houston.

[3]The fledgling party, founded by Dr. Gutierrez in 1969, characterized itself as an independent political mechanism determined to separate from the likes of mainstream Latino organizations they saw to be too closely allied with Anglo influence and domination. The idea of escape from the abuse and manipulation of the white establishment spread quickly throughout the southwest to Colorado, New Mexico, California, and elsewhere. A principal party objective was to organize around electing Chicanos to public office, targeting priority positions on local school boards, city councils, and county commissions.

- Exertion of undue pressures on Mexican-American teachers who might show sympathy or support for student protest activity;
- Alleged inequities in payment of taxes by business interests as they apply to support of public education.

A major earlier protest issue involved a challenge by Latino students against a system of selecting the annual homecoming queen. The event, sponsored by the ex-students association, was said to have been conducted in a manner that virtually eliminated Mexican-American girls from consideration. At a school board meeting a month before the boycott, appeals were successful in convincing the board to prohibit use of school facilities to accommodate the affair because it was discriminatory on its face and should not be sanctioned by the school. At that same meeting the board agreed to explore other grievances at the next regular session in early December. When the time came, however, there was an apparent reversal of intention and the complainants were denied recognition to make their presentation. It was this development that was seen to have contributed significantly to the protest support base.

Inflamed by the school board's seeming intransigence, a student delegation and their sponsors traveled to the nation's capital on December 18 to consult with federal civil rights compliance officials at the Department of Health, Education and Welfare (HEW), and with U.S. Senator Ralph Yarborough. The very next day, a team of investigators was dispatched to Crystal City to begin a preliminary review of the school districts policies and practices.

One of the most difficult obstacles to examination and resolution of issues had been the refusal of school authorities to recognize their young charges as legitimate parties with whom they were obliged to negotiate. Their position centered on an insistence that only parents, as taxpayers, were constituents and therefore the only appropriate parties to whom they were obliged to respond.

ENTER MULTIPLE THIRD-PARTY INTERVENORS

Having determined to offer an intermediary option to the parties, I was assigned with San Antonio field office conciliator Tom Mata as a biethnic team to explore ways in which we might be able to help ease tensions and move past the stalemate. (My partner had several days earlier visited the site to assess community unrest, make preliminary contacts, and recommend whether CRS should intervene).

Given that the HEW Office for Civil Rights was already being drawn into the dispute and was scheduled to send a four-man task force to the site on the very day of our decision to explore entry, my first action was to reach their task force leader (dispatched out of the Dallas regional office) to explain our intended role and seek their agency's endorsement. We weren't sure that these particular investigators were generally familiar with the CRS mission nor could we know how they would feel about a coordinated interagency effort to bring matters to a successful conclusion. As it happened, they were quite aware of our functions and recognized that their third-party part would likely be seen as the stick (enforcement), and ours the carrot (voluntary resolution), creating a useful tandem.

Upon our arrival in Crystal City we began prearranged separate and private meetings with the Superintendent of Schools, John C. Billings, and then with School Board President Edward F. Mayer. To each was explained in detail the nature of our conciliation involvement, the authority and role of our agency, possible availability of neutral technical resource assistance, and other related matters. Within a few hours, after consulting with other members of the board, the president notified me that they would accept our assistance and would be available on and after December 29 to engage in whatever procedures we presented. We already had been provided important background information and briefings on community relationships by several local sources of our independent choosing.

A meeting was then held late on the same evening of our arrival with three boycott spokespersons (Severita Lara, Mario Trevino, and Diana Serna), along with some twenty other interested students, all participants in the current walkout. The three leaders were fresh with spirit and confidence, having just returned from their highly productive trip to Washington, and then San Antonio, where they were able to muster further support for their cause from several notable Latino organizations and, most importantly from their perspective, the Spanish-language media. Orientations similar to those earlier provided school officials regarding our identity and role and the nature of our agency's mandate provoked probing questions and some degree of skepticism. The meeting adjourned with a decision on whether to accept CRS as an intermediary to be made within the following few days. Shortly thereafter, we received word of final approval from the student delegation that we could proceed with efforts to help reach a negotiated settlement.

On December 29 a series of shuttle meetings between representatives of opposing factions centered on reviewing and refining several of the more complex issues in contention. Critical scrutiny was given to the lingering question of who would be accepted by the school board representatives as negotiators for the students. After much messaging back and forth, using us as their communication linkage, it was finally agreed that five student participants in the walkout and five parents, each of whom had at least one son or daughter among the protesters, would constitute a complainant negotiating committee. Each such member would also have a named alternate available as a replacement in the event of unavoidable absence from joint meetings of the primary committee members. The respondents would be represented by at least four of the seven-member school board, along with the school superintendent. A three-member group of citizen observers acknowledged as impartial by both sides was to be invited to attend all joint sessions.

The issue of amnesty for student strikers would be given first attention because, unless that question was satisfactorily resolved, there would be no basis for settlement. It was agreed that the CRS representatives would preside at meetings, establish procedural guidelines, and have the authority to decide all matters regarding the process to be employed.

At this point, before joint sessions were arranged, the San Antonio field representative for the U.S. Civil Rights Commission (USCRC) contacted the CRS team seeking reaction to a tentative plan by his agency to hold hearings in Crystal City in a month or so. Its intent would be to explore the causes of student unrest, to determine what kinds of remedial measures might be most effective and, generally, to document the entire conflict in order that other communities in similar circumstances might benefit from the lessons learned in Zavala County. After consultation with legal and operational staff at Washington headquarters, we responded with affirmation of the proposal but with the proviso that no such hearing would be initiated until CRS-coordinated negotiations were completed, with or without success.

This latest injection of another agency into the mix of involvement raised concerns about possible threats to orderly process. It was suggested that there was a clear need for interagency coordination if there was to be a further multiplicity of resources entering the scene. It was proposed that the three federal agencies now involved (CRS, HEW, and the Civil Rights Commission), along with any of several private agencies (namely the Mexican-American Legal Defense & Education Fund [MALDEF] and possibly one or more other organizations heavily engaged in Hispanic affairs) meet for purposes of coordination.

The CRS team returned on December 30 to meet with school officials. Discussion reverted back to the subject already thought to have been settled—the questionable legitimacy and legality of an elected body dealing in any formal way with parties who were not tax-paying patrons. Renewed reluctance to embrace a negotiation process was said also to hinge on the failure of an earlier arrangement under which the Texas Education Agency had offered their good offices to deal with the problems at hand, a course that was soon abandoned for unstated reasons.

Recognizing that this exchange with the respondents was likely to determine whether or not the negotiation proposal would go forward, it was here that our persuasiveness would be tested. Toward the end of turning these vacillating attitudes among some school board committeemen to a more positive and receptive position, we directed their attention to a number of key considerations:

- Channeling student activism into constructive pursuits and toward useful methods of confronting problems can serve as an antidote to desperation measures;
- Other school districts in Texas and around the country had found that administrators giving students a reasonable voice in educational program decision-making has paid worthwhile dividends;
- The Crystal City student clamor for reform has been implemented in an unusually responsible way thus far, without violence, without known threats of personal injury or property damage. This apparent exercise of restraint can be compared with many parallel situations in which hostile aggression and sometimes rampant disorder are the consequences of perceived authoritarian rejection. To permit a deterioration in relationships between the providers of education and those who are its beneficiaries is to invite greater frustration and possible resort to more threatening devices;
- The use of nonparticipating local citizen observers is likely to keep student demands within reasonable bounds (later agreed upon to consist of one individual selected by each side and a third chosen by mutual agreement of both sides);
- Use of meeting facilities other than on school property will help eliminate any feelings of intimidation or discomfort on the part of students in addressing their concerns (later agreed upon to be conducted in a convenient local church with satisfactory meeting accommodations);
- Any reneging on the earlier agreement regarding the composition of the protest group will be seen by the students, and by many in the community, as evidence of lacking good faith on the part of school officials. (The earlier provision to have five students and five parents participate was ultimately adopted.)

An afternoon session with student team leaders extended into the early hours of the following morning. This phase of prenegotiation preparation dealt with a complete and detailed review and refinement of each issue proposed for an agenda. The students were, in effect, made to defend or support each grievance with specific illustrations and to explain their rationale where appropriate. They showed no resistance or displeasure at our probing, recognizing that they needed to examine their complaints as objectively and dispassionately as possible in order to strengthen their positions. The original list of twenty-three separate contentions was reduced to seventeen, largely through eliminating overlapping problems and combining others.

Part of the earlier orientation process with students had emphasized the need for going beyond defining problems by proposing possible solutions. A key CRS input during this session was an introduction to the "ombudsman" concept[4] and its possible usefulness in

---

[4]A mechanism popular in Sweden, New Zealand, and elsewhere that provides for an appointed specialist on the staff of an organization or institution to receive and investigate complaints, report findings, and assist with achieving equitable solutions.

framing a proposal for an effective grievance process. It was offered as an adjunct or substitute for a parents' advisory committee for which student leaders had initially given high priority status.

It is germane at this juncture to point out that the CRS entry into this case in late 1969 was well before we, as an agency, had considered the need and potential for a formalized, structured mediation process in accomplishing our mission. It was the fortuitous circumstances of this case, as much as in any other, that sparked our launching a thorough investigation of the mediation option that eventually became a major program thrust for our agency. Here we were, inadvertently applying many elements of what would later become some of the basic substance of our training and codification of field procedures.

LEVELING THE PLAYING FIELD

The first joint meeting between the parties was held on the morning of New Year's Eve, 1969. Following introductions around the table (most had not met before and were about to be in direct dialogue with one another for the first time), my preliminary comments as chair of the meeting included:

- Recapitulation of past barriers to effective communication between the parties; difficulties arising from judgments made based on rumor, second-hand reports, and media releases;
- A call to seek equitable solutions to issues of merit and to discard those that fail to reflect legitimate grievances;
- Need to minimize emotional reactions and to strive for objective and rational conclusions;
- Ground rules for participation in joint sessions, including: (a) each issue to be considered separately and independently from all others; (b) when reasonable basis for the merit of an issue has been established, response to be directed toward corrective measures, avoiding sidebar opinions or other inappropriate commentary; (c) prerogatives of the chair set forth and discussed covering normal procedural requirements, floor recognition, judgments of order, and so on; (d) explanation and encouragement of recess/caucus usage.

Student spokespersons made clear at the outset that any agreement reached between the two sides would have to be ratified by a substantial number of boycotting students and their parents, probably at a meeting called for that purpose. The stipulation drew no objection from school team members. It was further agreed that any document of resolution would be presented in writing and signed by the principal participants.

The agenda moved then to the first three of seventeen issues (amnesty, grievance procedures, and biracial/bicultural programs). Resolution was reached on each of these three questions, all ranked by protest forces at the highest level of priority. The full text of the agreement sets forth these and fourteen other issues, and related actions agreed upon.[5]

During a two-day recess before the next scheduled joint meeting on January 3, I received a phone call from Severita Lara, one of the established student leaders, but one who had not participated in the CRS-sponsored developments to that point in time. She stated that I was not to return to Crystal City to continue conducting negotiations. She offered no reason that seemed credible, given her absentee status. My only reasonable

---

[5]See addendum Z: Agreement text ending school boycott, dated 1/4/70.

recourse was to reach several of those students who had been involved and with whom I had been dealing from the outset. I learned from them that there was an obvious disagreement within the student leadership as to whether the CRS-introduced process should continue and, if so, under what circumstances.

It was quickly agreed that I would meet with the split factions together before any resumption of negotiation sessions. The expectation was that various dissatisfactions, suspicions, and misunderstandings could be aired in an attempt to bring about a better climate of understanding and trust. At a meeting held just hours before the scheduled resumption of negotiation proceedings, a candid exchange of views led to a substantially improved comfort level regarding the role and conduct of the chair. The primary reason for the contention, it was revealed during the discussion, related to a falsely drawn conclusion that I had told the school board president about the split in student ranks and that there was a resulting weakening of their effectiveness in negotiating positions.

That rumor, like so many that typically circulate under such circumstances, had no basis in fact. To have been guilty of the allegation would have been an unacceptable breach of trust and the antithesis of serving the neutral third-party role. Fortunately, the concerns of those students who raised the charges were set aside once the matter was aired and a degree of my integrity restored.

Shortly after the meeting, I had a visit in my motel room from Jose Angel Gutierrez (identified earlier in this account and who had not been openly involved with developments to this point), reputed to be the behind-the-scenes advisor and strategist to the protest coalition. His intention appeared to be based on a need to be personally assured of my innocence regarding the rumored allegations. That private exchange seemed to allay his misgivings.

The second joint session was convened on the evening of January 3. In keeping with a request by students, my colleague, Tom Mata, chaired this meeting. It was perhaps a message to me, I thought, of a lingering mistrust of an Anglo intermediary. Or possibly it was no more than an understandable preference for having the chairmanship occupied by a Latino with the ability to occasionally switch to Spanish language exchanges when circumstances warranted (although dissuaded in orientation guidelines out of fairness to non-Spanish-speaking participants). Also in attendance as observers, with the consent of the parties, were the two representatives in town from the U.S. Civil Rights Commission staff, preparing for their later planned hearing.

Turning to the next issues at hand, the first two (testing inequities and ethnic isolation) were settled with minimal debate or undue differences in positions. The third subject on the table, however, became the focal point for an impasse that threatened to negate all the promising and substantial gains that had thus far been made.

The sticking point centered on questions regarding methods by which certain student positions are determined (cheerleaders, sweetheart of athletic teams, prom servers, twirlers and drum majors, etc.). Many surprisingly complicated factors were involved, and it appeared that the school board would not back down from its proposal to settle the matter, one that failed to meet the prime objective of the students. For the first time, Mata and I called for a caucus with the respondent team. We felt it had become necessary to try to influence one of the parties to reconsider a hardened stand. With the three community observers present and offering opinions, a sometimes heated discussion lasted over an hour. The observers had aligned themselves with our position that the board needed to show more flexibility in a matter of such seemingly innocuous substance, yet of considerable importance to students. Finally, in a split vote taken during the caucus, our combined persuasiveness prevailed. The original student demand was accepted.[6]

---

[6]Ibid, issue VI.

The third and final negotiation session on January 4 turned on the remaining eleven issues. Step-by-step attention through to the last topic brought resolution twelve hours later to all remaining grievances. The basis for a document of reconciliation had been achieved.

Upon adjournment, several persons from each side (including the school board president, two students and two of the community observers who had attended the meetings) were named to join Mata and myself to finalize the wording of a written agreement, signed by the respondents but held in abeyance for student signatures until presentation and anticipated ratification at a mass meeting of protest constituents the following day.

The ratification assembly, held in a large hall that overflowed its capacity, drew an estimated 600 people. The document was read in both English and Spanish. Most segments, as they were presented, received generous ovations. It was apparent to all that the Mexican-American community had achieved virtually all the objectives they sought.

At one point, questions arose over a section referencing the action to be taken by teachers in cooperating with students seeking to make up lost school work during the boycott. Exception was taken to the wording "be expected to" in terms of their related instructions from the administration. In response to this concern, we suggested an immediate effort be made to contact school officials in order to modify the phrasing and eliminate the objections. The assembly was promptly recessed while a student spokeswoman, Diana Serna, joined my CRS colleague in a visit with the school board president. They accomplished their purpose and returned to the waiting throng at the hall. Soon afterwards, the agreement was signed by the appropriate protest principals before television cameras and all who came to witness what was seen to be an historic milestone in south Texas educational reform. Statewide media coverage was extensive throughout the marathon negotiations, culminating with the ratification event.[7]

Within hours after the celebratory crowd dispersed, and before we departed Crystal City, there was an incident connected to implementation of the agreement that sparked a fresh round of rumor, suspicion, and skepticism. A phone call to the superintendent of schools brought reasonable explanation of what had transpired. We reported back to the complaint source and a near-calamity was averted. As it turned out, not surprisingly, the action in question was not at all a commitment violation by school authorities, but rather a faulty communication that quickly deteriorated into unfounded hearsay.

The episode underscored the urgency for creating a temporary mechanism for immediate utility that would be able to deal with any and all communication problems and other situations requiring third-party investigation and evaluation. Such an arrangement would remain in effect until a grievance apparatus could be established, as provided in the agreement. In our parting activity, we made appropriate contacts with key individuals from all involved segments and steps were promptly initiated to activate a clergy group to serve this need during the interim period.

Although we left Crystal City with a high degree of satisfaction for the way our intervention achieved success, there were the inevitable uncertainties and uncontrollable developments that, sooner or later, were likely to threaten lasting amity. We knew, for example, that many of the remedies agreed upon would depend to a significant extent on the availability of funding to facilitate execution of reforms. Outside technical assistance might be required in some areas of administrative realignment.

Some changes would require longer time frames than were foreseen during negotiations. It would be of great importance that all parties be able to distinguish between legitimate delays and intentional obstruction. Given the ingrained attitudes of enmity and ethnic/class distinctions between many Anglos and "Tejanos," especially by student factions

---

[7]See addendum AA: *San Antonio Express-News*, 1/4/1970 and *Dallas Morning News*, 1/6/1970.

toward school authorities, the disposition to overreact to various real or perceived misdeeds could pose a constant threat to ultimate execution of the full agreement. The clergy committee, formed to provide a trusted local resource to put out fires before they became destructive, was seen to be the best hope for a stabilizing influence and as an instrument of community cohesiveness.

BY THE SEAT OF OUR PANTS

For my agency, the Community Relations Service of the U.S Department of Justice, this case was more than just one of many in which we engaged with similar components. It was, in fact, an experience that led me to urge our Washington headquarters staff to thoroughly examine the potential for adopting a more structured and disciplined process of negotiation that we could introduce to parties in conflict. We had, in Crystal City, inadvertently and without related training, applied some of the most basic precepts of mediation practice. There were invaluable lessons learned. Among them, before bringing the parties together for face-to-face interaction:

- Establish among the parties a full understanding of the role of the mediator and the mediation process with its promises and limitations and confirm the personal integrity of the individual in whom they are to place their trust as a fair and neutral third party;
- Require a comprehensive assessment to determine whether conflict issues and conditions are likely to benefit from a negotiation format before deciding on the appropriate CRS response;
- If necessary, review, clarify, refine, and prioritize issues of the aggrieved party and develop proposed solutions as part of an agenda that is likely to be readily understood and subject to affirmative response from the answering party;
- Emphasize and explain the critical and often adverse effect aggressive media coverage can have on progress toward settlement;
- Introduce the use of, and the rationale for, having nonparticipating observers as a part of the negotiation process;
- Describe the requirements of settlement, including elements of the instrument of written agreement, the degree to which it may or may not have enforcement potential, and recognition of the respondent's capacity to comply;
- Identify possible outside technical or professional resources who may be able to contribute to resolution and explain the conditions under which they may be called upon to participate;
- Recognize the substantial importance of creating a postagreement mechanism to deal with matters of compliance, rumor control, and open communication, vested if possible in a local third party individual or group that enjoys the trust and acceptance of the contestants.

THE BOTTOM LINE

One has only to contemplate the course of events as they unfolded after the boycott and settlement to recognize the full impact of this microcosmic uprising. Political changes were about to occur that would have been earlier considered far beyond probability. Within months, the previously referenced La Raza Unida Party was formed and seemed to be carried by the wave of enthusiasm and intrepidity created by the success of the boycott. Before the year was out, the reputed mastermind of the walkout, Jose Angel Gutierrez, won election to the school board and later became its president. Some three years later he was at the pinnacle of local political power, serving for five years as county judge of Zavala County.

The shift in power from Anglo to Mexican-American control was marked by ethnic turnover in the composition of virtually all key functions of municipal and county government. Severita Lara, one of the leading student protest voices, by 1986 became the first Hispanic county judge in all of Texas, occupying the same seat held more than a decade before by her mentor. Years later she was elected to the town council of Crystal City and thereafter chosen by her council colleagues to be mayor.

Before 1970, with only one exception, there were only Anglos hired as Crystal's city manager. From 1971 through the 1980s, only Mexican Americans held that position. Similarly, superintendents of schools until 1971 had all been Anglo. For the next two decades, all were Tejano.

The battle for reform in Crystal was seen by many to have been the launching pad for Chicano self-determination and political muscle throughout the state of Texas and beyond. Face-to-face negotiation had been embraced as a source of empowerment. Protest leaders recognized an opportunity to take better control of their lives and to repudiate a local government they saw to be oppressive and insensitive to their needs. Today, the gradual but certain increase in Mexican-American participation is self-evident at all levels of government, from the national capital to the main street city hall. Some part of that evolution, many would say, was rooted in a small town in south Texas where a group of high schoolers and their parents went the distance.

A DISPUTE SETTLEMENT CENTER
FOR DALLAS, TEXAS

The Courts of this country should not be the place
where the resolution of disputes begin. They should be the place
where the disputes end—after alternative methods . . .
have been considered and tried.

—Former U.S. Supreme Court Justice
Sandra Day O'Connor

The personnel of our agency's neutral conflict interveners and peacemakers were guided by the parameters of our mandate, described elsewhere in this text. That framework, however, allowed for considerable latitude in how we might carry out that commission. This was a service that had no precedent in the federal establishment. If our supervisors and policy-makers in Washington headquarters saw a proposal by a field office contributing to our basic objectives in resolving conflict, they were likely to approve our involvement. I have chosen to include in this anthology an illustration of notable departure from the norm in our modus operandi. It was an initiative that drew us into a *catalyst* mode intended to pre-empt conflict escalation, rather than our more typical role as interveners in already existing and threatening conflict conditions.

WITHOUT RECOURSE TO COMPULSION

The 1970s were a time when the search for alternatives to traditional litigation remedies was gathering steam. Legal scholars and others had long been seeking ways to make the adjudicative process more accessible, more affordable, and more responsive. Now they were being joined by an array of citizen resources outside the legal profession, representing business, educational, and religious institutions, neighborhood and civic organizations, and other centers of interest. Throughout the country, coalitions largely drawn from these sources were going about the building of new mechanisms to deal with community dispute settlement.

Their primary program targets were neighborhood problems that caused rancor and unease (property infringement or misuse issues, nuisance conditions, student dissension, consumer complaints regarding defective merchandise or unsatisfactory customer relations, family and interpersonal quarrels, disagreements between landlords and tenants, etc.).

A significant proportion of these sorts of squabbles would wind up in small claims courts or in the hands of lawyers catering to petty civil and sometimes minor criminal actions. Always there was a winner and a loser. The community dispute resolution center concept was providing an opportunity for more fruitful results by bringing the parties together in a less contentious environment to seek common denominators and avoid an imposed finding.[1]

Changes in personal, family, institutional, and community values, and a host of other societal developments over the previous three decades or so, influenced markedly the ways in which adversaries confronted one another. The family physician, the pastor, the teacher with special interpersonal skills and sensitivities, the parent or close relative, the police officer on a walking beat—seldom do these erstwhile stabilizing, problem-solving intervening resources function as they once did. No longer are these and similar peacemakers as readily sought out, nor are they likely to be as easily available to help overcome the family feud or to help mend other troubled relationships. Such persons, even when they were more accessible, too often were poorly equipped to perform as objective interveners. Normally, they were not trained for such roles nor were such obligations necessarily central to their perceived responsibilities. Beyond these considerations, the changes from neighborhood cohesiveness and closer ties by virtue of proximity and common interests to more diverse residential patterns, mobility and transiency, and a tendency toward anonymity, if not isolation, had further contributed to a more volatile climate of individual and group interaction.

Over the preceding decade, this emerging interest in the United States in these alternative approaches to dispute processing, surprising perhaps only in the sense of synchronicity, was being given serious attention in other locations, and among other cultures around the world.

So here again, as described in preceding chapters but in other contexts, we are focusing on another approach to removing disputants from the adversarial climate of the court room. As in most conflict situations, it is recognized in this milieu that dissension frequently stems from faulty perception, poor communication, simple misunderstanding, or all three. It attempts to overcome the inhibitions (foreboding to many) to the traditional legal proceeding that calls for public disclosure, the threat of sanctions, compelled and sworn testimony, rules of evidence, cross-examination, and other accessories of jurisprudence (all requirements to ensure due process, protect the innocent and determine guilt, but not necessarily to resolve the problem to the satisfaction of all). Although the community dispute settlement center deals largely with cases of relatively minor seriousness in terms of civil or criminal culpability, those who seek its services can be relieved of consequences that often produce painful stress and frustration and even bring about an escalation of their problem to more disagreeable proportions.

---

[1]The American Arbitration Association opened one of the first such projects in Philadelphia in 1972. It became a prototype for similar initiatives in Rochester, NY, San Francisco, New York City, and elsewhere. The Night Prosecutor Program in Columbus, Ohio, was established in 1971, one of the first attempts to deal with interpersonal conflict before the parties became litigants. The Institute for Mediation and Conflict Resolution in New York City, created in 1970, was another pioneer in this field, one of the earliest to offer research and training (we at CRS among its trainees), its roots planted in the labor-management arena. By 1980 there were estimated to be almost 100 local dispute settlement centers in the United States.

By the end of the 1970s, according to various estimates of the number of independent, nongovernmental community mediation and arbitration services established in the United States (depending upon whose figures were relied upon), there were 100 more such programs established. Major cities represented in those precursory times, in addition to those already referenced in this chapter, included Los Angeles, Chicago, Detroit, Pittsburgh, Washington, DC, Boston, Cleveland, Akron, Cincinnati, San Jose, Wilmington, Jersey City, Trenton, Schenectady, Albany, and Portland (Oregon). None was reported to have been established in Texas or the southwest, although Houston was known to have begun investigating program feasibility. Tucson and Denver had come on line soon after the turn of the decade.

By this time, national conferences on legal reform were considering how changes in the judicial system might be best applied. At one such conference in 1976, a task force was appointed, headed by Judge Griffin B. Bell, soon to become Attorney General of the United States. Early the next year, the new attorney general would create within the Department of Justice a special office to promote and develop new ways to adapt an inertial legal structure to the new challenges of a restless and discordant society. Their objectives were virtually indistinguishable from those who organized community centers for mediation and conflict resolution already in operation. But their subsequent pilot projects in Atlanta, Kansas City, and Los Angeles contributed substantially to the body of knowledge and experimental variations that would eventually constitute core operational guidelines for other programs. Moreover, it was another noteworthy indication of the nation's commitment to judicial innovation.

Further evidence of national attention to non-judicial remedies was demonstrated by the American Bar Association. By the late 1970s, the ABA had created a special committee on alternative dispute resolution. Leadership in the legal profession had increasingly shown an awareness that the traditional litigation process is sometimes too costly and too time consuming to serve the ends of justice. This was seen to be especially true when the contested issues were of relatively modest content, as in terms of personal injury or property damage. Inordinate delays in processing both civil and criminal cases had been widely cited by prominent members of the bar as impediments to the effective resolution of many disputes that clog lower court dockets in America's cities.

THE RISE OF COMMUNITY MEDIATION IN TEXAS

In 1980, Dallas had been my home for some 25 years, long before I entered federal service. I had worked there during my early career in employment that was at the periphery of the still relatively dormant racial divide that limited equal opportunity in job placement, public accommodations, housing, education, and other privileges of citizenship. I knew the city well.

During my early years with CRS, being stationed in the agency's Dallas regional office, there were opportunities to develop relationships with many who had a hand in guiding that city's stewardship—city and county government, minority organizations, public and private organizations devoted to social services and intergroup relations, the business community, law enforcement agencies, clergy leadership, and so forth. Consequently, my contacts in Dallas were far more extensive than in any other location to which my assignments would take me.

I was struck by the fact that by the late 1970s, this city of legendary "can do" reputation was not among the major American population centers that had connected to the community justice center movement. I knew the needs there were at least as great as in any other city of its size and complexity. It took little persuasion to convince my superiors that we would be true to our mission by devoting time and energy to initiatives that would bring Dallas into the community dispute resolution orbit.

The preparation before any overt activity could begin took several weeks of exploration and research. One of my earliest contacts in January of 1980 was with Larry Ray,[2] Staff Director for the ABA's Special Committee on Resolution of Minor Disputes. He was able to bring me up to date on dispute resolution programs around the country, providing me with much valuable documentation. I would be working closely with him throughout the Dallas project.

A second early and important ally was Frank G. Evans, Associate Justice of the Court of Civil Appeals in Houston. He had become the sparkplug in that city to investigate and make recommendations to the Houston Bar Association as to the feasibility of establishing a justice center there. We would be in frequent communication of mutual assistance, sharing ideas, contacts and information.

By early February, I had prepared a 33-page concept paper titled "A Survey to Probe Potentials for a Dispute Mediation Center in Dallas." The document was sent to 89 selected representatives of government, the legal profession, the judiciary, business, law enforcement, public education and civic/social service organizations and agencies. They were asked to review and evaluate the proposal and to indicate whether they would be interested in attending one or more exploratory meetings leading to the later establishment of a steering committee to undertake initial planning and organization. The response was enthusiastic far beyond expectations.

The first two briefing sessions were held on March 10 and 11, attended by a total of 55 participants.[3] The duplicate programs at each of the meetings featured the two previously identified consultants, Judge Frank Evans of Houston and Larry Ray, on the staff of the American Bar Association in Washington, DC. The two guests led discussions that included options for organization issues, sponsorship, funding, staffing, program features, and interagency relationships. Clear consensus had now been reached: Dallas would benefit substantially from the creation of an alternative dispute resolution program. Forty-two "participation/leadership survey" forms were returned indicating various levels of interest and availability for further involvement. Others, including some who were unavoidably absent from the briefings, were later added to the planning group roster.

From these opening developments came the appointment of a seven-person interim coordinating committee composed of the executive director of the Dallas Citizens Council,[4] a county and a district court judge, a Dallas County commissioner, a black justice of the peace, the chairman of the criminal justice committee of the Greater Dallas Council of Churches, and a senior partner of a prominent local law firm. Two large supporting groups were divided into differing levels of participation. One pledged time commitments of up to ten hours per month until first-stage organization was in place and an official policy board appointed. The second, because of other priorities precluding a fixed time commitment, offered intermittent participation and availability for consultation in problem areas related to their particular backgrounds or expertise.

The next major step along the road to implementation was a full-day workshop held at Southern Methodist University on April 19. The program was funded by the Law Enforcement Assistance Administration (LEAA) through the Criminal Courts Technical Assistance Project at the American University in Washington, DC. Three prominent con-

---

[2]In that new position for only a few weeks, Ray was previously attorney-director of the Night Prosecutor's Program in Columbus, Ohio (already referenced in footnote 1 of this chapter).

[3]Each event was limited to no more than 30 participants seated at a large conference table.

[4]Membership of top business executives, often characterized as Dallas' oligarchic power structure and by others as the city's most influential source of progress and beneficence.

sultants[5] were featured on an agenda to examine current developments in the field of non-traditional conflict resolution and to more thoroughly explore options available for the formulation and implementation of a dispute mediation program in Dallas.

Professor Dan McGillis provided a national overview of program models; Edith Primm described lessons from the demonstration project she headed in Atlanta; Richard Evarts addressed the topic: "Getting Started — Frustrations and Rewards." Many questions raised at the March meetings were laid to rest. Dr. McGillis later prepared a detailed summary of workshop discussions that was printed and distributed to variously interested parties, in Dallas and around the country, by The American University Institute for Advanced Studies in Justice

With the completion of this seminar, sustained enthusiasm for the project seemed clearly to reflect the will to move forward toward implementation. Response to committee assignment invitations had been overwhelming. The planning council roster listed 78 individuals, including many key governmental, business, professional, church, and civic leaders serving on eight committees. Another group of 24 became a project support group with commitments to provide consultation and limited participation. It was time for next steps toward actualization.

The first committees to be called together were those concerned with project organization, dealing with incorporation, tax status, funding strategies, sponsor relations, preliminary staffing, site alternatives, interagency relationships, and so forth. Houston's Judge Evans continued to work closely with our project, especially in connection with the legal work necessary to create the organizational structure. An LEAA[6] grant application to fund organizational activity was prepared and submitted in early May.

By now, momentum was intensifying in the Texas legal community for engagement with the alternative dispute resolution concept (by then commonly referred to as ADR). The State Bar of Texas established a committee to study the issue, inviting me, a nonlawyer, to its membership. Endorsement of the new option to replace judicial remedy was becoming a legitimate parcel of the legal profession.

The first phase of the project, program exploration and mobilization of community interest, was completed by the end of September 1980. The second phase, funding and pre-operational preparation, was under way. The third and final phase, program implementation, was targeted for early 1981.

Promising forward movement now came from Texas Governor William P. Clements, Jr. In response to an appeal for funding assistance sent by Planning Council Coordinating Committee member, Nancy Judy,[7] the governor was laudatory in his support of the Dallas project and reported that the staff of the Texas Department of Community Affairs agreed that the proposal had great merit. He said in his letter that he was particularly impressed by the level of local support that had been generated as a prelude to seeking financial backing. Half of the first year's budget, he said, could be made available.

Exploration of prospects for foundation and other philanthropical sources of funding continued. Federal cutbacks in criminal justice spending left us with little choice but to seek out local benefactors. Preliminary steps were taken to identify candidates for initial staffing and volunteer positions (mediators, administrative assistants, outreach speakers, etc.). The legal committee chair submitted proposed articles of incorporation and bylaws,

---

[5]Dr. Daniel McGillis, Research Associate, Criminal Justice Center, Harvard University Law School; Richard Evarts, Executive Director, Denver Conciliation Services; Edith Primm, Executive Director, Neighborhood Justice Center of Atlanta.

[6]Law Enforcement Assistance Administration, a part of the U.S. Department of Justice, either through state agencies or directly from its own discretionary disbursement pocket, contributed to many local dispute center start-ups until about the time the Dallas project was being launched, soon after which it was dismantled.

[7]Dallas County Commissioner.

along with a draft application for exemption from federal income tax. Temporary letter-heads for the Dispute Mediation Service of Dallas (DMS) displayed its new ten-member board of directors (all members of the previously designated interim coordinating commit-tee) with me as provisional project coordinator to serve until permanent staff was employed.

By the time we had reached this stage of development, the Houston Neighborhood Justice Center had hired staff and was then in the process of training mediator volunteers. They had been among the last of LEAA grant recipients before that agency closed its doors, sacrificed to federal budget reductions.

As project coordinator, I prepared a final comprehensive proposal, dated January 1981, to serve as the principal funding package. In addition to a program narrative that included an historical background summary, program characteristics and objectives, antic-ipated referral systems, and organizational projections, eleven exhibits referenced budget estimates, organization rosters, letters of support/endorsement representing community leadership, the originating concept paper and workshop agendas, legal papers, organiza-tion chart, case flow chart, and diagrammatic processing sequences. The document was forwarded to the Texas Department of Community Affairs as part of our submission to them to receive one-half the first year's budget, already tentatively approved. It was also sent to selected foundations for matching and subsequent financial support with regard to second- and third-year requirements. Long-term funding through enabling state legisla-tion was being undertaken by the Texas Bar Association through initiatives taken by Houston's Judge Evans, in which our board of directors collaborated.

In late March of 1981, the Texas Senate Committee on Intergovernmental Relations voted unanimously to approve a bill authorizing counties with over 500,000 population to levy a fee on civil litigants for the sole purpose of funding alternative systems of dispute resolution. Principal testimony in achieving that result was provided by Judge Evans and two Dallas representatives, along with two Texas Supreme Court justices, and others. At the time, only two other states, California and Florida, had similar enabling legislation.

Meantime, the interim DMS president[8] was busy contacting private area foundations in search of complementary funding and, in addition, probing corporate and legal commu-nity prospects for such participation. Soon, the charter board of directors took office, with Louis J. Weber, Jr., a senior partner with an influential Dallas law firm, becoming the first elected DMS president. New appointments expanded the number of board directors from eleven to thirteen. It was a veritable "who's who" of public service in "Big D."

Shortly thereafter, a major grant of $65,000 from the Meadows Foundation was received (half of the first year's budget to be matched with a grant in the same amount from the Texas Department of Community Affairs, in addition to smaller cash gifts from the Texas Industries Foundation and the Pollack Foundation to go toward the second year's operations). We were ready to open a bank account and begin administrative operations.

The expectation that the state legislature would pass the proposed bill to provide per-manent funding arrangements to sustain dispute resolution programs in Texas' largest cities turned out to be premature. Some suggested the bill fell victim to unwarranted polit-ical bickering.[9] Later on, however, those who opposed the measure would reverse their positions after objectives were clarified and misconceptions eliminated.

Richard Evarts,[10] after several visits to Dallas for a series of interviews, assumed duties in early August to become the inaugural executive director. He was one among some forty applicants. His first priority, after hiring support staff, was to launch a training program

---

[8]Wallace Savage, former mayor of Dallas, prominent attorney and bank executive.

[9]See addendum BB: Editorial, *Dallas Times Herald* dated 6/3/81.

[10]Formerly founder and administrator of the Center for Dispute Resolution in Denver (later renamed CDR Associates), past president of the Society of Professionals in Dispute Resolution.

for volunteer mediators and then to begin case processing by October. More than a dozen applications from eager would-be mediators were already on hand, to be part of the first class of no more than 40 that would take the intensive minimum 40 hours of training. Ultimately, those first 40 were selected from among 72 applicants. Among the first contingent of trainees were attorneys, teachers, psychologists, clergy, and other professionals. Others were business managers, local government officials, civic organization leaders, sales people, and retirees. A program of monthly in-service training would provide ongoing refinement of intermediary skills and deeper insights into mediation dynamics.

With the appointment of a full-time DMS director, my role as facilitator and temporary coordinator of the project was at an end. In my final communication addressed to 100 or so of the original planning council members, current directors, and others who participated in and contributed to the effort over the previous 18 months, I summarized developments, recounted funding projections, and expressed personal appreciation for the phenomenal support given the initiatives provided by our office.[11] I continued my connection with the new enterprise by accepting appointment to the board of directors on which I served until my retirement from federal service to pursue a business opportunity in the private sector in late 1984. During that same period, I continued serving on the Special Committee for Alternative Methods of Dispute Resolution of the Texas Bar Association.

FROM INFANCY TO MATURITY—ADR IN DALLAS AND THE NATION

The Dallas Center marked its 25th anniversary in 2006. During the intervening years it closed almost 45,000 cases, processed by more than 250 trained volunteer mediators. It currently provides dispute resolution services to the Family District Courts and Justice of the Peace Courts, the Dallas Housing Authority, a women's recovery center, and the Dallas Police Department. Conflict resolution training is offered to a variety of youth and adult organizations. Key staff members boast tenures of over 20 years, offering evidence of the compelling appeal of the ADR movement to those who seek careers in the helping professions.

Along with Houston's precursory program, the Dallas initiative helped provide stimulus for other Texas communities to join the parade of alternative dispute resolution (ADR) community-centered systems. By 2006, almost three decades after the Houston and Dallas operations came on line, many of the state's major population centers, and a number of smaller communities, had established programs—seventeen in all. Some had been launched on a shoestring by enthusiasts who had no significant advanced financial support from governmental or private benefactors. A variety of support organizations had been formed by then to provide umbrella technical assistance and to mobilize resources that would contribute to the rapidly developing professionalization of the neutral intervener.

As in a growing number of other states, Texas mediators wasted no time in establishing their own organization, the Texas Association of Mediators (TAM), that would provide for collective action in promoting the use of mediation, enhancing communication among mediators, setting standards of ethics and practice and sponsoring continuing education. Later, TAM would add additional programs such as a member locator service for the public to find qualified mediators and a grievance procedure for mediation clients to address complaints of unsatisfactory performance.

The Texas Mediator Credentialing Association established ethics and practice standards to apply to its members, along with training and experience requirements. The Texas

---

[11]See addendum CC: correspondence dated 8/11/81.

Mediation Trainer Roundtable was formed in the early 1990s to further refine standards and practice and to achieve the highest degree of professionalism among those who offered to train others. On the national scene, well into the 1980s, as late-comer Texas was sprouting its fledgling community-based centers, there were already estimated to be as many as 180 such operations across the country. By the turn of the century that figure was said to be more than 550, utilizing almost 20,000 trained and active volunteer mediators. There was, of course, also a corresponding profusion of support organizations at the national level. Founded in 1993, the National Association for Community Mediation was created solely to serve the institutionalized segment of dispute resolvers, looked upon by many as the voice of the community mediation movement in the United States. With members in 45 states, U.S. territories and other countries, it provides an array of information services, training and technical assistance, and seeks to bring the community mediation remedy to wider public attention.

The American Bar Association Section on Dispute Resolution had its origins in the mid-1970s. Its program began with a rather narrow focus on minor civil and criminal issues, later delving into cases involving more serious conditions. As reported earlier in this chapter, it was their staff director who gave significant assistance in the early development phases of the Dallas project.

Today, the number of resource organizations and internet expedients (excluding those in higher education offering academic credit, estimated at over 300 institutions in North America alone) with programs aimed at serving the evolving class of peacemaking professionals is staggering. One recent count put that number at about 90 separate and distinguishable entities.[12] The explosive expansion was buoyed by a chorus of voices from some of the nation's most prominent practitioners in the legal community and from academia.

"For many citizens, the urban judicial system is a foreboding, somewhat mysterious institution whose costs and arcane workings make it practically inaccessible. If the citizen steps into this system, he may find that the costly adjudication process moves at a disturbingly slow pace and that the control of events falls into other hands. Any sense that justice has been delivered is often overwhelmed by feelings of frustration and powerlessness; that one has been dealt with by strangers rather than served by a segment of the community."

Whatever description might be most widely accepted, the institutionalization of the community conflict abatement concept has brought new strength to social organization. Citizen advocacy groups, schools, churches, and businesses, as well as individuals and families, had found a new and promising way to effectively address discord.

As for the condition of the Dallas Mediation Service on the 25th anniversary of its founding, the activity report for fiscal year 2005 showed well over 2,000 cases opened and more than 900 mediation sessions conducted, with a settlement rate of 59%. That notable level of activity was accomplished by 216 active volunteers who devoted more than 3,000 hours to the task. A dozen on-site community service programs offer outreach to meet a variety of public needs. Over the first 25 years of its existence, DMS logged 46,646 cases, serving a total of 156,909 Dallas area residents.

By any measure, DMS has succeeded in its mission. There are few community mobilization efforts that exceed those associated with this project.

---

[12]See addenda DD and EE: selected listings of academic and nonacademic programs.

THE NEUTRAL INTERMEDIARY
AS FACT FINDER

There is nothing makes a man suspect much,
more than to know little.

— Sir Francis Bacon (1561-1626)

I have described in earlier chapters the two principal operational formats used by our agency's field personnel. One, conciliation, was shown to involve such somewhat unstructured activities as (a) serving as a courier in facilitating intergroup liaison and useful communication between adversaries; (b) coordinating initiatives to bring about dialogue and greater understanding of opposing positions and perspectives; (c) establishing controls over the development of damaging rumors; and (d) providing policy guidance to public officials, institutional administrators, business and civic leadership, and so on, regarding support for healthy community relations, citizen equity, and violence prevention.

The second procedural format, mediation, was characterized as a more formal *negotiation* process in which the disputants are brought together by the neutral intervener, typically in joint sessions for face-to-face interaction, to seek a settlement of differences through an established conformance that included a written, signed resolution agreement. The basic tenet here was to help the parties develop their own formula for reaching accommodation.

As a result of new circumstances and experiences in applying these two foundation categories of intervention, there arose a third program approach—that of fact finding and conflict analysis. In my experience, such assignments were referred by federal courts in cases dealing with school desegregation. That is not to say that fact finding is seen to be within the exclusive domain of court-related referral. To the contrary, there are many circumstances under which this approach may be applied to cases completely outside any litigation context. But, for a variety of reasons, fact finding is likely to take on special significance in terms of its appeal as an option for the courts to exercise when conditions are favorable. Nor is there an especially significant attachment to school desegregation issues. The process has similar application in other arenas such as corrections, police-community relations, government policy protest, and so forth.

Conflict analysis, performed by an impartial third party acceptable to both sides in a dispute, can go a long way as a prelude to mediation in clearing the air regarding faulty assumptions and misunderstood positions.

THE NATURE OF THE INQUIRY

Fact finding can be defined as a process used to assist in the compilation, analysis, and evaluation of the origins, perceptions, and settlement prospects of issues in contention. It involves the intervention of a neutral, voluntarily agreed upon by the parties (or enlisted by a court of law, sometimes without party endorsement) who undertakes to examine all aspects of a dispute and draw observations and recommendations as a result of such inquiry.

Fact finding may be applied to situations in which mediation appears to be a suitable method of seeking resolution but where party positions appear to be separated to some extent by lack of information and/or differences in interpretation of facts or circumstances upon which the dispute is grounded. It may precede or substitute for mediation in an effort to bring about reconciliation without entering into a structured negotiation proceeding. An exploration of the issues and the perceived differences between the parties may be sufficient to bring about a settlement once the findings have been shared with all concerned. Simply stated, fact finding is an attempt to put things in proper perspective—to provide a reality basis for review and evaluation of dispute issues. It is an attempt to separate fact from fiction and rational thinking from emotion.

Under normal circumstances, fact finding results in the preparation and release of a written report that is not binding on the parties. Otherwise, in effect, it would be essentially an arbitration proceeding. If the parties were to agree in advance to be bound by the fact finder's recommendations, then indeed, they would have opted for arbitration.

PROCESS NUTS AND BOLTS

How often have we heard a mayor, a police chief, a school superintendent, or other institutional spokesperson say "I don't know what 'they' want." Or sometimes ". . . They are misinformed. They know nothing about what it would take to agree to their demands." On the other side of the coin, the protest leader or the aggrieved complainant often charges that the respondents are unwilling to listen, deliberately hide or distort the facts, fail to take legitimate and necessary action, and so forth. Repeated lessons over the years very often reveal that hostilities and bitterness are matters of perception. They are, in part at least, sometimes the result of poor communication between the parties, more often than not fed by suspicion, distrust, and stereotyping by each side of the other.

It is when such conditions have surfaced that fact finding is most useful. The parties recognize that there are wide disparities between their respective views of the issues, not to mention how a solution might be achieved. Under such circumstances, the choices for resolution are typically limited to litigation or other adversary action (e.g., filing a complaint with a regulatory agency or some kind of direct protest initiation). It is when these elements of contention are present that the fact-finding option should be made known and available to the contestants.

Although it may be possible to proceed with fact finding without the assent of the contesting parties, it is likely that such an undertaking would be severely hampered. Much of the information to be collected and synthesized must necessarily come from the parties themselves. Without their full cooperation, the task becomes much more difficult, if not impossible.

When used as a preparation tool prior to engagement in mediation, a well-constructed fact-finding report can be a real asset in developing a negotiating agenda. It can save the parties untold time and effort in seeking out information that may not be as readily available to them as it is to the neutral researcher. It can help avoid unnecessary delays during mediation because the information needed already has been collected, compiled, and disseminated.

Turning to a more subtle observation, it can be argued that fact finding should appeal particularly to public officials facing constituency discontent. Some may suggest that the astute elected officeholder might well be able to parlay fact finding into a political asset. For one thing, it may be seen as a chance to transfer the focus of protest to a third party, buying time for preparation to respond to problems presented. If the political figure sees positions to be grossly misunderstood by dissidents, fact finding may very well be seen as the best possible course to follow

Finally, there is the statesmanship image that most politicians cherish and pursue. They know that the public, in general, looks for a willingness by its elected officials to subject themselves and their administrations to external scrutiny (given confidence in the fairness of the research authority) as evidence of honesty and transparency. Fact finding provides a forum for that purpose. A readiness to take on such an exercise may also be seen by voters as evidence of spending restraint, saving tax dollars by avoiding expensive litigation.

Procedures employed by the examiner will vary from case to case as circumstances dictate and as style diversity among individuals influence varying approaches. In general, the following steps might be considered typical:

1. The parties are contacted and informed of the fact-finding option. Separate meetings are convened with each principal group or their representatives, at which time a thorough explanation is given of the proposed process with an opportunity for discussion and questions. Once it is agreed to use the procedure, the parties are asked to describe the issues as they view them. They are also requested to identify every known group or individual they think may be in a position to contribute insights or information regarding background factors, demographic data, conflict parameters, perception differences, and so forth. The fact finder records pertinent information, including the names of all known resources, their areas of knowledge or expertise, and how they can be contacted.

2. All sources of related written documentation (print media articles, governmental records, library reference materials, party correspondence/records, etc.) are searched, reviewed, and selectively extracted for possible later use in report preparation.

3. An outline of projected report headings is prepared, tailored to the nature of the inquiry. In addition to introductory observations, report sections might include a *background summary* describing the environment in which the case is found. A more detailed section may be devoted to *characteristics of the parties* in terms of their socioeconomic/educational status, history of organizational affiliations and past relationships with the disputants and with other tangential parties, their roles and reputations in the community, professional/vocational identities, and so forth. Questions as to who is being most adversely affected by the issues being examined and the extent to which victimization patterns are found to exist, may also be included in this segment.

A third component might be an analysis of *party positions* and how each is perceived, including possible remedies. In some cases, it may be appropriate to explore peripheral influences that bear on the dispute but are not directly related to the parties themselves or the objectives they seek.

Finally, there is the matter of *external perceptions . . .* how the issues affect elements in the community-at-large and how such groups and individuals perceive the conflict. A thorough exploration of carefully selected contacts in this connection can be useful in helping to formulate problem analysis and assessment, as well possible remedies.

The outline thus prepared becomes a skeleton upon which to add the flesh of inquiry. As information is gathered, it is organized under the aforementioned or other appropriate section headings, later to be reviewed, sorted, and extracted for inclusion in the final report. Supporting documentation is collected at the same time, and made subject to later selection as exhibit material to supplement the main body of the report.

4. At the discretion of the fact finder, subsequent meetings with the parties may be arranged, separately or in joint sessions. At that time, those portions of information collected from the principals that may require clarification or further elaboration can be presented and discussed. Such an occasion can also provide an opportunity for the parties to make any necessary corrections or additions and, generally, to further support their positions before a draft of the final report is prepared.

5   Once a draft of the document has been prepared, especially if the fact finding is being conducted under court auspices, those portions of the content that originated with the parties should be distributed to them for review and possible further revision. This provides those who are most concerned with the report a chance to react to the accuracy and completeness of its content. It is not an invitation otherwise to alter the findings in terms of the kinds of information that should be included or what portions are considered by one or another party to be inappropriate for use. The fact finder may choose to invite broader comment than that limited to correction of errors or omissions, but he/she does so at some risk to the integrity of the process.

6. Preparation of the final report requires the usual organizational and writing skills necessary to produce a cohesive and useful document. The end product must be seen as credible and sufficient to be used as a tool in the search for resolution. It is after the main body of the text is drafted that the researcher turns attention to conclusions and recommendations. In many respects, that final section is the most difficult to construct. Surely, it is the most sensitive and subjective part of the findings. Inescapably, it requires judgmental deduction, always a detriment to neutrality. It will be the part most likely to be given close scrutiny by the parties, the media, and others interested in the outcome. It is the part that is likely to have the most significant impact on events to follow.

It is this salient summation that raises obvious questions:

What is the range of remedy options? Has every possible avenue of settlement been pursued? What previous efforts to find resolution have been attempted and with what results? What untried creative approaches can be identified? What new ideas have surfaced that the parties have not yet considered? Are conditions essentially as described by the complainants or are there apparent discrepancies? Are there extenuating circumstances that must be clarified or overcome and, if so, what are they?

Do the parties show good faith intentions to settle their differences voluntarily? Has there been significant new information uncovered by the fact-finding process that could constructively affect party positions or attitudes? If so, what are they? Does the dispute have implications that are likely to impact nonparticipants in the community at large? Can any observations be made that would be helpful in distinguishing questionable rhetoric from legitimate grievances?

Answers to questions such as these can provide the makings of a reasoned explanation of the reporter's conclusions and recommendations.

In considering the total report, but particularly the concluding summation, *it is of paramount importance, to the greatest extent possible, that the investigator avoid statements that are clearly judgmental.* It is not the proper task of the inquiry to determine guilt or innocence. The process is aimed at dissecting the problem(s) at hand and getting the parties to reexamine their views, motivating them to search more diligently for areas of mutual self-interest and acceptable solutions. It is an attempt to expose root causes of conflict, as opposed to superficial symptoms. The concept holds that such an undertaking can best be accomplished through a detached third party, with appropriate intervener skills, who can be seen by all participants to be fair, thorough, and professional.

7. Release to the media of the final report is another consideration that will vary with circumstances. In general, when prepared under a court mandate, it is understood that the final report will be made public. Virtually all matters before a court of law, after all, are subject to public access. It is doubtful that this process would warrant any exception.

Under conditions in which there is no court involvement, the question should be put to the parties at a very early stage of deliberations. From the standpoint of the fact finder who is interested in pursuing resolution of the contested issues, public release of the report can be an additional tool in bringing pressure for settlement. If, however, the principals are strongly opposed to public disclosure, it is possible that they would reject the entire proposal if such a stipulation were mandatory. Ultimately, it is the prerogative of the fact finder to decide on preconditions or ground rules, given awareness of the possible risk of a loss of accession to proceed.

THE SEARCH FOR INFORMATION

It is well to point out that there are no useful guidelines for identifying the most productive sources of information. It is largely a matter of trial and error. The fact finder decides on what types of information are most useful to accomplish the task (e.g. census data, sources of financial support, past research on the subject(s), media features or news accounts related to case issues, attitudes and opinions of appropriate observers, etc.). Obviously, a corrections case would lead to different sorts of information needs than would one in education. Likewise, law enforcement issues would have very different kinds of information requirements than would health services or employment.

Typically, as the fact finder pursues a particular line of inquiry, one source will uncover or suggest another. The more the inquirer learns about the case environment, the more new avenues to search will become apparent. Determinations as to which particular information sources should be utilized by and large are made as a result of familiarity with community structures and resources and with the availability of informed local contacts.

Information sources can also suggest elements for inclusion in the report that may not have occurred to the investigator. Individuals with established connections and relationships are sometimes in a better position than the examiner to know about certain areas worthy of inquiry. Interviews should not be limited to preconceived notions about the source's expertise, depth of knowledge or potential contribution.

The question of how many information sources will be sufficient to produce the necessary yield is also difficult to predict. The time frame within which the task is to be completed will certainly influence that decision. The wishes of the court and/or the parties in terms of expectations for use of the end product are also factors that will bear on the extensiveness of the inquiry. Perhaps the most important measure in this regard is the assurance that every substantive element of the issues to be examined is included in the data collection framework.

An example of information need determination might be based on the following circumstances:

A dispute centers on allegations of serious police abuse directed against minorities, primarily the unnecessary and excessive use of force. Inquiry areas might include:

1. Analysis of local firearms policy with comparisons to other police departments of similar size and environment;
2. Compilation of incidents involving local police use of force with details of case circumstances, community protest reaction, administrative/legal action taken, and so forth; comparisons of resulting profile with those of other analogous police agencies; identification of areas of apparent dissimilarity among case histories and solicitation of explanations from appropriate interviewees;
3. Interviews with various persons, from inside the department and from without (e.g. civil service board, city commissioners, and/or staff, etc.) who are responsible for reviewing and adjudicating allegations of misconduct;
4. Interviews with complainants and their legal counsel, if applicable, regarding perceptions of alleged wrongdoing;
5. Interviews with police officers who have been accused in the past of wrongful use of force and, if appropriate, with supervisors, to establish the essence of their views regarding past incidents (avoiding references to any specific cases that may be pending legal or administrative disposition);
6. Review of related elements of academy or in-service training;
7. Review of past and present community relations programs and minority recruiting efforts, if any, giving achievements as well as obstacles and disappointments, with rationales for each.

Any of these lines of inquiry might lead to extensions of the data initially uncovered or to entirely new areas of interest. Such a ripple effect is not uncommon.

Finally, there is this additional observation regarding information source utilization: The scope of grievances under inquiry has everything to do with the extent of report development. If, for example, a dispute centers on a narrow educational issue such as discipline, it can be safely assumed that the information canvass will be substantially more confined than if the subject matter encompasses a range of educational elements (e.g. curriculum content, desegregation effectiveness, transportation requirements, student activities, etc.). We can generalize, therefore, that the depth of the information sampling process will be in direct proportion to the dimensions and complexity of the problem(s) under examination.

IMPEDIMENTS TO SUCCESS

In fact finding, just as in mediation or any form of conciliation that requires voluntary participation by the disputants, willingness to use the process is tied firmly to self-interest. It is that perception of self-interest that must be influenced constructively if the concept is to be applied successfully. It may be useful to consider some of the problems that are likely to surface in this regard.

First, it is essential to determine need (or, in effect, party self-interest). Just how is each party likely to benefit by agreeing to proceed? If local officials see no need to pursue the fact-finding objective, cooperation is unlikely to be forthcoming. Local government officials traditionally resist outside assistance because it may make it appear that they are unable to handle problems themselves. Some are especially reluctant to call upon a federal agency for assistance, particularly if there is no monetary incentive attached. Such a move sometimes is perceived as a sign of weakness or dependence to be avoided at all costs if political or career survival are seen to be threatened.

So it is incumbent on the fact finder in exploring case success potentials to do the necessary homework—the precontact investigation—that will either confirm or contradict the bare facts initially collected and may reveal personal agendas of some of the primary participants. Do appropriate spokespersons acknowledge the problem exists and do they show evidence of willingness to address the issues? If not, is there an opportunity to uncover information that may cause local officials to reconsider their positions and recognize the consequences of inaction or neglect of responsibilities?

A second area of difficulty arises out of the limitations often found among available sources of information. There are many reliable and accessible sources for certain types of information retrieval, of course. Libraries, universities, media reports, government agencies, foundations, and a variety of civic/professional/special interest organizations are frequently able to produce valuable data or research findings. It is the more subjective input sought by the fact finder that should be treated with reservations.

When opinion is sought from certain individuals considered knowledgeable in the area under inquiry, responses as to the cause of a problem or the best way to correct it are all too often influenced by established biases or loyalties, unrelated personal experience, or simple self-interest. It therefore becomes very important to select input sources in a way that will assure the most balanced collective result possible. If the parties to a dispute differ markedly in their views of the differences between them, it is probable that those who see the conflict from some distance will be even more diverse, uncertain, or confused in their interpretations.

Yet, fact finding does require that the broadest possible spectrum of contribution to the analysis be assured. That means, in most instances, having to seek enlightenment from observers of the problems, not themselves conflict principals, who have special related backgrounds or expertise.

A third possible difficulty revolves around the inability of the parties themselves to find the wherewithal to research their own positions or, less commonly, to research their responses to complaint allegations. When either party is a well-financed and well-staffed agency or institution, the problem is minimized or is nonexistent. But when either party is a group of individuals or an organization with few resources, it can become a burden to respond effectively to the inquiry. If, for example, a minority organization with no paid staff and little or no budget, is asked to produce a documented account of a complex past experience regarding the grievance(s) under inquiry, it may be that it is too impractical for the task to be undertaken. There simply may be no one available on a voluntary basis with the time, the ability, and the willingness to respond.

Another problem area has to do with the very nature of information gathering. In order to collect enough valid content, one must invariably assemble considerably more documentation than can possibly be used in the final preparation. Typically, it is not at the point of collection, but at the time of review, that determinations can be made as to what will ultimately be selected for inclusion. Such being the case, the researcher is frequently faced with sorting out and evaluating a great deal more material than can be absorbed. So the process can take substantially more time than might be anticipated.

FACT FINDING SCENARIOS

1. A public school district stands accused by a coalition of minority organizations of failure to comply fully with a court-ordered desegregation plan. Allegations center on inequities in physical plant facilities, curriculum deficiencies, and classroom ethnic composition in a number of racially identifiable schools. Administration and elected officials vigorously deny the charges. The matter has been taken to federal court and a preliminary hearing has been held. The judge is known to be interested in facilitating a pretrial settlement but attorneys for both sides have shown no willingness to try mediation. The court needs a practical means of ascertaining hard facts outside a courtroom proceeding. A fact finder is engaged.

2. A major city police department has had an unusual number of citizen fatalities arising from street confrontations. Protest forces are gathering momentum. Demands are escalating for reform, including wholesale revision of certain operating policies and the establishment of a citizens' review board to investigate and/or adjudicate charges of abusive conduct. Statements that are diametrically opposed to one another are being given to the media by the two sides. It is clear that contrasting positions could not both be sound. It is also apparent that the contradicting perceptions have probably grown out of wishful thinking, clouded or distorted judgments, exaggeration, or worse. The mayor and police chief, weary of persistent unrest and unhealthy race relations, have recently shown some interest in finding new ways to address the problem. They see no useful purpose in opening a mediated dialogue because demands are based on what they see to be faulty assessments of actual conditions, but they would agree to some mutually acceptable resolution process that both sides could comfortably endorse as fair and objective. Fact finding by an independent and reputable resource appeared to be an acceptable option.

3. A group of mostly female employees in a division of a large corporation have organized a grievance committee to confront administrators with widespread complaints about unfair employment practices said to affect training, promotion, pay scales, and work assignment patterns, among other issues. The dissident employees have been unable to get access to company personnel records to document their charges, claiming management is covering up a multitude of sins. The respondents claim that records being sought would make clear that they are guilty of no wrongdoing, but that such records must be held confidential to protect innocent parties and to comply with state law. The matter has come before the corporate board of directors who are dismayed at these developments and seem uncertain as to how to go about finding resolution to the dissension. The introduction of a fact-finding process is found to be in order.

4. A medium security state prison has had incidents of serious inmate unrest. A series of law suits by convicts has been filed over a period of years seeking relief from allegedly unconstitutional living conditions, some of which the plaintiffs claim could be corrected without large expenditures. Priority issues revolve around visiting hours restrictions, mail privileges, kitchen sanitation, recreation, and medical services. Prison officials have repeatedly denied that the complaints are valid and have had confirmation of their position by various outside sources of their own choosing. The governor's office has indicated concern over growing tensions behind institution walls, urging immediate

steps be taken to avoid an all-out violent uprising. Intermediary fact finding is pursued.

The above case conditions describe only a few among many types of disputes to which fact finding can be applied.

DEVELOPING TRENDS ACROSS THE LAND

The emergence of minority elected and appointed officeholders to local, state, and federal government offices has come to be a growing phenomenon characterizing the national political scene. With each election year, from small southern hamlets to major U.S. cities, and from county, state and federal seats of government, competent, largely well-educated people of color are making their way into the highest levels of authority and public responsibility. To many observers it has been a breathtaking ascent of minorities (and women, as well) to levels of equal achievement opportunity at a pace unforeseen even by those who authored the landmark civil rights legislation of the 1960s or in the celebrated dream of Martin Luther King, Jr.

Indicative of what many would like to credit the inbred compassion and sense of fairness in the American psyche, these trends have brought on little antipathetic backlash from racists who, in our sullied past, have been known to stand in the way of human rights and equality.

Like all conditions of social change out of which conflict can arise, however, the fact-finding formula may be useful. If, for example, a newly installed minority mayor, city manager, police chief, school superintendent, or other principal officeholder is inclined to take a fresh look at community relations, he or she may welcome the availability of a reputable and trusted outside resource to help evaluate priorities and establish program parameters. This might be especially true if preceding occupants of the position were characterized by neglect of minority community needs and aspirations. Whatever the need might entail—identifying pressure points, evaluating levels of deprivation, defining or clarifying issues, measuring attitudes—all would likely call for scrupulous objectivity in the discovery process, a goal that can be best delivered by a detached third party.

CHARACTER DISTINCTIONS OF INTERMEDIARIES

It is worth noting that the attribute requirements of the fact finder differ in some respects from that of the mediator or the conciliator. The differences lie in terms of temperament, work environment preferences, and career objectives, among other personal characteristics.

Most apparent, perhaps, is that the nature of the fact-finding mission eliminates the need for the third-party intervener to deal directly with the conflict parties in a confrontational or negotiation setting. The mediator and the conciliator are expected to influence communication effectiveness between adversaries who are typically unprepared emotionally to engage in placid and patient dialogue. They seek to modify attitudes between antagonists through direct interaction: convening and chairing joint meetings, shuttle caucusing, bringing resources to bear in moving disputants toward settlement, influencing changes in posture by harnessing external pressure sources, and so forth. These activities call for the ability to exercise a high degree of persuasiveness in interacting with individuals as well as with groups. Dominance of personality is often a key to success.

The fact finder, on the other hand, approaches the resolution objective from quite a different direction. Contact with people is oriented toward seeking cooperation with the fact finder rather than inducing adversaries to cooperate with one another. As such, the task calls for an individual with research and writing skills more than it does verbal and interactive talents. It requires something of a more cautious and organized temperament than that of the more flexible and adventurous colleague who enters the fray and becomes part, albeit a neutral part, of the struggle for resolution.

IN CONCLUSION

- Collecting conflict-related information and drawing appropriate determinations from the assembled material is an assignment best performed by an objective third-party neutral. Only such a resource can be expected to apply the necessary balance and impartiality that will preserve the integrity of the fact-finding process and deserve the confidence of all participants. Information sources, furthermore, are more likely to respond to the fact finder with greater willingness and candor than they would to a representative of one of the parties or to someone otherwise identified with one faction or another.

- Among the key objectives of fact finding are:
    1. To investigate and report to the parties and/or the court all aspects of a dispute including history of relationships, characteristics of the parties, causes of discord, factual conditions underlying complaint allegations, influencing circumstances on party behavior, any external hegemonic impact on conflict issues;
    2. To present a document that is supported by available evidence and is a fair and accurate representation of findings;
    3. To reflect without bias party positions, perceptions and special interests;
    4. To encourage the disputants to moderate differences and to provide alternatives for possible settlement.

- The success of fact finding depends to a large extent on emphasizing *remedies*. It is essential that judgmental observations, conclusions, or recommendations be scrupulously avoided. Under no circumstances should the investigator suggest or imply the guilt or innocence of one side or another of a conflict under inquiry.

- Fact finding differs from arbitration in that, like mediation, there is no final and binding decision rendered as to the merit of contested positions or which party should prevail. It produces, rather, in addition to a compilation of pertinent case-related information, a document that recommends one or more options for settlement. Neither the court nor the parties have any legal obligation to accept the results of the inquiry, but strong pressures often come into play from public opinion when the fact finder's report is released and given high visibility. It differs markedly from mediation in that an *evaluative* report is the end product (in contrast to a written, signed voluntary agreement), a feature that would be the antithesis of a mediation format.

- It is the nature of fact finding that parties who have taken an unyielding stand during earlier stages of negotiation or public positioning (perhaps during pretrial proceedings or in public hearings before governmental bodies) may later be looking for a way to back down without loss of face. Fact finding can provide that opportunity. If the fact finder's recommendations are persuasive, party leadership can tell constituents that they did their best in bilateral negotiations but that once findings and recommendations were made by an well-regarded third-party neutral, they felt obliged to accept the results or risk damaging consequences from the media or other channels of public opinion.

- The language of reporting is all-important to the fact finder's task. Care must be taken to avoid unnecessary criticism of any disputant or respective positions. Typically, the findings will favor one side or another, although there is often a range of disclosures, some of which favor one party and some the other. Rarely will one party prevail on all issues. In any event, the choice of words in setting forth determinations of fact, as well as resultant conclusions, can achieve the same results with sensitivity and moderation.

- Fact finding is not a viable process in many conflict situations. It might be said that the greater the requirement for pure value judgment, the less appropriate fact finding is going to be. Obviously, if an issue centers on whether or not the respondents have committed some allegedly wrongful act(s), fact finding would not be at all appropriate. Determination of civil or criminal liability has no place here. There is not the capacity to investigate such evidence. Such a requirement can be satisfied only through investigative channels that can access sworn testimony, cross-examination, and other legal devices. It would be unwise to step across that line in fact finding, for to do so would jeopardize the essence of neutrality and compromise the fact finder's nonadversarial posture.

- Another observation relates to the enforceability question. Theoretically, the fact finder's recommendations will serve as the basis for agreement. In a court-referred case, if there is an agreement, provisions can be incorporated in a consent decree, thus eliminating any doubt about enforcement. In other instances, however, an agreement, just as in mediation, may be dependent upon the good faith of the parties, public pressures for implementation, or going to court in a civil action to force fulfillment of a contractual obligation. In the latter instance, much would depend on the applicability of state law and whether or not the agreement met the necessary legal requirements for a valid contract.

- It is well to point out that the parties may accept only portions of the fact finder's recommendations, leaving the unresolved residue to another form of remedy. That is a right that the parties should not be expected to sacrifice. The fact finder is a facilitator, not a dictator.

- Once a fact-finding report is completed and distributed, there may be considerable reaction from the court, from the media, or from the parties. It may be favorable and supportive, or it may be unfavorable and critical. If valid criticisms do surface, the fact finder may decide to reconsider portions of the report and later issue a supplement or addendum. In it, either new information can be introduced, possibly calling for modification of certain conclusions or recommendations, or clarifications can be offered where there was confusion.

- Care must be taken when setting forth citizen perceptions that such statements are identified as just that—perceptions. A disclaimer is worthwhile that differentiates between findings of verifiable fact and those that are essentially matters of opinion, speculation or attitude. The reader must understand that such portions of the report are not based on established fact and that they may flow from personal biases or stereotyping. It should also be made clear, however, that such subjective input is nevertheless important to consider since it does reflect conditions that can have considerable impact.

- Fact finding holds great promise as a practical tool in conflict resolution. Like all tools, it will need ongoing application in order to determine where refinements and improvements can be made and standards further established. There is much yet to be learned about its potential as well as its limitations.

A RETROSPECTIVE ON THE CLIMATE OF RACE RELATIONS IN DALLAS, TEXAS DURING THE BIRTH OF THE CIVIL RIGHTS ERA[1]

They will react to a specific incident often with a vehemence and an anger
out of proportion to that incident because it grows from a lifetime
of rage, frustration, aggravation and grievance.

— Roger W. Wilkins, Author, Professor of History,
former Assistant U.S. Attorney General

It was said by many in the mid-1960s that Dallas enjoyed a healthy climate of racial and ethnic relations. There had been little "trouble." Organized protest in those earliest days of civil rights awakening was rare in "Big D". Visible signs of unrest were seldom seen.

Business and civic leaders had been notably successful during prior years in quietly but effectively helping to bring about desegregation of public facilities and accommodations. Many Dallas employers had made commendable progress in overcoming exclusion barriers in order to provide non-traditional jobs for minority employees. Stanley Marcus, chief executive officer of Dallas' Neiman-Marcus flagship emporium and icon of luxury retailing, had led the way in demonstrating nondiscriminatory hiring practices. African-American children, in limited but gradually increasing numbers, were attending school in racially mixed classrooms.

It was not unreasonable to conclude that the city had escaped the urban disruption that had shaken so many other cities with civil strife and intergroup hostility.

Some said that such a conclusion deserved close examination. Prominent civil rights advocates were suggesting that racial peace does not necessarily equate with racial justice. They had only to point to the countless deep south communities of recent years where there was never a voice raised against the most severe forms of injustice and denial of opportunity. There had been relative peace between the races in Southern Rhodesia and in South Africa, but they were in that time hardly exemplary societies in which there was equality before the law.

---

[1]This chapter is an adaptation from a paper prepared by the author in April of 1967. It was an attempt to set forth a viewpoint of the then current status of intergroup relations in that city and to focus on specific problem areas that were seen to be potential threats to community stability.

The *Reader's Digest* in October of 1964 had published an article on "How Los Angeles Eases Racial Tensions." That city by then had developed what was thought to be one of the more sophisticated human relations programs in the nation. Then, the following summer, there was the unprecedented eruption of civil disorder—the turmoil of Watts.

In the aftermath of the Watts turmoil, Los Angeles leadership took a fresh look at their own complacency. They recognized that there had been neglect of new problems and disregard for new aspects of old problems. Times were changing, they concluded, but the tools and techniques for dealing with community conflict had not kept pace. It was a costly lesson. Other cities were enduring similarly painful revelations.

There was little intent by critical observers to compare Dallas with Johannesburg, or with Los Angeles, for that matter. But the point was illustrative.

Questions were raised. Does Dallas have serious problems of overt discrimination and/or disadvantage based on race or ancestry? If so, can they be resolved, or at least relieved, with proactive initiatives? Upon whom would the responsibility rest to seek such remedies?

Dallas was unique in that day in that it had no public or private human relations organization with a primary accountability and the wherewithal to investigate and try to relieve minority community tensions. There was no agency inclined or equipped to examine effectively the extent to which discrimination or inequities existed and to recommend and implement corrective measures when necessary.[2] Among urban centers most appropriately compared with Dallas, this city stood alone as the only one without such a resource.[3]

So it was that proactive advocates of improved human relations were increasingly convinced of the critical need to establish a program to inventory, assess and address racial/ethnic conditions in "the can-do city of the southwest."

Progress in healthy race relations, it was said, would require the ability to audit the human relations balance sheet of assets and liabilities. Reliance on speculation, wishful thinking, rumor, or information otherwise likely to be faulty could only damage the best of intentions.

Conceding that civic and governmental leadership in Dallas was genuinely and completely committed to the elimination of every injustice and disadvantage rooted in racial, ethnic or religious bias, the question was posed as to how remedial reforms could be justified and expected to win public support for the investment of resources to accomplish the goal. The answer seemed evident enough. One needed only to examine the pages of the national press, popular magazines, or the television screen to be aware of the continual, persistent protest sweeping across the land, although not yet significantly invading the streets of Dallas.

Discontent over alleged discrimination in employment, in education, and in housing was not unknown locally. Upon this tripod of fundamental inequities, acknowledged or otherwise, rested countless other areas of grievance and sources of frustration, manifested mostly in the poorest, underserved enclaves of urban America. Denial of equal protection of the law, unsatisfactory coverage of minority issues by the news media, lack of access to public health and welfare services, consumer inequities, disorganization in the indigenous minority community, unavailability of municipal services and facilities, obstacles to proprietorship, exclusion from civic participation and contribution—these were among the issues that simmered in the shadows of latent protest, and in some places already erupting in street violence and defiance of law. From these and other causes of unrest came the

---

[2]Typically a municipal commission or a private council on human relations or some similarly designated agency.
[3]Those with such established mechanisms, ranking in population at that time from 6th to 24th, generally in the range of 500,000 to 1,000,000 inhabitants, among which Dallas ranked 14th, included such major southern cities as Atlanta, Houston, San Antonio, Baltimore, and New Orleans..

impetus for Dallas voices favoring preemptive initiatives to overcome centuries of irrational psychosocial conditioning.

The focus became one of determining how to somehow relate these national exigencies to the Dallas environment before it became a reactive necessity. Clearly it would be worthwhile to find out to what extent, if any, potentially volatile conditions were indeed present in this community as compared with other cities of similar size and composition. But, as already noted, Dallas was without the wherewithal to pursue an objective and searching probe.

In lieu of organized means for comprehensive self-examination and appraisal, the situation seemed to call for an independent initiative that might provide some thought provocation and stimulate further exploration. Consequently, our newly created Dallas CRS regional office, of which at that time I was a staff of one with a secretary, was given a green light to see what might be done to attract community interest in facing up to issues of maintaining racial harmony.

My first effort was the preparation and carefully selected distribution to influential Dallasites of a monograph titled *Race Relations and the Intergroup Climate in Dallas, Texas*. It was written as an analysis and commentary on the nature of the city's community relations problems from one who had labored there for more than a decade in activity surrounded by the consequences of living in a segregated society.

The paper was presented in a format of questions in various problem areas—employment and training, education, housing, police-community relations, community intergroup organization, and health/welfare/public services. The questions were intended to call attention to specific elements of inquiry that might be undertaken, given the creation of a suitable apparatus to pursue improved conditions. Much of the content in these queries might seem shopworn in today's civil rights vernacular, but in the mid-1960s, they produced considerable anxiety and defensiveness among those many seen as targets for reform.

The following is a sampling of points of inquiry posed.

Employment and Training

1. What is the actual rate of local unemployment among Anglo-Caucasians as contrasted to Latin Americans and Negroes?[4]
2. What is the average head-of-household income for each of these groups?
3. What local programs exist, if any, to relieve hard-core unemployment, especially among minority young adults and working age adolescents? If no such resources are available, how can such a program be designed and implemented?
4. Are minority employees in Dallas often found performing work at virtually the same or higher performance and/or responsibility levels as white coworkers, but at lower wages and/or under less desirable working conditions?
5. What potential lies in assisting women of low income families (many of whom provide sole support) to become better prepared for work and then to find suitable employment? Can a job development program be created to attack this special problem?
6. What apprenticeship programs are being offered in the Dallas area? Do each of them reflect nondiscriminatory practices in screening, admitting and training applicants?

---

[4]Identification terms in popular use in that day.

7. Do most Dallas employers provide opportunities for assignment, promotion, transfer, training and use of facilities without regard to race or national origin?

8. To what extent have noteworthy breakthroughs in nontraditional minority employment been given appropriate attention in the disadvantaged community in order to motivate young people and encourage "believability" among those already conditioned to obstacles and exclusion? What is the prevailing attitude in the Dallas minority population regarding the reality of equal job opportunity for all?

9. There have been reports of local projects designed to provide special training for *underemployed* minority individuals in an effort to upgrade their potentials for optimal utilization in the workplace. What agencies or groups have carried out such programs? What has been the nature of their efforts? Were their objectives and experience worthy of broader application?

10. What recourse, other than federal intervention, is available to minority employees with legitimate grievances concerning allegations of job discrimination? Does the absence of a local mechanism to deal with such problems contribute to intergroup tensions?

Commentary followed this series of questions:

"Various groups of Dallas citizens have recently investigated and considered a number of program possibilities for improvement of minority employment opportunities. Among these have been proposed affiliations with at least two reputable national organizations—the Urban League[5] and the National Institute of the Occupational Industrialization Center of Philadelphia . . . the fact that they have been successfully established in so many cities across the country is reliable testimony to the contributions they have to make. . . . Most knowledgeable observers agree . . . that the impact of manpower effort to date has been too modest. The emphasis has been on training or placing *qualified* applicants. Serious attention has yet to be properly directed to relieving the plight of the unqualified individual—the men and women who have the least to offer an employer. These are among the most needy and who present the real challenges to innovation. It is they who contribute most to instability and unrest in the minority community."

Education

1. Can constructive steps be taken to more nearly bring about compliance with the spirit and intent of the law as it has evolved since the 1954 U.S. Supreme Court decision on school desegregation?

2. To what extent is there persistent racial isolation among students attending public schools in Dallas?

3. Has there been any noteworthy integration of public school faculty and administrative personnel? If not, what have been the major obstacles to progress and what can be done to help overcome them?

4. What measures have been taken to prepare teachers and administrators for a healthy and desirable transition to racially mixed classes and integration of normal school activities?

5. What are the problems of teachers and administrators in predominantly Negro schools as the prospect of an integrated system is anticipated? Is anything

---

[5]At the time of this writing a biracial committee had begun exploring affiliation with the National Urban League. Later in the year, what is now the Urban League of Greater Dallas completed funding arrangements and staffing. The organization currently operates four service centers throughout Dallas County.

being done to help them compete for new assignments or to turn their skills and interests toward new vocational or career opportunities?

6. Do textbooks used in Dallas public schools reflect Negro-American and Latin American history in proper and fair perspective? Are outstanding contributions from minority personalities of the past—in science, education, social welfare, literature and the arts—give appropriate attention?

7. What are the comparative public school dropout rates among Negroes, Latins, and Anglos? Is there an effective way to analyze the dropout problem as it affects the minority child and then work to overcome it?

8. What are the present regulations and procedures for transfer from one school to another? Do such regulations tend to facilitate or inhibit desegregation?

9. Have there been any interracial incidents among children attending schools with Negroes in attendance for the first time? Have effective remedial or preventive measures been taken to avoid or correct such problems?

10. Are all school facilities, services, events and activities, including participation in athletic, social and other extracurricular programs, seating arrangements and locker assignments, use of materials, bus transportation, and so forth, provided on a nondiscriminatory basis?

11. To what extent do nonwhite individuals have access to Dallas area private schools in which trade, business, technical, and other vocational courses are offered? Which schools deny admission to Negroes?

The foregoing questions regarding opportunities in education are but a few among many that could indicate a useful line of inquiry. Without forthright answers there can be no meaningful evaluation of problems. To the extent that there are honest answers to such questions, unless and until they are effectively communicated and understood in the minority communities, they will continually contribute to building resentment and deteriorating confidence toward those who carry the responsibility for assuring equitable educational opportunities.

Housing

In one of the many trenchant statements of his presidency on the course of civil rights legislation, Lyndon B. Johnson had this to say: ". . . Today the subject of fair housing is engulfed in a cloud of misinformation and unarticulated fear. . . . The task of informing the minds and enlightening the consciences of those who are subject to these fears should begin at once . . ."

1. The term "ghetto" has been used to describe racial isolation in housing. It connotes, among other things, involuntary restriction of residence within certain neighborhood boundaries. To what extent are Negroes in Dallas unable to live outside artificially prescribed areas? In what census tracts and in what proportions are neighborhoods composed of persons of the same racial or ethnic background?

2. Is there a sufficient number of adequate low-cost housing units to meet the needs of families whose income is below a reasonable level of subsistence?

3. What has been the trend of changes in racial composition of residents in the Dallas central city as contrasted to the surrounding suburbs?

4. What has been the experience in Dallas of neighborhoods into which Negroes have moved for the first time? How have property values been affected? Have

any such neighborhoods been successfully stabilized for any significant peri-od of time? If so, what lessons can be learned from those experiences? Would it be fruitful to explore parallel developments elsewhere?

5. Is there any agency or focal point of interest and concern in the community that can or should devote primary attention to problems of housing inequities and unfair practices?

6. What opportunities exist for obtaining federal resources to improve housing conditions? What private resources? Have the potentials been fully explored and, if so, what conclusions have been drawn?

7. How does availability of public transportation between poverty areas and downtown Dallas (near health and welfare offices, job markets, etc.) compare with other sections of the city?

8. In what areas are there located major employers who might otherwise attract qualified professional, technical and other skilled Negroes but for the fact that convenient, affordable housing is not available?

9. What are the policies and established practices of builders, realtors, and lend-ing institutions regarding the sale, rental, and financing of housing, as such transactions affect minority buyers? To the extent that such policies and prac-tices may contribute to hardship and inequality of housing access, what can be done to help overcome these conditions?

10. What are the most formidable obstacles to an open housing market in Dallas? Is there any educational effort being undertaken to examine this critical issue and to bring about public enlightenment?

The problem of segregation in housing is often said to be the most critical obstacle to resolution of the entire dilemma of racial discrimination in America. Segregated housing produces segregated schools, which result in inferior education, which in turn denies sat-isfactory preparation for earning a living. Restricted livelihood completes the full cycle back to the inability to afford adequate housing. Whether the process is lineal or cyclical in nature, surely discrimination in housing must ultimately be overcome before we will see truly meaningful progress in the overall commitment of the nation to provide every citi-zen with equal access to the fruits of our society.

Police-Community Relations

1. What is the general image of the police in the minority community? Does the average disadvantaged person perceive the police officer as a symbol of protec-tion or as a threat to his own security? To the extent that this image is found to be negative, what constructive steps can be taken to change such perceptions?

2. To what extent is appropriate intergroup or human relations training provid-ed to Dallas police officers?

3. Are minority offenders apprehended and processed by police officers in the same manner as other law violators? Are contacts between law enforcement officers and the public made with the same courtesies, regardless of the race or ethnicity of the subject?

4. What process is available for citizens to seek a hearing and redress of com-plaints against police officers for alleged wrongdoing? Is there a remedial process that tends to mitigate fears of reprisal and which is likely to assure thorough and impartial investigation, judgment, and corrective action, when justified and necessary?

5. What is the minority composition of the police force? Are such officers found in numbers reasonably reflective of their proportion in the general population? If not, what problems exist in attracting and selecting such applicants for police careers?

6. What efforts have been made to recruit proactively promising candidates for careers in law enforcement? With what degree of success? What have been the most difficult obstacles to greater progress in minority utilization in the Dallas police department?

7. Are nonwhite officers assigned for duty without regard to the racial or ethnic composition of the neighborhoods in which they work?

8. Do poverty areas of the city receive approximately the same patrol coverage as do middle-class and more affluent sections?

9. To what extent have minority officers succeeded in progressing through the ranks to supervisory and other positions of higher responsibility? Are such officers assigned to a broad cross-section of departmental functions?

10. To what extent are nonwhite officers assigned to work in biracial units or teams? Are all duty assignments made entirely without regard to racial or ethnic considerations?

11. Are there occasional or frequent incidents in the minority communities in which misconduct charges are made? Are these incidents fully and equitably investigated? If so, by whom and with what pattern of results? Are the findings fully disclosed and discussed with indigenous leaders in order to minimize misinformation and misunderstanding?

12. Are minority individuals employed in the clerical, administrative, and other nonsworn positions? If so, to what extent?

13. To what extent has the department investigated and availed itself of available grant funds for initiating or improving training programs in police-community relations?

14. Has any independent evaluation been made of the Dallas police department by a competent professional resource in terms of its effectiveness in the field of intergroup or human relations? If so, what were the results?

Organization in the Minority Community

1. To what extent are there local organizations which effectively seek improvement of social, cultural, educational, economic and/or political conditions that tend to disadvantage citizens because of race, religion, or ancestry? Do such groups offer programs geared to establish and maintain meaningful channels of communication and to promote orderly change in overcoming discriminatory practices?

2. To what extent has minority representation been reflected in municipal and county governmental bodies that set public policy and affect the daily lives of all citizens? Have such persons been encouraged to take part in civic, cultural, religious, business and professional clubs and organizations?

3. Have Dallas decision makers sought opinion and reaction from a wide cross-section of the minority community with regard to identification of problems and approaches to resolution?

4. What has been the reaction of Dallas community leaders to past expressions of peaceful and lawful protest? Have such occasions been carefully examined and evaluated in order to gain optimal insight and benefit from those experiences?

5. Does Dallas leadership and the community at large understand the function of a municipal commission to deal with interracial/ethnic problems? Has the proposal to establish such a commission been fully investigated and given fair consideration?

Health, Welfare and Public Services

No person in the United States shall, on the ground of race, color, or national origin, be excluded from participation in, be denied the benefits of, or be subjected to discrimination under any program or activity receiving federal financial assistance.

—Section 601, Title VI, Civil Rights Act of 1964

1. What is the name and program objective of each local public and private agency engaged in providing services designed primarily to relieve problems of illness and disease, unemployment, financial distress, substandard housing, hunger, family disorganization, legal aid and other manifestations of impoverishment? What evaluations of their programs have been made and with what results? Are they reasonably accessible to most prospective clients?
2. Do all hospital and other health care facilities in the Dallas area admit patients on a nondiscriminatory basis? Are staff positions with such institutions open to all qualified physicians and technicians without regard to race, religion, or ancestry?
3. What progress has been made in establishing comprehensive, multipurpose neighborhood centers in disadvantaged areas where all community services can be disbursed and coordinated?
4. In what ways and to what extent are Negroes in Dallas disadvantaged with regard to ambulance service, funeral and burial arrangements, home care nursing, retirement facilities, and so forth?
5. Are local municipal services such as street repair, garbage collection, traffic control, park and recreation amenities, library facilities, and housing code enforcement provided to residents of poverty areas at the same level of responsiveness as in more affluent sections of the city?

White Dallas, as white America, has been generally conditioned to acceptance and perpetuation of the "place" of Negroes, and to some extent, Mexican Americans. The mass of those who have lived lives of exclusion and denial as a condition of birth have themselves become resigned. To many such individuals, full and equal access to promising jobs, to quality education, to decent housing—to the pursuit of happiness, in the words of our founding fathers—are only distant expectations for future generations, if indeed, they are foreseen at all.

And so it may be said that as a result of this conditioning to which most of us have been exposed for so long, we fail to see our environment as it is. We are inclined to rationalize that our neighbors who suffer deprivation are lacking in talent, ambition, or intelligence and therefore are not destined for successful lives. We are less inclined to recognize what is more often the fact—that artificially, we place certain of our citizens in a society which can and does deny opportunity to develop the personal resources necessary to compete.

It should be emphasized that there is no singularly effective tool or approach to overcoming generations of discrimination and disadvantage. Those who look to a municipal human relations commission, or to any other community organization, public or private, to deal with these problems, must be aware of their limitations. Such resources are of value only to the extent that they are capable of implementing constructive programs to bring about meaningful social change. To do so, adequate financing, skilled and dedicated staff, and the positive support and influence of political, economic, and civic leadership structures must be available. Without any one of these elements, progress can be impeded rather than advanced.

The Bottom Line

Dallas, as might be said of many other large U.S. cities, is like a large house with many closets in some of which lie smoldering inflammable materials—human frustration, defeat, and hopelessness. Given the right conditions, the spark to ignite fuse and explosives already in place, there is little defense against tragedy.

It is not reasonable to argue that we really cannot overcome discrimination or prevent violence or civil disruption through taking preventive measures. To do so is to say that we continue to have crime and corruption and we therefore need no laws or enforcement agencies to combat them. Also analogous is to suggest that our fire departments should limit their responsibilities to extinguishing fires, giving no attention to enforcing regulations and inspecting property in an effort to prevent or reduce their number and severity. Somehow, most communities in this country have failed to take the forthright measures necessary to grapple with racial injustice until after the wrench of frustration and aggression could no longer be contained and the situation becomes a threat to stability. Then, attention having been forcefully and dramatically drawn to the problems at hand, more often than not we're more likely to deal more seriously with harsh reality.

Dallas has intelligent, resourceful, and dedicated leadership. Given reliable information and sound justification, it has traditionally made the right choices and responded to recognized community need. Thus far, however, with regard to the condition of minority community relations, at least as seen by those who have dedicated themselves to meaningful reformation, there has been little determined effort to bring about meaningful change. The experiences of other cities in somewhat parallel circumstances have been largely disregarded.

Grass roots interest and activity toward developing an appropriate agency to deal with these issues have been mobilized in recent months. Civic, religious, and professional groups have investigated, evaluated and reported their findings regarding available options. There has been unprecedented biracial involvement from many quarters of the city. Still, the most influential power centers have not responded to the degree necessary to achieve significant progress.

Racial tensions in Dallas may never erupt into destruction or mob lawlessness. We hope not. Leaders in other places have said, in effect, "It can't happen here. 'Our people' are not inclined that way." They were right until, one day, they were wrong.

THE REST OF THE STORY

The foregoing excerpts were taken from a paper that was written in April of 1967, one of my first intergroup relations projects after opening the Dallas regional office as the lone representative of the U.S. Community Relations Service. It was intended as an interest stimulant to community leadership in bringing about an improved interracial/ethnic climate in the city and in promoting multicultural understanding. It was distributed through appearances before civic and church groups and many private consultations with minority organization leaders, business, governmental and social service agency figures likely to participate in mobilization initiatives. The degree to which its distribution may have resulted in achieving those objectives is beyond knowing. It was only part of a larger effort shared by others to introduce Dallas to a proactive position in preparing for social change and meeting the challenges of the new civil rights era.

In January 1969, a privately funded, nongovernmental Greater Dallas Community Relations Commission became a reality. By the following June, after almost six months of organizational preparation, strategy development, and interfactional compromise, a budget was subscribed, staff appointments finalized, and program activities begun. Sometimes muted opposition, sometimes strident defiance, from various influential business and political elements were largely overcome. The inevitability of a new dawn in human rights and the suppression of divisive social mores was gradually but surely sinking into the consciousness of those who harbored racial biases. The combined initiatives of our office and the various partnering community organizations[6] had come to see coordinated efforts reach fruition.

The commission functioned for more than 35 years, eventually taking on a variety of "activist roles" in the late 1980s that ultimately helped lead to its demise. Key programs centered on assisting public housing residents become more engaged in property management, advocating political reform in favor of single-member-district city council elections and, probably most controversial, leading efforts to strengthen citizen involvement in reviewing allegations of police misconduct. The latter activity became a "lightning rod" in attracting strong opposition. Eventually, public support and funding sources declined. In May of 2005, the commission was disbanded.[7] Another chapter in the history of intergroup relations in Dallas was closed.

---

[6]Including the Greater Dallas Council of Churches, the local office of the National Conference of Christians and Jews, Dallas Citizens Council's Biracial Committee, the newly formed Dallas Urban League, NAACP and the Dallas Clergy Coalition (organized by CRS following release of the Kerner Commission Report calling for responsive community effort to implement recently enacted federal civil rights legislation), and Black Citizens for Justice, Law and Order.

[7]Information regarding later year GDCRC developments was provided by Elizabeth Velasquez who served the commission as executive director from 1987 until her resignation in 2002.

ADDENDA

A   Chapter 5, Louisiana State Penitentiary: copy of a bulletin sent by the inmate mediation team to the prison population announcing the plan to negotiate issues pending in litigation.

TO THE INMATE POPULATION

This bulletin is to inform you of a series of meetings between officials of the Department of Corrections and a team of prisoners. The purpose of this meeting is to present and attempt to solve the problems of this institution as they are seen from the prisoner's point of view. Disciplinary policies and medical care will be the two areas under discussion. These meetings are the result of an attempt by Federal District Judge E. Gordon West to resolve the many problems in these two areas that prisoners are expressing concern about. He has invited an agency of the federal government to act as mediators (referees) in these discussions. The team of prisoners will consist of four prisoners who are here in Angola now and one ex-convict. The prisoners were selected by the Federal Agency from among the heads of the inmate organizations and from among the inmates who presently have writs pending in Judge West's court.

All of the members of this team are aware of the existing problems in these two areas. Every member of this team will represent to the best of his ability the interest of the entire prison population. None will bite their tongue or otherwise avoid the real issues. Every prisoner no doubt wishes to speak for himself, but obviously this is impossible. We will do out utmost to present the solutions that every prisoner believes are needed, in the two areas to which the discussions will be limited.

If you have had any experience in either of these two areas whereby you feel that you were treated unfairly or harshly we would like to use your experience in bringing these problems to the surface and attempting to deal with them. You may remain anonymous if you wish. But by all means be honest about your experiences. You can write a brief statement of your experience on the back of this bulletin and put it in the box in front of the dining hall for minimum security prisoners, both new prison and out camps. All maximum security prisoners give your statements of experience to the Hall Boy and they will be picked up Thursday.

The prisoner team will consist of :   Frank Bagala   -   Magnolia
                                       Leotha Brown   -   Pine
                                       Nathaniel Stewart -   CCR
                                       Robert Matthews   -   CBC

Nothing is promised except that we will do our very best.

October 6, 1972   Angola, Louisiana
                              Louisiana State Penitentiary

FINAL SETTLEMENT AGREEMENT BETWEEN THE NEGOTIATING TEAMS FOR THE
LOUISIANA STATE PENITENTIARY AND PRISONER REPRESENTATIVES.

The following is agreed between the undersigned parties:

1. The following hours shall prevail for access to shower
    facilities in the dormitory:

    Open from 5:00 A.M. to 7:00 A.M.
    Open from 10:30 A.M. to 1:00 P.M.
    Open from 3:30 P.M. to 9:30 P.M.

2. There shall be a committee appointed by the two teams jointly
whose responsibility it will be to prepare and submit revisions to the
existing inmate rules and regulations. Recommendations from this committee
shall be designed to eliminate arbitrary and unnecessary rules and
regulations and to incorporate such rules that are found to be necessary
additions for proper management of the institution. Institution
committee members shall be: Lloyd W. Hoyle, Jr. (Chairman), Associate
Warden H. J. Dees, Associate Warden William Kerr; Alternates -
James Stephens and Colonel Robert Bryan. Prisoner team members shall
be: Leotha Brown (Chairman), Frank Bagala, Robert Mathews, and Frank
Williams.

(Note: The word "Arbitrary" means a rule which is not related to a
valid purpose for which it was intended.)

It is agreed that the committee will report back to a joint session of
both teams on December 4, 1972. The committee will give particular
attention to the following rules enumerated in the prepared agenda for
the joint sessions begun on October 2, 1972: Rule II-15, II-16,
rule regarding "refusal to work", and rule regarding "improper work."

After promulgation of this code, nothing will be punishable as an
offense which is not stated in the rules and regulations. These
rules and regulations may be ammended from time to time by the Warden
and/or Director of the Department of Corrections.

3. Rule II-01 is amended to read as follows:

"II-01. FAILURE TO OBEY ORDERS. All inmates shall obey orders given
them by employees of the penitentiary. Failure to do so may result
in up to ten days in isolation and failure to earn more than sixteen days
good time per month.

No inmate shall be required to carry out an order which requires him to
perform a function which is properly an employee duty. No inmate shall
be required to carry out an order when doing so would place his well-
being in jeopardy. A reasonable explanation of the refusal, or the
invalidity of the employee's order, shall provide a complete defense."

4. The following paragraph will be included in the foreword of the Inmate Rules and Regulations: "Upon a determination that the inmate is not guilty of the offense charged against him, he shall be exonerated and the accusation stricken from the record."

5. Rule V-01 Waste of Food is amended to read as follows: "Inmates shall not be permitted to carry food from the Mess Hall."

6. Penitentiary directive number 7 in the rules and regulations entitled "Inmate Correspondence" is amended to read as follows:

"The following rules are established regarding inmate correspondence.

1. A. All mail orders must be sent through the office of the Chief of Security for approval.

   B. All orders for hobbycraft must be sent through and approved by the Director of Recreation.

   C. All subscriptions to newspapers, magazines, and other publications must go to the office of the Director of Education for processing.

2. The envelope must be clearly addressed to the person to whom it is being mailed and no designs or pictures are to be drawn on the envelope. In the upper left hand corner of the envelope, inmate's return address must be given as follows:

EXAMPLE

Inmate's name	John Doe
PMB #	PMB #84177
Dormitory, Camp of Cellblock	Walnut 4
City and State	Angola, Louisiana 70712

Inclusion of PMB and prison number is necessary to avoid delay or loss of mail, especially in cases where there are two or more persons in the institution with the same name.

3. All letters are to be posted unsealed for inspection except those letters to the Governor, Director of the Department of Corrections and her staff, inmate's attorney, sentencing judge, district attorney, sheriff, probation and parole officer, and the attorney general.

4. The safety and security of a correctional institution requires the careful examination of all incoming and in certain instances, outgoing correspondence and the careful examination of all packages. No inmate shall be permitted to send or receive communication or a package of any nature until he has signed the required form consenting to the opening and examination of the contents for contraband. This form is signed by the inmate when he is first admitted to the institution.

5. No packages except those containing periodicals or other approved items will be permitted through the mail.

6. Only checks or money orders will be accepted for deposit to an inmate's account and must be mailed to the Cashier, Louisiana State Penitentiary, Angola, Louisiana 70712. A note must accompany the check or money order giving the inmate's name, number, and location. Deposits should not be placed in an envelope addressed to the inmate. Checks and money orders should be made payable to the inmate but mailed to the Cashier.

7. The collection and distribution of mail is never to be delegated to an inmate. Neither is the mail to be dropped on the table or other convenient place for each individual inmate to come and look for his own." (End of Penitentiary Directive #7 relating to Inmate Correspondence).

7. Rule VI-o3 (Haircuts and Mustaches" shall be amended to read as follows:

"RULE VI-03 HAIR STYLES AND FACIAL HAIR. Hair length (including facial hair) shall only be regulated in order to comply with necessary and reasonable health (sanitation) and safety factors. Judgements of what constitutes a health (sanitation) or safety problem shall be made by the responsible official and justified through explanation of the hazard involved. Standards are to be set and decisions made regarding these factors by appropriate consultation with the Director of Industries, the Culinary Manager, and/or the Hospital Administrator. All inmates received in the Admission Unit shall be clean shaven for the purpose of identification photographs.

8. RECORD OF IMPASSE. (Lockdown-Exercise)

The inmate team proposed that one hour of outdoor exercise in lieu of indoor exercise be provided for inmates who are in Lockdown in CCR and the cellblock. The matter was found unacceptable by management for these basic reasons: (1) It is discriminatory in terms of comparable rights and privileges in non-lockdown status. (2) The exercise should be coupled with a work program. The matter of outdoor exercise will be examined and a recommendation made if a practical solution can be found.

Management made the following counterproposal: Prisoners incarcerated under lockdown conditions in the cellblocks and in CCR should be required to work a full day. In return, they would receive privileges commensurate with those that are enjoyed by prisoners in the general population. Management recognized that there are security and physical limitations which would excuse the work requirement. Inmates who fall in that category would receive one hour of outside exercise (weather permitting).

An impasse was reached because the prisoner team found the proposal unacceptable. Reasons for these conclusions were: (1) That the outdoor exercise option is considered a right and not a privilege; therefore it should be considered separately from any condition of work.

It was stated by the prison team that there is no reasonable distinction between lockdown imposed by law (Deathrow inmates) and lockdown imposed by administrative order (CCR and cellblock lockdown). The inmate team felt that equal provisions for exercise should be provided irrespective of the reason for lockdown.

9. Prisoners incarcerated in the cellblocks who are not in lockdown and who are on work schedules shall be entitled to the same yard privileges as the rest of the population.

10. ADMINISTRATIVE LOCKDOWN. Administrative lockdown (including isolation at the Reception Center) shall be followed by a hearing no later than 72 hours after detention, except in the event of a three day holiday or in case of delay when returning from satellite locations. Upon presentation of a reasonable need for a continuance to prepare for hearing, the Disciplinary Board shall grant same for a period of up to five days. Any period of time spent in administrative lockdown as a result of the continuance shall be credited as time served. Location of confinement of the inmate in preparing his defense shall be determined at the discretion of the hearing board.

11. ADMINISTRATIVE LOCKDOWN - CREDIT FOR TIME SERVED. The period of confinement of administrative lockdown (or isolation at the Reception Center) pending a hearing on a disciplinary report shall be credited toward the serving of the actual sentence imposed by the Disciplinary Board.

12. LOCKDOWN - INDEFINITE SENTENCES.

A. Penitentiary directive number thirteen dated April 12, 1972, (Subject - "Lockdown") shall be incorporated in the document containing rules and regulations. (Note: The word review is construed to mean a hearing).

B. An inmate confined to Lockdown is entitled to written reasons for denial of release at the time of the hearing.

13. ELIMINATION OF ISOLATION CELLS AT C.C.E. (RED HATS). The C.C.E. isolation cells (the Red Hats) shall be closed. The institution will utilize the thirty cells that are now being used for Administrative Lockdown. Six of these cells will be utilized as Administrative Lockdown. The remaining cells will be utilized as isolation or punishment cells. Necessary renovations will commence as soon as possible and transfers are expected before the end of October.

14. <u>LOCKDOWN - ISOLATION CELLS.</u> Inmates in isolation cells will be allowed the following rights:

    A. To receive correspondence.

    B. To originate correspondence only to communicate with the courts and legal counsel.

    C. Inmates will be allowed to communicate by telephone with their families and legal counsel only in emergency situations (collect).

    D. Inmates will be permitted to have visitors in keeping with necessary security precautions.

    E. Inmates will be issued clean coveralls daily.

    F. Inmates shall be permitted to take daily showers.

    G. Inmates shall be allowed to have toothpaste and toothbrush in the cells. The institution shall furnish towels and soap (outside of the cells).

    H. Inmates shall be provided with three meals in accordance with the American Correctional Association standards.

    I. Corridors shall be appropriately lighted. Individual cells will not have light fixtures.

    J. Sufficient heating for all cells shall be provided.

    K. Inmates shall be provided a clean mattress. If necessary two mattresses will be placed in each cell. Mattresses shall be issued after countdown at approximately 9:00 P.M. and removed at approximately 5:00 A.M. daily.

    L. A mattress cover will be made available to each cell as soon as they are purchased and received. Inmates shall be issued a clean mattress cover upon entering isolation.

    M. Blankets will be washed or cleaned as often as possible in order to maintain reasonable standards of cleanliness.

    N. Under normal circumstances, isolation cells will not be occupied by more than three persons.

    O. Inmates confined in cells will be allowed to engage in conversation within the limitations of Rule II-04 governing language.

15.   LOCKDOWN - ABUSE. The right of inmates to hold and express religious and political beliefs shall be observed and respected. It is understood that written materials in the possession of inmates must be in keeping with state and federal laws.

16.   LOCKDOWN - INVOLUNTARY TRANSFERS. Before an inmate may be involuntarily transferred to lockdown, he shall first be placed in Administrative Lockdown. He shall be given a hearing as is provided in the rules governing Administrative Lockdown.

17.   LOCKDOWN - VISITING PRIVILEGES. All inmates who are incarcerated in cellblocks A, B, C, D, and CCR shall be allowed to visit in the "A" Building visiting room unless it is determined that they are security risks by the Shift Supervisor.

18.   LOCKDOWN - TELEVISION PRIVILEGES. Television privileges will be made available to those inmates in lockdown situations upon receipt of a sufficient number of television sets. (Inmates in isolation will not be allowed television privileges).

19.   ACCESS TO PRODUCTS IN GLASS CONTAINERS. Suitable plastic containers shall be made available in the Inmate Canteen to be used to store food purchased originally in glass containers.

20.   MEDICAL ATTENTION. Specific reference is made to rule #33 which was alleged to be poorly enforced in the past. Management will take steps to assure that the rule is properly enforced. Rule #33 of the employee handbook reads as follows: "Correctional Officers are not trained in medical science. However, they should be able to recognize the basic characteristics of certain types of illness. The determination of whether a man is ill will be made by the medical staff. No man will be denied medical treatment and will be sent to the hospital when he becomes ill."

21.   PHYSICIANS ORDERS. Employees of the prison shall not act or cause an inmate to act contrary to the orders of the physician and/or the medical department. Should an employee question the validity of a physician's order, the employee shall take no action other than consultation with the physician for further judgement.

22.   FIRST AID. First aid equipment and supplies (as soon as available) shall be located at critical points within the prison. Certain employees shall be instructed in the provision of first aid for the critical injuries of the nature typically sustained by inmates. At least one trained employee shall be on duty in the area.

23.   MEDICAL AND DENTAL EXAMINATIONS. Bi-annual medical and dental examinations shall be available to inmates provided there is sufficient medical staff available.

24.   SICKCALL ON CELLBLOCKS. Under normal conditions, an
appropriate technician will make sick call in the Cellblocks (including
isolation and CCR) on a daily basis. The officer in charge of the unit
will make an announcement when the technician arrives for sick call.

25.   ON CALL EMERGENCY SERVICE. Management shall provide 24 hour
on call emergency services provided the medical staff has at least two
physicians employed.

26.   MEDICAL TECHNICIAN TRAINING. Exploration will be made of the possibility of introducing medical technician training at the institution
through contact with State and Federal agencies.

27.   INMATE GRIEVANCE COMMITTEE. A mechanism to provide prison
management with communication on grievances and inmate problems shall be
established. The Chairman and Vice-Chairman of both negotiating teams
shall consider and prepare a suggested grievance procedure to be
recommended at the joint session of the negotiating team on December 4th.

28.   The foreword of the inmate rules and regulations to be revised
will include the following statement:

"In the event of emergency conditions, the Warden or his
delegate may suspend any and all rules and regulations until the
emergency situation has ceased."

_____   _____
Mrs. Elayn Hunt, Chairman   Leotha Brown, Chairman
Negotiating Team, Louisiana State Pen. Negotiating Team
Director of the La. Dept. of Corrections   Prisoner Representation

_____   _____
Warden C. Murray Henderson, Vice-Chairman   Frank Bagala, Vice-Chairman

Page 8   Angola, Louisiana   October 6, 1972
                     Louisiana State Penitentiary

Lloyd W Hoyle Jr.   _Robert Matthews_
Deputy Warden Lloyd W. Hoyle, Jr.   Robert Matthews

Hayden J Dees   _Nathaniel Stewart_
Associate Warden Hayden J. Dees   Nathaniel Stewart

Robert Bryan   _Frank E Williams_
Colonel Robert Bryan, Director of Security   Frank E. Williams

E. C. Day (Alternate) (Hospital Adm.)   Colonel Bolt (Alternate)
William Kerr (Alternate) (Assoc. Warden) Roosevelt Hill (Alternate)
James Stephens (Director of Class.)   Grover Wooten (Alternate)

                                          Dudley Spiller, Legal Counsel

WITNESS:
Robert F Greenwald
Robert F. Greenwald, Mediator   OBSERVERS:
Community Relations Service
U. S. Department of Justice   Reverend Jack Allen, Chaplain
                                          Herman Smith, Legal Office
                                          John Whitley, Classification Off.
James Freeman
Corrections Specialist
Community Relations Service
United States Department of Justice

UNITED STATES DISTRICT COURT
Eastern District of Louisiana
400 Royal Street
New Orleans, Louisiana 70130

JACK M. GORDON
Judge

August 29, 1974

Mr. Robert F. Greenwald, Regional Coordinator
United States Department of Justice
Community Relations Service
Southwest Regional Office
1100 Commerce Street
Dallas, Texas 75202

Re: Jefferson Parish Jail case

Dear Mr. Greenwald:

We have now concluded the trial and I have issued my
opinion relating to the issues which remained unresolved after
your most fruitful mediation efforts.

I am enclosing for your information a copy of my opinion,
which I have sent to West Publishing Company for publication in due
course.

You may be interested to note that I devoted a substantial
portion of the opinion to outlining the mediation efforts and the
manner in which they were carried out, as well as commenting upon
my views as to their efficacy in such situations. I felt that issu-
ing the opinion in this form would be as good a way as any of acquaint-
ing others with the success we met in this case. No small part of
this success was due to the perspicacity which you and your associates
with the Community Relations Service brought to this matter, and I
should again like to express my deep appreciation for your assistance.

Sincerely,

Jack M. Gordon
United States District Judge

Encl.

Joel Wade FRAZIER et al.

v.

Thomas F. DONELON et al.

Civ. A. No. 72-814.

United States District Court,
E. D. Louisiana.

Aug. 23, 1974.

Civil rights action by inmates of parish jail alleging that refusal and censorship of their mail and alleged curtailment of their right to read certain material abridged their constitutional rights. The District Court, Jack M. Gordon, J., held that jail authorities had right to open and read mail to and from inmates, that jail's policy of reading letters from inmates to and from attorneys and judicial officers violated inmates' constitutional right, and that refusal to allow inmates to read magazine which contained sexually stimulating reading matter did not violate their constitutional rights.

Order accordingly.

1. Prisons ⊂4

Generally, federal courts adhere to the tenet of not interfering in internal affairs and administration of correctional systems, except in those extraordinary instances when available administrative remedies within penal system are of no avail to its inmate inhabitants.

2. Convicts ⊂1

Lawful incarceration brings about necessary withdrawal or limitation of many privileges and rights, a retraction justified by considerations underlying penal system.

3. Convicts ⊂1

Although incarceration of an individual may require circumscription and deprivation of certain rights afforded to his or her free counterpart, one who is incarcerated is not stripped of all constitutional guarantees but maintains those constitutional protections that are not at variance with needs and objectives of correctional facility.

4. Prisons ⊂4

Prison administrators' regulation of inmate mail was valid if mail restrictions were justifiable and implementation of restrictions necessitated a minimum degree of discretion.

5. Prisons ⊂4

To justify mail censorship, prison authorities must establish that regulation authorizing such censorship covers a substantial governmental interest, such as the security and discipline within correctional institution and that questioned regulation is worded so as to minimize any resulting constitutional transgressions.

6. Prisons ⊂4

Prison regulations involving inmate correspondence cannot be promulgated for self-serving purposes such as to suppress uncomplimentary, defamatory or critical language contained in letters.

7. Prisons ⊂4

Once prison authorities decide to censor major portions of a letter to or from an inmate or to reject in toto the letter, minimal procedural safeguards should attach and authorities should notify sender of decision with accompanying explanation for action and sender should have available some avenue of review if he believes that his or her product is outside the pale of the restrictions.

8. Prisons ⊂4

Prison administrators have the authority to open and review most incoming and outgoing inmate mail.

9. Prisons ⊂4

Exigencies in operation of a penal institution dictate the loss or minimal deterioration of certain constitutional rights during confinement, inter alia, right to mail letters uninspected and unread by third party.

10. Prisons ⊂4

A cursory inspection of envelope and contents therein of letter received or sent by inmate is justified in order to prevent flow of contraband, weapons and narcotics and to detect possible escape plans.

11. Constitutional Law ⬌90.1(1)

Restrictions on prison inmate's written correspondence to the courts and to attorneys does not violate First Amendment freedom of speech. U.S.C. A.Const. Amend. 1.

12. Constitutional Law ⬌272
Criminal Law ⬌641.12(1)

Prison policy condoning indiscriminate reading of inmate correspondence to and from attorneys and judicial officers violates inmate's rights under Sixth and Fourteenth Amendments. U.S.C.A. Const. Amends. 6, 14.

13. Constitutional Law ⬌90.1(1)

Prison authorities' termination of distribution to inmates of local newspapers donated to prison, necessitated by financial difficulties of prison, did not violate the First Amendment right of inmates who were not deprived of right to subscribe to newspaper at their own cost. U.S.C.A.Const. Amend. 1.

14. Constitutional Law ⬌90.1(1)

Refusal to allow prison inmates to read magazine which contained sexually stimulating reading matter that had tendancy to disrupt internal discipline of prison did not violate inmates' First Amendment rights. U.S.C.A.Const. Amend. 1.

William D. Treeby, and Michael R. Fontham, Stone, Pigman, Walther, Wittmann & Hutchinson, New Orleans, La., for plaintiffs.

Alvin R. Eason, Parish Atty., Robert I. Broussard, Lionel R. Collins, Asst. Parish Attys., Gretna, La., for defendants, President of the Parish of Jefferson and Councilmen of the Parish of Jefferson, Louisiana.

Russell J. Schonekas, Tucker & Schonekas, New Orleans, La., for defendants, Alwynn J. Cronvich, Sheriff of the Parish of Jefferson, and Roland J. Vicknair, Warden of the Jefferson Parish Prison.

JACK M. GORDON, District Judge:

Plaintiffs, on behalf of themselves and other inmates of the Jefferson Parish Prison, instituted this action pursuant to 42 U.S.C. § 1983 and 28 U.S.C. § 1343,[1] against Thomas F. Donelon, the President of Jefferson Parish, Louisiana; all councilmen of Jefferson Parish;[2] Alwynn J. Cronvich, the Sheriff of Jefferson Parish; and Roland J. Vicknair, the Warden of Jefferson Parish Prison. In their complaint, plaintiffs challenge a number of the practices, rules, and regulations of the Jefferson Parish Jail as constitutionally violative of the First, Sixth, and Fourteenth Amendments.

Plaintiffs maintain that certain illegal procedures are in operation at Jefferson Parish Jail and accordingly, plaintiffs

---

1. Title 42, United States Code, Section 1983 reads as follows:

Every person who, under color of any statute, ordinance, regulation, custom, or usage, of any State or Territory, subjects, or causes to be subjected, any citizen of the United States or other person within the jurisdiction thereof to the deprivation of any rights, privileges, or immunities secured by the Constitution and laws, shall be liable to the party injured in an action at law, suit in equity, or other proper proceedings for redress.

Title 28, United States Code, Section 1343 reads in pertinent part as follows:

The District Courts shall have original jurisdiction of any civil action authorized by law to be commenced by any person:

*   *   *   *   *

(3) To redress the deprivation, under color of any State law, statute, ordinance, regulation, custom or usage, of any right, privilege or immunity secured by the Constitution of the United States or by any Act of Congress providing for equal rights of citizens or of all persons within the jurisdiction of the United States;

(4) To recover damages or to secure equitable or other relief under any Act of Congress providing for the protection of civil rights . . . .

2. The defendant president and councilmanic members of Jefferson Parish filed a motion to dismiss prior to trial; this motion was unopposed by plaintiffs and accordingly was granted by the Court.

contest these procedures as enumerated in the following allegations: (1) prison officials assert the right to open, inspect, read, and censor all correspondence to and from prison inmates; (2) prison officials sometimes refuse to mail inmate correspondence containing complaints about prison conditions; (3) mail arriving at the prison occasionally is delayed without reason; (4) visiting hours for inmates are limited arbitrarily and the present visiting facilities are substantially inadequate; (5) visiting regulations are applied in a discriminatory fashion; (6) usage of the public telephone is denied capriciously to some inmates; (7) inmates are not allowed access to newspapers, books, magazines, and other publications; (8) many inmates arbitrarily are denied the right to attend religious services conducted in the institution; and (9) prisoners have been refused the right to designate spokesmen to inform prison officials of the complaints of the inmate populace.

[1] Generally speaking, the federal courts have adhered to the tenet of not interfering in the internal affairs and the administration of correctional systems, except in those extraordinary instances when the available administrative remedies within the penal system are of no avail to its inmate inhabitants. *See* Procunier v. Martinez, —— U.S. ——, 94 S.Ct. 1800, 40 L.Ed.2d 224 (1974); Robinson v. Jordan, 494 F.2d 793 (5th Cir. 1974); Granville v. Hunt, 411 F.2d 9 (5th Cir. 1969); Jackson v. Godwin, 400 F.2d 529 (5th Cir. 1968). *Cf.*, Haggerty v. Wainwright, 427 F.2d 1137 (5th Cir. 1970); Eaton v. Capps, 348 F.Supp. 237 (M.D.Ala.1972), aff'd, 480 F.2d 1021 (5th Cir. 1973). This non-intervention approach by the courts stems principally from judicial recognition of the sui generis nature of problems inherent in the formulation and execution of policies in a correctional environment. A complementary supportive factor in the development of judicial restraint with respect to the correctional area is the reticence of the federal courts to administer the functions of state institutions. Manage-

381 F.Supp.—58

ment of state penal institutions should at the very least be deferred to state courts and at the very best to the appropriate prison authorities. *See*, Preiser v. Rodriguez, 411 U.S. 475, 93 S.Ct. 1827, 36 L.Ed.2d 439 (1973).

The tasks that administrators of penal facilities perform are not easy or envy-engendering ones; these responsibilities include, inter alia, the maintenance of frequently overcrowded institutions, the preservation of internal order and discipline, guarding against escape and preventing the infiltration of various contraband, such as weapons and narcotics, all without infringing the personal rights of the inmates. It is not very surprising, therefore, that problems surrounding incarceration are complicated and usually are not susceptible of ready resolutions. Accordingly, extensive research, planning, and expertise in correctional affairs must be employed when attempting to discover viable solutions. It would not seriously be questioned that the courts, vis-à-vis other branches of government, are the least equipped governmental organ through which to ventilate and resolve inmate grievances because inherent in the juridical operation is the necessity that courts view each issue in black and white terms. By its very nature, a court's ruling is antithetical to the attainment of striking a judicious medium between the parties. Cognizant of the undesirable result produced by such a "one or the other" approach when dealing with inmate assaults upon the regulations of correctional institutions, this Court attempted to avoid resolution of the present complaint by judicial fiat. It is the opinion of this Court that resolution of disputes by litigation, due to the combatant win or lose attitude of litigants, generally has the effect of driving the parties further apart instead of bringing them together. Thus, the Court preferred to yield to the less stultified process whereby judicial involvement in correctional problems hopefully would be eliminated or perhaps minimized substantially.

Consistent with the above stated philosophy of avoiding, when possible, a tripartite confrontation between the inmates, the prison administrators, and the judiciary, this Court concluded that a non-judicial remedial system for inmate grievances would constitute a more preferable approach. Therefore, the Court sought to employ some means whereby the inmates and the administrators could negotiate the complaints in the instant case without judicial interference but subject to court review if warranted. Such a negotiating structure must be both flexible in its operation and independent of the system that it seeks to modify.

As would be expected, this form of collective bargaining also requires the presence of some impartial individual or agency, trained as a mediator, who can assist the parties in the creation of a suitable format. Not only must this neutral consultant be able to delineate to the respective sides the sundry, conflicting interests and needs of their bargaining opponent, but the mediator must be able to serve as the necessary catalyst in helping the parties develop possible solutions to their mutual problems.

Inasmuch as collective bargaining within the correctional parameters is a relatively novel approach which many persons, including judges, still consider to be in an embryonic stage, the Court felt that it would be instructive to detail the fundamentals of the negotiating system that the Court employed in this case, and, more particularly, how such a system developed and functioned.

Initially, the Court informally requested the parties to the suit at bar to agree to keep the litigation in abeyance while the mediation progressed, in recognition of the fact that litigation is often incongruous with the forward movement of mediation. The litigants voluntarily consented to the unrecorded stay order and concurred with the Court in its desire to provide an alternative remedy to the judicial process. Of course, the first task was to select a competent mediator. The usage of the Community Relations Service (hereinafter referred to as "CRS"), a division of the United States Department of Justice, proved most formidably to satisfy this need. After contacting the Regional Coordinator of the CRS, arrangements were made whereby the Court personally explained to the CRS representative the existing issues of conflict. As an aside, the CRS representative informed the Court that the CRS had prior experience in mediating inmate grievances and recently had achieved success in performing mediation services in a nearby state correctional institution. Once the CRS representative understood the inmate grievances, the Court scheduled a conference in chambers with the CRS representative, the attorneys for the inmates, the Sheriff of Jefferson Parish, the Warden of Jefferson Parish Prison, as well as their attorneys. From that juncture until the completion of the arbitration processes, the Court's involvement was strictly de minimis. During the Court's conference the CRS representative presented some tentative ground rules for the forthcoming discussions and posed a plan for the selection of members of the respective negotiating teams. The inmate body of Jefferson Parish Prison designated their bargaining agents,[3] which included the inmates' counsel, while the so-called prison management side consisted of the Sheriff, the Warden, various correctional officials, and attorneys for the Parish.

Upon the selection of the negotiating committees, the CRS representative secured a meeting place where the discussions could occur with a substantial degree of privacy. These sessions were scheduled so as to allow an adequate amount of time for each conference as well as to permit ample time between

---

3. The prison team and management team selected alternates. As would be expected, the jail population has a quick turnover due to the fact that it is used as a holding place for inmates who are scheduled to be transferred to penitentiaries or for those convicted individuals who are sentenced to a relatively brief period of incarceration.

sessions; the parties thus had sufficient time to fully air their views at each encounter and concomitantly enjoyed enough time between sessions to digest the conversations and results of the previous session as well as to obtain feedback on the different issues from their respective represented bodies.

As reported to the Court by the CRS representative, the negotiating meetings were highly productive. Although these sessions were intended to focus on the inmate grievances contained in the complaint, the parties were not limited in their discussions to any specific boundaries. In a remarkably short time, a certain camaraderie between the two factions surfaced and soon thereafter concrete compromises were perfected on a plurality of the issues that were in dispute. The fruits of these mediation sessions culminated in a binding agreement entered into by the parties on the following matters: access to religious services; public telephone service; grievance procedure; and visiting privileges. For illustrative purposes, the Court has appended to its opinion (identified as Appendix A) the final settlement agreement between the prison authorities and the inmates. In addition to the formal agreements, the Court clearly appreciates certain fringe benefits that resulted from this series of negotiations; among these valuable extras are a higher level of rapport between the authorities and the inmates, and, of no small import, the indoctrination of mediation to both sides as a potentially viable and permanent alternative to the courts in resolving the complaints of inmates.

Due to the mediation discussions, only the following two contested issues remained: the right of the prison authorities to open, inspect, read, and censor prisoner correspondence[4] and the inmates' accessibility or lack thereof to reading materials. Since the parties were unable to reach a compromise on this pair of issues, the Court scheduled this portion of the case to be tried. Having heard the testimony of the principal protagonists and a number of interested parties, equally representing the views of the correctional authorities and the inmates, supplemented by the legal memoranda submitted by counsel, the Court is prepared to rule and to outline the procedures that should be implemented with respect to prisoner correspondence and inmate access to reading matter.

The inmate plaintiffs contend that the perusal and periodical censorship of their mail coupled with the alleged curtailment of inmate reading material abridge their rights protected by the First, Sixth and Fourteenth Amendments to the United States Constitution. Specifically, the inmates argue that the actions of the prison officials infringe upon the inmates' rights of free speech and personal privacy and impair free access by the inmates to the courts and to counsel. The prison authorities, quite naturally, defend the contested restrictions as appropriate means through which certain penal objectives can be achieved. Of paramount concern among the administrators' goals are the maintenance of security and inmate discipline.

At the outset, it is incumbent upon the Court to state certain findings of fact garnered from the testimony during trial. With respect to prisoner correspondence, the normal routine of distribution of mail can be capsulized as follows: all incoming mail is initially routed to the Sheriff's office, situated within the institution, where a member of his staff inspects the mail to filter out any contraband of weapons, narcotics, or currency. Incoming mail is subject to being read, but, as a practical matter, the staff member only intermittently reads a few letters, randomly selected, to serve as a spot check. The Warden testified that the incoming mail of inmates,

---

4. In the pre-trial order submitted to the Court, the parties stipulated to the fact that all incoming and outgoing inmate mail is subject to being opened, inspected, read and censored. This practice was confirmed by the testimony elicited during trial.

who are considered by the authorities to pose security risks, is regularly read as a safety precaution.[5] Outgoing mail is collected daily from the inmates and likewise is subject to being read and censored by the Warden or his Chief Deputy. Objectionable outgoing mail is returned to the author or may be mailed once the offensive portions are deleted. The inmates contend, but the Court found no credible evidence to support the fact, that some prison guards, without authorization, occasionally read mail written by the inmates.

At trial, the Court also learned that written correspondence is not the only means of communication by an inmate. Alternative channels of communication are available and these include use of the public telephones and visitation privileges with family, friends, and legal counsel. As previously indicated, these alternative means of communication substantially have been improved, both quantitatively and qualitatively, due to the recent mediation efforts.

The availability of reading material to the inmates is a considerably narrow issue. After hearing all of the testimony, this Court has only been able to discern two complaints and each is very specific in nature. The first focuses on the termination of the gratuitous distribution among inmates of the local morning newspaper. A newspaper dealer previously had been donating extra copies to the Jail provided someone from the Jail picked up the newspapers each morning. For purely budgetary reasons, that is, the increased cost of sending someone to collect the free newspapers, the administrators discontinued this service. Parenthetically, the authorities did express in open court that they would attempt to renew this service to the inmates as soon as the necessary fis-

cal arrangements could be completed. It is significant to note that at no time did the temporary stoppage of free newspapers impair the right of the inmates to subscribe, at their cost, to the local newspaper or to any other news journal.

The second inmate complaint is founded on certain limitations of inmate reading matter imposed by the Jail authorities. Although a number of former and present inmates testified, the only prohibited periodical that could be identified was Playboy Magazine.[6] The authorities responded that their policy of screening out all prurient literature is predicated on the belief that sexually stimulating reading matter has a tendency to disrupt the internal discipline of a penal institution; the correctional authorities reported to the Court that written descriptions and pictorial displays of nudity and simulated sexual acts constitute valuable contraband within the prison culture, and consequently, possession of these items frequently becomes a source of inmate competition and agitation.

[2, 3] Beginning its restricted evaluation of correctional policies, the Court, in formulating its views, acknowledges the oft-repeated, though less heeded, principle that "[l]awful incarceration brings about the necessary withdrawal or limitation of many privileges and rights, a retraction justified by the considerations underlying our penal system." Price v. Johnston, 334 U.S. 266, 285, 68 S.Ct. 1049, 1060, 92 L.Ed. 1356 (1948). *Accord,* Wolff v. McDonnell, — U.S. —, 94 S.Ct. 2963, 41 L.Ed.2d — (1974); Jones v. Connors, 496 F.2d 82 (5th Cir. 1974); United States ex rel. Tyrrell v. Speaker, 471 F.2d 1197 (3rd Cir. 1973). *See also,* Cruz v. Beto, 405 U.S. 319, 92 S.Ct. 1079, 31 L.Ed.2d 263 (1972); Brown v. Wainwright, 419

5. Jefferson Parish Jail authorities related to the Court some of the ingenious methods that inmate correspondents have employed in their attempts to convey contraband to the inmates; for example, contraband has been discovered by the authorities under postage stamps, on the glue of envelopes, and sand-

wiched between a photograph and its cardboard backing.

6. It is germane to this criticism to recognize that a prison library, containing a variety of books and magazines, is available to the inmates in addition to any private subscriptions of periodicals.

F.2d 1376 (5th Cir. 1970). Although incarceration of an individual may require the circumscription and deprivation of certain rights afforded to his or her free counterpart, this is not to suggest that one is stripped of all constitutional guarantees upon passing through the prison portals. Rather, an inmate maintains those constitutional protections that are not at variance with the needs and objectives of the correctional facility.[7]

The inmate plaintiffs asseverate that their rights under the First, Sixth, and Fourteenth Amendments should not be one scintilla less than those of citizens who are not behind bars. Adhering to the procedure recently followed by the Supreme Court in a similar factual context, *see* Procunier v. Martinez, *supra,* this Court elects to resort to a narrower basis for decision instead of resolving the whole gamut of prisoners' rights. In *Procunier,* the Supreme Court recognized that two factions, the inmates and "those who have a particularized interest in communicating" with the inmates, have an interest in securing written communication free of censorship. Whether sender or recipient, an inmate's correspondent suffers an infringement of his or her First and Fourteenth Amendment rights when the correctional authorities choose to censor prison mail, albeit that such a constitutional abridgement is merely an unintentional by-product of a superficially licit administrative function. Unlike *Procunier,* this Court need not decide the validity of specific penal regulations controlling correspondence; however, not unlike *Procunier,* this Court must determine if the mail policies at Jefferson Parish Jail constitute a proper standard of review.[8]

[4–6] Paralleling the guidelines opined by the Supreme Court in *Procunier,* this Court approves of the Jefferson Parish Prison administrators' regulation of inmate mail provided the authorities demonstrate that any mail re-

---

7. *See, e. g.,* Haines v. Kerner, 404 U.S. 519, 92 S.Ct. 594, 30 L.Ed.2d 652 (1972); Cruz v. Beto, *supra*; Gilmore v. Lynch, 319 F. Supp. 105 (N.D.Cal.1970), aff'd. 404 U.S. 15, 92 S.Ct. 250, 30 L.Ed.2d 142 (1971); Cooper v. Pate, 378 U.S. 546, 84 S.Ct. 1733, 12 L.Ed.2d 1030 (1964); Ross v. Blackledge, 477 F.2d 616 (4th Cir. 1973); Sostre v. McGinnis, 442 F.2d 178 (2nd Cir. 1971); Brenneman v. Madigan, 343 F.Supp. 128 (N.D.Cal.1972).

8. It does not appear to the Court that any well-defined written regulations currently exist governing the correspondence of inmates in Jefferson Parish Prison. Clearly the Court could not and would not uphold such a nebulous degree of personal latitude on the part of the authorities caused by the lack of specific rules. However, in keeping with this Court's philosophy of minimizing the extent of judicial intervention in correctional affairs, the Court will defer to the parties the responsibility of formulating the permissible standards through which inmate mail can be regulated. These standards should closely conform to the guidelines described in this opinion. Though not suggesting that the parties adopt verbatim the mail policy of the Federal Bureau of Prisons, the recitation of the federal criteria may prove helpful. Policy Statement 7300.1A of the Federal Bureau of Prisons prohibits the following material in inmate correspondence:

(1) Any material which might violate postal regulations, i. e., threats, blackmail, contraband or which indicate plots of escape.

(2) Discussion of criminal activities.

(3) No inmate may be permitted to conduct his business while he is in confinement. This does not go to the point of prohibiting correspondence necessary to enable the inmate to protect the property and funds that were legitimately his at the time he was committed to the institution. Thus, an inmate could correspond about refinancing a mortgage on his home or sign insurance papers, but he could not operate a mortgage or insurance business while in the institution.

(4) Letters containing codes or other obvious attempts to circumvent these regulations will be subject to rejection.

(5) Insofar as possible, all letters shall be written in English, but every effort should be made to accommodate those inmates who are unable to write in English or whose correspondents would be unable to understand a letter written in English. The criminal sophistication of the inmate, the relationship of the inmate and the correspondent are factors to be considered in deciding whether correspondence in a foreign language should be permitted.

strictions are justifiable and that implementation of these restrictions necessitates a minimum degree of discretion. To justify mail censorship, the authorities must establish that the regulation at issue furthers a substantial governmental interest, such as security and discipline within the correctional institution, and that the questioned provision is worded so as to minimize any resulting constitutional transgressions. Hence, regulations involving inmate correspondence cannot be promulgated for self-serving purposes, that is, to suppress uncomplimentary, defamatory or critical language contained in the letters. Nor can the enumerated exceptions of overriding interest be identified in such ambiguous terms that they encourage unbridled discretion in their application by the authorities.

[7]   As previously mentioned, censorship of inmate correspondence has a dual effect—it concerns the inmate as well as the inmate's correspondent. Therefore, once the authorities decide to censor major portions of a letter or to reject in toto the letter, minimal procedural safeguards should attach, and it does not seem unreasonable that the authorities notify the sender of this decision with an accompanying explanation for their action. Moreover, if the author believes that his or her product is outside the pale of the restrictions, then the writer should have available some avenue of review.

[8-10]   Implicit in the Court's above discussion regarding the censorship of inmate correspondence is the entitlement of jail authorities to open and read most incoming and outgoing inmate mail. *See*, Wolff v. McDonnell, —— U.S. at —— 94 S.Ct. at 2984-2985. To summarize briefly, the exigencies in the operation of a penal institution dictate the loss or

minimal deterioration of certain constitutional rights during confinement, inter alia, the right to mail letters uninspected and unread by a third party. It is axiomatic that a cursory inspection of the envelope and the contents therein is justified in order to prevent the flow of contraband weapons and narcotics and to detect possible escape plans. This result is consistent with the formula earlier stated by the Court whereby the particular societal interests are measured against the particular regulation at bar.

[11, 12]   The second phase of the plaintiffs' attack on the mail regulations is directed to inmate correspondence to the courts and to attorneys. Plaintiffs argue that restrictions on written correspondence with members of these two groups violates the First Amendment (freedom of speech), the Sixth Amendment (attorney-client relationship), and the Fourteenth Amendment (access to the courts). With respect to the First Amendment issue, this Court reiterates its refusal to broaden First Amendment rights inside a penal institution in light of controlling governmental interest, especially when higher courts unmistakably have endorsed the same approach. *See*, Wolff v. McDonnell, *supra*; Procunier v. Martinez, *supra*. The Sixth [9] and Fourteenth [10] Amendments do appear to conflict directly with the present restrictions that condone indiscriminate reading of inmate correspondence to and from attorneys and judicial officers. The Court must strike a balance that will accommodate the constitutional guarantees of the inmates while concurrently recognizing the need to preserve internal security. Bearing in mind this goal, the Court proffers the following guideposts. All incoming mail marked as originating from a judge or court personnel should be opened in the pres-

9.   It is important to recognize that the basis of a Sixth Amendment consideration is strictly to protect the relationship of attorney and client in criminal matters, although if the Court grants relief pursuant to this argument, the net effect would protect all

written correspondence between attorney of record and client.

10.   *See e. g.*, Johnson v. Avery, 393 U.S. 483, 89 S.Ct. 747, 21 L.Ed.2d 718 (1969); Ex parte Hull, 312 U.S. 546, 61 S.Ct. 640, 85 L.Ed. 1034 (1941).

ence of the inmate or of an inmate representative to determine if contraband is enclosed. The correspondence then should be delivered to the addressee absent unreasonable delay; prison authorities should not read this mail.[11] Outgoing mail to the courts should not be opened or read. It should be visibly marked as inmate correspondence and placed in the mail.[12] Correspondence from attorneys should be afforded the same procedural privilege as the mail from the courts except that as a condition precedent to the initiation of this privilege of unfettered correspondence the attorney should be obligated to communicate to the jail authorities the existence of an attorney-client relationship with the designated inmate and counsel's name and address. Similarly, if an attorney's name and address has been listed with the authorities then the authorities only should identify the origin of the outgoing mail to that attorney—nothing else. Otherwise, correspondence between an inmate and an attorney should be treated as normal personal correspondence with the authorities' concomitant rights to inspect and read the contents.

[13] The controversy over inmate reading material is the second of two remaining issues post mediation. The problem can be subdivided into the inmates' contention that they are entitled to receive any periodical, including Playboy Magazine, and that the authorities

improperly have terminated the distribution of free local newspapers. Starting with the latter complaint, the Court previously has stated that financial difficulties of the Jefferson Parish Prison caused discontinuance of the newspaper service. However, the inability to deliver free tabloids in no way affected the inmates' option to subscribe to the newspaper. Such a grievance definitely cannot activate First Amendment or other constitutional protections and its ultimate resolution should rest with the prison authorities. *See*, Jones v. Connors, *supra*.

[14] It is somewhat difficult for the Court to address itself to the inmates' complaint that they are prohibited from receiving certain publications since both their allegation and the related testimony are considerably vague on this averment. Despite the Court's belief that the inmates' asserted *right* to read Playboy Magazine borders on frivolity,[13] the Court has concluded that the authorities have demonstrated that the interests of internal order and discipline require suppression of Playboy Magazine and other periodicals with similar sexual formats. Plaintiffs have been unable to prove any arbitrariness or capriciousness on the part of the defendant authorities in the suppression of this magazine. Should the inmates decide to challenge subsequent reading bans, then it likewise is obligatory upon the authorities to justify these particularized

---

11. *Accord*, Adams v. Carlson, 488 F.2d 619 (7th Cir. 1973); Smith v. Robbins, 454 F.2d 696 (1st Cir. 1972).

The record in the instant case reflects that approximately thirty to forty letters are received daily at Jefferson Parish Prison. This influx of mail includes personal correspondence and mail from courts and counsel. The Court thus believes that this procedure could be executed quickly and efficiently and that such a format would not unduly burden the administration of the institution.

12. Exemplary of this concept is the Federal Bureau of Prisons policy which stamps on prisoner mail the following language:

Federal Correctional Institution

(Location of Institution)

Date ———

The enclosed letter was processed through special mailing procedures for forwarding to you. The letter has neither been opened nor inspected. If the writer raises a question or problem over which this facility has jurisdiction, you may wish to return the material for further information or clarification. If the writer encloses correspondence for forwarding to another addressee, please return the enclosure to the above address.

13. *See*, Kaufman, Prison: The Judge's Dilemma, 41 Fordham L.Rev. 495 (1973).

restriction.[14] *See,* Jackson v. Godwin, *supra; see* generally, Royal v. Clark, 447 F.2d 501 (5th Cir. 1971); Northern v. Nelson, 315 F.Supp. 687 (N.D.Cal.1970), aff'd, 448 F.2d 1266 (9th Cir. 1971).

Accordingly,

It is ordered that the defendant, Sheriff Alwynn J. Cronvich, shall formulate new regulations governing inmate mail in accordance with this opinion, and serve the proposed regulations on plaintiffs' counsel and concurrently file them with the Court on or before October 1, 1974. Plaintiffs shall have until October 10, 1974, to respond to these submitted regulations. Meanwhile, this Court reserves jurisdiction of this lawsuit until properly formulated regulations have received this Court's approval.

APPENDIX A

FINAL SETTLEMENT AGREEMENT BETWEEN NEGOTIATING TEAMS FOR THE JEFFERSON PARISH/LOUISIANA PRISON AUTHORITY AND REPRESENTATIVE PRISON INMATES

New Orleans, Louisiana   June 27, 1973

The following is agreed between the undersigned parties:

I.   ACCESS TO RELIGIOUS SERVICES

A.   The Catholic and Protestant prison chaplains will be expected to inform inmates, and particularly new arrivals, as to the time, place, and day denominational religious services are to be available.

B.   Each Sunday, or whatever other day may be set aside for such services (i. e. special holidays), at approximately thirty minutes before the scheduled time to begin, announcement on the public address system will be made for the purpose of: 1) alerting inmates to be ready to proceed to the appointed place if they choose to go; 2) notifying the hall boys to circulate the call-out list. Those who indicate a desire to attend services will affix their names to a call-out list made available by the hall boy.

A second announcement on the public address system will be made approximately fifteen minutes before the scheduled time for services to begin. This final reminder is designed to help assure that all who wish to attend services are aware of the hour and can be prepared to leave promptly when called.

Those inmates who have signed the call-out list will be called forth by a prison guard or other official when it is time to depart. Any inmate who fails to respond will be passed over and called again after the list is completed. Any inmate who had signed the call-out list and then declines to go, or fails

---

14. Application of this rule must be done against the backdrop of the well-settled doctrine that control of prison mail is generally a matter within the scope of the prison administrators' discretion and good faith. *See* Brown v. Wainwright, *supra;* Comment, Prison Mail Censorship and the First Amendment, 81 Yale L.J. 87 (1971).

to respond on time, shall have his name lined out and the opportunity to initial the change. If the inmate declines to initial the change, an appropriate note to that effect shall be entered by the hall boy.

C.   Each inmate will be entitled to attend one denominational service of his choice on any given day on which the services are made available. The aforementioned call-out list will be used to provide a record of attendees and to assure that no inmate attends more than the one service to which he is entitled.

D.   All inmates will be extended the opportunity to attend religious services, regardless of security status, the nature of his offense, or the condition of his incarceration, with the following exceptions reserved:

1.   Those inmates confined to lockdown, unless prior approval has been granted by the warden.

2.   Those inmates known to have a history of behavior problems of such nature as to make their attendance at general group religious services an undue security risk or otherwise inadvisable. It is understood, however, that any inmate so denied will have the right and the opportunity to appeal such a decision directly to the warden.

E.   Prison chaplains will be given access to the upper floor for purposes of conducting services for those inmates who are not permitted to attend general services. Such arrangements will be made in keeping with evidence of need, availability of chaplain's time, and the orderly operation of the institution.

II.   PUBLIC TELEPHONE SERVICE

In order to reduce congestion, facilitate easier access, and improve administrative control over use of public telephones, the following changes will be implemented upon concurrence from appropriate officials of the South Central Bell Telephone Company:

A.   Have installed a public telephone on the upper floor and another in the annex.

B.   Sheriff Cronvich, as soon as possible, will direct a letter to the telephone company requesting the additional pay station units. A copy of said letter will be sent to the attorneys for the inmate team. It is understood that the negotiating team will be consulted in determining the precise locations for the new instruments. It is further understood that the inmates' team attorney or his designee may seek directly any explanation from the telephone company as to difficulties or reluctance in responding affirmatively to the request.

(Note: A letter from Sheriff Cronvich addressed to the telephone company, written shortly after the session at which this issue was resolved, is attached to this agreement. The new phones were, in fact, installed on May 11.)

922   381 FEDERAL SUPPLEMENT

C. Inmates will be generally allowed at least two outgoing phone calls each week. Urgent need will be given favorable consideration for additional usage.

D. If urgent calls cannot be completed by an inmate during hours at which the phone is available, arrangements will be made by prison authorities to determine when the party to be contacted can be reached within the hours the institution has made the telephones available to the inmates. Such information will be communicated promptly to the inmate.

III. GRIEVANCE PROCEDURE

The recently established inmate council is considered a satisfactory mechanism for use in helping to resolve grievances. At the request of the inmate team, it was agreed that the warden shall attend all inmate council meetings unless otherwise specified by the council. If the warden is unavailable, the meeting is to be rescheduled at a time when he can attend.

IV. VISITING PRIVILEGES

A. Visiting hours will henceforth be as follows:

Saturdays: 12:00 – 3:30 P.M.

Sundays: 12:00 – 2:30 P.M.

B. To the extent possible, and consistent with manpower availability, additional visiting days during the week will be arranged at the warden's discretion to meet individual special needs or circumstances.

C. Each inmate will be entitled to have not more than three visitors on any given visiting day. The number allowed in the visiting room at one time will be determined by the total number of visitors on hand.

D. A maximum of three persons who are not members of the inmate's immediate family will be authorized to be included among visitors, provided they are approved in advance by the institution authorities. A record of such authorizations will be maintained by prison officials to facilitate recognition and approval upon such visitors' arrival at the prison. Changes in the names of such pre-approved visitors may be made by the inmate after the name to be removed has been designated for a period of not less than two months.

E. Acoustical materials will be installed on the ceiling of the visiting room in order to help reduce sound problems.

F. The institution will prepare a statement of general regulations regarding matters covered by this agreement for distribution to newly arrived prisoners.

G. Parish authorities were said to be already in the process of investigating the availability of more satisfactory power phones used in the visiting room for communication through the partition. It is understood that the parish will undertake whatever measures are necessary and practical to im-

FRAZIER v. DONELON   923
Cite as 381 F.Supp. 911 (1974)

prove the communication equipment and/or to reduce present sound problems in connection with conditions in the visiting room.

For the Institutional Team:

(s) Alwynn J. Cronvich
    Sheriff Alwynn Cronvich, Chairman

(s) Richard Tompson
    Richard Tompson, Vice Chairman

Lionel R. Collins, Assistant Parish Attorney
Russell J. Schonekas, Attorney for defendants in federal court
Roland J. Vicknair, Warden, Jefferson Parish Prison
Captain John Weber, Administrative Officer, Sheriff's Department
Robert Broussard (alternate), Assistant Parish Attorney

For the Inmate Team:

(s) Erwin K. Brewer
    Erwin Brewer, Vice Chairman

(s) William D. Treeby
    William D. Treeby, Attorney for Inmate Team

(s) Michael R. Fontham
    Michael Fontham, Attorney for Inmate Team

* Francis Jacobs, Chairman
Frank Chicarelli, Negotiator
John Huber, Negotiator
Ulysses Bazille, Alternate Negotiator
Vernon Betsch, Alternate Negotiator
Alexander Ferguson, Alternate Negotiator

Witness:
    (s) Robert F. Greenwald
        Robert F. Greenwald, Mediator
        Community Relations Service
        U.S. Department of Justice

                    (s) James W. Freeman
                        James W. Freeman, Admin. Justice
                        Spec. Community Relations Service
                        U.S. Department of Justice

* Transferred to the La. State Penitentiary prior to the execution of agreement.

ARKANSAS GAZETTE, Wednesday, September 28, 1983

Private Meetings Allowed In School Suit Negotiations

By GEORGE WELLS
Gazette Staff

Federal Judge Henry Woods decided Tuesday to allow negotiations to settle the Pulaski County school consolidation suit to proceed behind closed doors, but he took under advisement a request to permit the affected school boards to discuss the proceedings in executive sessions.

The three Pulaski County school districts asked him Tuesday to issue an order permitting the closed sessions with Robert F. Greenwald, a federal mediator that Judge Woods called in to try to resolve the lawsuit out of court. A meeting is scheduled at 9 a.m. today.

The districts wanted Judge Woods to allow them to ignore the state Freedom of Information Act and meet separately in executive sessions to discuss the proceedings. He will rule later on that request.

Judge Woods also agreed, at the request of the districts, to allow any documents generated by the mediation sessions to be withheld from the public and to make Greenwald the sole spokesman for the proceedings.

Meetings between representatives of the three districts and Greenwald should be closed to the press and the public to enhance a potential settlement, Judge Woods decided. Only one school board member from each district will meet with the mediator.

The Little Rock School District sued the North Little Rock and Pulaski County School Districts last year to force consolidation of all or parts of the three districts to eliminate what the Little Rock District considers the last vestiges of segregation.

The Little Rock District also asked Judge Woods Tuesday to order the county district to respond to requests for information pertaining to the location of new schools. The Little Rock District contends the new schools were located "to promote white flight," and thus increase the percentage of blacks concentrating in the Little Rock District.

In a separate filing, the Little Rock District also said that the trial should not be divided into two parts, as the Pulaski County District has requested. The county district said a separate hearing should be conducted on whether it or the North Little Rock District actually caused any of the Little Rock District's problems. If the defendant districts are found to be at fault, then, under the county district's motion, a separate hearing would be conducted on what remedy would be appropriate.

The Little Rock District said Tuesday that the supposed efficiency to be derived from dividing the trial into two parts was "largely illusory." Such an action would only delay the ultimate solution, the Little Rock District argued.

The three districts asked for the ruling on open meetings after reading an article in the *Gazette* quoting Attorney General Steve Clark as saying that mediation sessions should be open to the public, according to one of the attorneys for the Pulaski County District.

The state Freedom of Information Act requires all school board meetings to be open to the public except for certain kinds of personnel actions.

Kathlyn Graves, an attorney for the county district, drafted the motion that was also signed by attorneys for the other two districts and the state Board of Education, which is also a party to the suit.

The motion said that closed sessions of the school boards "may well be indispensable if mediation is to have a chance of success. A body that is a party to a lawsuit can hardly conduct settlement discussions in public."

A federal judge has authority to issue such an order under common law and under the doctrine of federal supremacy, the motion argued.

FILED

IN THE UNITED STATES DISTRICT COURT
EASTERN DISTRICT OF ARKANSAS
WESTERN DIVISION

MAY 6 1983

CARL R. BRENTS, CLERK

By: _____

LITTLE ROCK SCHOOL DISTRICT   PLAINTIFF Dep. Clerk

V.   NO. LR-C-82-866

PULASKI COUNTY SPECIAL SCHOOL
DISTRICT NO. 1, ET AL   DEFENDANTS

ORDER

The Court has requested the Community Relations Service, United States Department of Justice to provide assistance to the parties to this litigation and to the Court in the attempted mediation of the subject matter of plaintiff's complaint. Mr. Robert F. Greenwald of the Community Relations Service has agreed to perform this function for the Court.

Mr. Greenwald will be making "fact findings" in order to facilitate his mediation efforts. The parties are directed to cooperate with Mr. Greenwald in his efforts to secure the necessary factual data required by him to engage in meaningful mediation. These "fact findings" shall not substitute for the Findings of Fact to be entered by the Court in the event this matter proceeds to trial. Rule 52 Fed.R.Civ.P.

Evidence of mediation negotiations, including but not limited to statements of the parties and counsel at such negotiating sessions, shall not be admissible evidence in this or any other proceeding, see, e.g., Rule 408 Fed.R.Evid.

This 6 day of May, 1983.

HENRY WOODS, U. S. District Judge

ARKANSAS GAZETTE, Saturday, May 14, 1983

Arkansas Gazette.

Founded in 1819
Oldest Newspaper West of the Mississippi

WILLIAM E. WOODRUFF, Founder
J. N. HEISKELL, Editor 1902-1972

HUGH B. PATTERSON, JR., Editor and Publisher

CARRICK H. PATTERSON, Executive Editor

WILLIAM K. RUTHERFORD, News Editor
WILLIAM T. SHELTON, City Editor
JAMES H. JONES, State Editor
M. PATRICK CARITHERS, Wire News Editor
ORVILLE M. HENRY, Sports Editor
DAVID B. PETTY, Assistant to Executive Editor

JAMES O. POWELL, Editorial Page Editor
JERRY F. DHONAU, Associate Editor
ERNEST C. DUMAS, Associate Editor
LELAND DuVALL, Associate Editor

ROBERT S. McCORD, Forum Editor

C. THOMAS GRIFFIN, Advertising Director
W. E. SWOR, Circulation Director
RALPH B. PATTERSON, Marketing Services Director
MICHAEL C. ELDREDGE, Controller

A Mediator in School Suit

The school consolidation suit filed in federal court by the Little Rock School District has taken another interesting twist, even long before the trial that is scheduled for October 3. Judge Henry Woods, to the surprise of all sides, has called in a federal mediator to explore the possibility of resolving the suit through a negotiated settlement, thus making a trial unnecessary.

Earlier on, Judge Woods had said he might hire an expert to help him with the case should it go to trial, following a pattern set in a desegregation suit at St. Louis. Judge Woods has asked the parties to the suit to nominate education experts for his selection. The Little Rock and Pulaski County School Districts have complied, but the North Little Rock School District has formally objected to the naming of an expert unless Judge Woods rules that North Little Rock has contributed to the Little Rock District's racial imbalances.

In any event, the appointment of an expert to serve during a trial surely will be decided later.

In the meantime, the federal mediator has been introduced as Robert F. Greenwald of Dallas, a mediator from the Justice Department's Community Relations Service. He was appointed because Judge Woods says he (Woods) is a believer in mediation, having seen it work in the labor practice that he did before taking the bench. Judge Woods indicates that a mediator may speed up resolution of the case, which could take years if it goes to trial.

How does a mediator function in a case of this nature? Well, the role as outlined by Judge Woods appears to be consistent with a process of negotiation that the Little Rock District tried to get started with the other two districts, with the encouragement of the Eighth United States Court of Appeals at St. Louis, before the others rejected it. That rejection left the Little Rock District no choice but to file suit seeking consolidation to correct the racial imbalances in school enrollments among the three districts.

The mediator will be a fact finder for Judge Woods and any negotiations that may flow from the process will be voluntary. If the parties should somehow reach an agreement through mediation, the suit could be settled before a trial became necessary.

Certainly no harm can be done by the appointment of a mediator, and there is always a chance that a suitable agreement can be reached through this process. It might be a mistake, however, to expect too much, for the school boards that would have to make a three-way agreement answer to constituencies that might not be easily convinced. A mediator at least can provide the background information that can help Judge Woods in his own preparation for such an important and far-reaching case.

ARKANSAS DEMOCRAT • SUNDAY, JUNE 26, 1983 • • • •

Mediator sheds light on emotionally charged issue

BY CYNTHIA HOWELL
Democrat Staff Writer

Convincing representatives of the Little Rock, North Little Rock and Pulaski County school districts to sit down to a chat on merging their districts is not a task for the easily discouraged.

But apparently U.S. District Judge Henry Woods, who is presiding in the controversial consolidation lawsuit filed last November by Little Rock school officials against the other two districts, sees discussions as a way to speed the case along.

Last month Woods said he feared the suit would be the bane of his existence for the next two years, so he called on the U.S. Justice Department's Community Relations Service and Robert Greenwald, of Dallas, regional mediator, to wheedle and cajole the districts to give the talks a try.

The goal, Greenwald said in a recent interview, is to get a written, signed agreement among the districts to be used as a consent decree in October when the lawsuit is tried.

THE SUIT ALLEGES that the policies and practices of local and state agencies in the past have resulted in racial enrollment imbalances in the districts.

While the Little Rock School District is becoming increasingly black in enrollment, the other districts are predominantly white.

Greenwald is a mild-mannered, unpretentious man who lacks the brisk "official business" air associated with FBI agents, U.S. attorneys or others employed by the Justice Department. He has been with the Community Relations Service since 1968. Greenwald said 70 to 80 percent of the mediated cases result in a signed agreement.

Analysis

"It's not healthy for a community to have conflicts among important institutions," he said. "People want to resolve the conflicts if they can do so without sacrificing their best interests."

IN THE LITTLE Rock School District case, Greenwald has been appointed to act as a fact finder for the judge and to explore the possibility of mediating the suit for an out-of-court settlement. Since the middle of May, Greenwald has made periodic visits to Little Rock to compile information on demographics, the histories of the three school districts and the attitudes people have about the schools.

The districts have been helpful in providing the needed facts, and he now has a "ton of information" which he hopes to have synthesized into a report for the judge by late July.

Then, presumably, decisions will be made on who the participants in the mediation process will be (superintendents, school board members or attorneys), the ground rules will be set and the discussions will commence.

PARTICIPATION IN the mediation process is voluntary, Greenwald said. The parties are expected to proceed with it until they decide it isn't in their best interest. The Little Rock and Pulaski County school boards recently passed resolutions stating their willingness to cooperate with the court and Greenwald.

As a mediator, Greenwald said he will be the "facilitator of meaningful communication." In other words, he will chair the meetings, set the ground rules and act as a spokesman to the

public and the news media. The discussions will be closed to the public, officials say, so as to not limit conversation.

The one thing Greenwald will not do is try to get the parties to settle on one particular solution.

"We're one agency that doesn't tell folks what to do," he said. "It's not our job to solve problems, but to help parties come to a decision – not our decision, but theirs."

THE COMMUNITY Relations Service isn't very well known to most people, Arkansans included, although there was a branch of the Dallas regional office in Little Rock up until the 1970s.

"It is one of the albatrosses around our necks that people think of prosecutors and investigators when they think of the Justice Department," Greenwald said. "We do neither."

The agency was created as a part of the Civil Rights Act of 1964 to deal with racial problems or ethnic differences that have an impact on a community. The service has two main functions: conciliation, which includes fact finding for the courts and other activities to increase communication and reduce tension in a community, and mediation, where the disputing parties are brought to the negotiating table to discuss their differences.

GREENWALD SAID the agency, of which there are 10 regional offices across the country, gets involved not in the disputes of individuals, but in cases where a group of inmates may feel their rights have been violated by the prison system, or where a group of citizens feels a government agency is practicing discrimination or not spending federal funds for specified pur-

'It is one of the albatrosses around our necks that people think of prosecutors and investigators when they think of the Justice Department'

Robert Greenwald

poses.

The Community Relations Service frequently works in situations where deadly force has been used by police and the community is in an uproar.

The agency has surveyed communities to measure attitudes about law enforcement and worked to settle differences between Vietnamese and Americans about shrimping and fishing practices in the Gulf of Mexico.

ABOUT 50 PERCENT of the mediation talks involving Greenwald - the only mediator in the region encompassing Oklahoma, Texas, Louisiana, Arkansas and New Mexico - center on law enforcement; 30 percent on education-related issues; and 20 percent on matters such as unemployment, government services and prison systems.

In 1981 Greenwald offered to help then-Gov. Frank White reconcile differences with Aid to Families with Dependent Chil-

dren recipients who were upset about state ordered cuts to their benefits. He said he has also worked with community problems in Camden, Texarkana and Magnolia in Arkansas.

The Little Rock School District case will be unique for the Community Relations Service, Greenwald said, because three parties are involved, which will call for some shuttle negotiating and other modifications to the ground rules, and because all three parties are school districts instead of the typical setup where one party is a government agency and the other is a group of citizens.

Greenwald has already met with lawyers, superintendents and board presidents for the districts to tell them what his role will be and to get information from them.

It was about this time last year that Greenwald conducted a meeting in Little Rock for business leaders, media representatives, minority groups and

educators to discuss schools and integration. The meeting was designed as a catharsis for community leaders, and no decisions for action were made. Greenwald said he remembers the meeting, which received little or no press coverage, because 33 of the 35 people invited actually attended. He said he thought that was quite remarkable.

For his work in the consolidation suit, Greenwald will collect his regular government paycheck and will not be paid by the parties in the suit. He will not participate in the trial, nor will any of the discussions in the negotiations be used as evidence.

WHEN GREENWALD WAS appointed in early May, Judge Woods told representatives of the three school districts that he was a believer in mediation because he has seen some bitter labor disputes resolved through mediation. The consolidation lawsuit is not a labor dispute, but it is an emotionally-charged issue.

Greenwald is a native of the eastern United States and a graduate of George Washington University in Washington. He said he holds a degree in government, and now considers Texas where he has lived since 1950, to be home.

Before joining the Community Relations Service, Greenwald worked in a vocational rehabilitation center and then was a manager for several chambers of commerce in Texas and Oklahoma. Both jobs, the first of which was integrated and the second of which gave him experience working with structured organizations, prepared him for his work with the Community Relations Service.

School study says opinion obstacle to racial balance

BY CYNTHIA HOWELL
Democrat Staff Writer

Public opinion against consolidation of the three school districts in Pulaski County could be the biggest obstacle to resolving racial imbalances that exist in the districts, a study prepared by a federal mediator suggests.

Robert Greenwald, regional mediator for the U.S. Justice Department's Community Relations Service in Dallas, submitted the report last week to U.S. District Judge Henry Woods. The report contains statistical information about the three school districts and the perceptions of 23 community members regarding the pending Little Rock School District consolidation suit.

Greenwald's report does not draw any conclusions, but simply states facts or perceptions he found in discussions with people such as Hillary Rodham Clinton, Arkansas businessmen and women, legislators, educators and others known for their interest in education.

The lawsuit was filed last November against the Pulaski County and North Little Rock school districts. It alleges that practices and policies of local and state agencies resulted in a predominantly black enrollment in the Little Rock School District, while enrollments in the other districts are predominantly white.

Woods, who released the report to the press Wednesday, will preside over the case when it goes to trial Jan. 3. He has encouraged the districts to settle the suit out of court.

Obstacles to consolidation as perceived by the community members Greenwald interviewed include:

• The belief that the consolidation of the Pulaski County, North Little Rock and Little Rock school districts would benefit only the Little Rock district. The Little Rock School District has a black enrollment this year of about 70 percent, while the percentage of black students in the North Little Rock and Pulaski County districts has remained rela-

tively stable at about 35 and 23 percent, respectively.

The belief that any remedy to racial imbalances would be a "one-way street" is typically accompanied by the conviction that the Pulaski County district struggled for many years to attain a high level of educational quality, Greenwald said.

• Some view the Little Rock School District as placing a higher priority on finding a new tax base rather than correcting the racial imbalances. People "allege that the urban district is already spending more per pupil than its two neighboring districts, yet fails to offer a quality education sufficient to stem white flight," Greenwald said.

• A cooperative arrangement between the Little Rock and Pulaski County school districts to share computer facilities and personnel was ended last year when the Pulaski County district withdrew from the venture to start its own system. The county district took virtually all the experienced staff and left Little Rock with an unexpired lease. Greenwald reported that some believe the "divorce" was a deliberate attempt to create financial and administrative hardships for the Little Rock district.

• An overwhelming number of Pulaski County district patrons are said to be devoted to maintaining the existing boundary lines. A poll of patrons in 1980 showed that 75 percent were opposed to any changes.

In his discussions with residents of Pulaski County, Greenwald said he learned some factors favorable to cooperation among the districts or "unification:"

• A limited number of cooperative agreements have existed among the districts, such as the Little Rock-Pulaski County computer consortium, the North Little Rock-Pulaski County adult education program and the Metropolitan Vocational Technical School, where students from all districts may take classes.

• Many recognize that

money could be saved by the combined use of personnel among the districts, central purchasing, transportation, technical services and special programs, Greenwald said.

• The number of miles students travel to and from school by bus out of their neighborhoods could be reduced.

• Previously all-white subdivisions in the county are being quietly integrated without negative impact. As the neighborhood changes take, the likelihood of whites fleeing the public schools can be expected to moderate, Greenwald said.

On racial isolation attitudes in the schools, many white suburbanites resent implications that they are racist, Greenwald reported. They believe racial imbalances are the result of economic barriers rather than social exclusion, he said.

Greenwald also found:

• Some black leaders view consolidation as a potential threat to their hard-won level of influence in the Little Rock district.

• Some people believe that consolidation will result in more white flight to private schools.

• Black political participation in the Pulaski County School District has been virtually nonexistent, although changes in qualification requirements to seek election as a school board candidate in the district may change that.

• Some believe dividing the county into two school districts might cause additional segregation of schools.

ARKANSAS DEMOCRAT

THURSDAY, SEPTEMBER 8, 1983 •

ARKANSAS GAZETTE,   Thursday, September 29, 198

Negotiating the School Suit

Federal Judge Henry Woods has decided to allow negotiations to settle the Pulaski County school consolidation suit to proceed in private, as requested by the attorneys for the three districts, Little Rock, North Little Rock and Pulaski County. Judge Woods also has agreed to allow any documents of the districts generated by the mediation sessions to be withheld from the public and to make the court-appointed mediator, Robert F. Greenwald, the sole spokesman for the proceedings.

A legitimate case can be made for privacy during the court-sanctioned mediation sessions. Only one member of each school board will be present with the mediator and attorneys, and there is substantial question whether such a gathering would fall within requirements of the state's Freedom of Information Act. A federal judge presumably has authority to suspend application of a state statute, but the power should be exercised with great care.

This means that it would be grave error for the court to grant a second, sweeping request by the attorneys to permit the three school boards, in direct defiance of the letter as well as the spirit of the state FOI act, to discuss the case in executive sessions of the separate boards. For the public to be excluded from the deliberations of a public board on a matter of such profound importance to the community would be to make a mockery of full accountability.

To be sure, if a negotiated settlement can be devised, thereby avoiding a trial, it will need maximum public acceptance if it is to have long-term success in treating the problem that prompted the Little Rock district to ask for countywide consolidation in the first place: racial imbalances in the public schools.

It is difficult to imagine, frankly, how the goal of correcting racial imbalances, without massive and unacceptable disruptions, can be achieved short of forming a single, countywide school district. Such a district would be desirable for other compelling reasons as well — Arkansas should have one school district per county for maximum efficiency — but the issue in the federal court suit revolves around racial imbalances. The possibility that negotiators, working behind closed doors, will be able to work out a countywide consolidation seems as remote now as it would be desirable, but they deserve a chance to explore ways of reaching an out-of-court settlement.

Even so, the fact remains that the Little Rock School District brought suit only after extraordinary efforts to work out some arrangement had been met with hostility. Little Rock's district has a strong and compelling case for countywide consolidation on acceptable terms and it needn't feel that it is under pressure to accept less than countywide consolidation simply to avoid the full airing of a trial.

Arkansas Democrat

THURSDAY, SEPTEMBER 29, 1983

Consolidation meetings ruled priva

BY DAVID DAVIES
Democrat Staff Writer

U.S. District Judge Henry Woods ruled Tuesday that federal mediation proceedings between the three Pulaski County school districts may be held in private, but he put off a decision on the districts' request that their school boards be allowed to hold separate private meetings to discuss mediation efforts.

Woods also ruled that all documents generated in the mediation proceedings could be kept private.

Woods did not indicate in his court order when he would rule on the schools' request to hold closed board meetings.

The North Little Rock, Little Rock and Pulaski County school districts had asked Woods to allow them to meet in private, saying they would be unable to settle their differences if they were forced to meet in public.

The Arkansas Freedom of Information law prohibits public bodies from meeting in private except to review personnel matters.

The Little Rock School District filed suit against the North Little Rock and Pulaski County school districts to improve racial balance in the schools. The lawsuit seeks the consolidation of the three school districts.

Schools reject latest plan; talks collapse

BY DAVE WANNEMACHER
Democrat Staff Writer

Talks on school district consolidation in Pulaski County broke off Friday morning and federal mediator Robert Greenwald of Dallas is packing his bags and heading home.

The North Little Rock and Pulaski County school districts rejected the latest proposal, this one by Greenwald, to reach an out-of-court settlement in a lawsuit filed by the Little Rock district.

Little Rock is looking for an answer to racial imbalances in the three county school districts.

Because the districts are at an impasse, the lawsuit will go to trial Jan. 3 in federal court as scheduled unless the talks resume before then. But Greenwald, who has been working with the districts for several weeks, didn't hold out much hope for a resumption.

"We are now in what mediators call an indefinite recess," he said at an afternoon press conference to discuss the progress of the talks, which were held behind closed doors.

"The parties ... are back to an adversary setting, back to a litigation setting," he said. He called Friday's talks "the last thread of hope we had to get a consensus."

In recent weeks, the three school districts mulled over five different options in negotiations to reach a settlement. Representatives of the districts last met in October, but they rejected plans to consolidate, change boundary lines or adopt a student-transfer program.

The latest proposal, rejected Friday, called for each district to retain its separate boundary lines, but have each school in the county specialize in different curricula. Parents could send their children to any school in the county, but subsequent choices would have to be made if the school

See SCHOOLS, Page 6A

Schools

• Continued from Page One

was full or had already met a strict racial composition.

Little Rock is trying to merge its district with the others because its schools are predominantly black (about 70 percent). The North Little Rock district is the best represented district racially (63 percent white to 37 percent black), Greenwald said, and is in no hurry to disrupt a system that officials have worked hard to achieve. Pulaski County's district is mostly white (78 percent).

Greenwald said Thursday that his latest option was a "very, very long shot."

He said Friday that he developed it out of desperation. As it stands, the trial will begin after the new year in U.S. District Judge Henry Woods' court. If no settlement is reached by then, Greenwald said, a trial could take more than a year.

He said he had seen similar cases last for four to five years. "And then you have appeals," he said.

Friday's meeting was the seventh time the districts got together to work out a possible settlement. Greenwald began his press conference by saying that the number seven "is not a lucky number for the people of Pulaski County, in my opinion."

If a settlement had been reached, he said, it would have been to the advantage of the county's taxpayers.

Greenwald had no estimate on the cost of a lengthy court case, but indicated that it would be expensive.

Part of the problem with his proposal, Greenwald said, was financing and which district would pay for what. Representatives from the Pulaski County Special School District also questioned the voluntary versus involuntary role the students would have in making a choice on which school to attend.

"We played with that for a long time," Greenwald said. "If a kid couldn't go to one school, the one he wants, then any other choice is not voluntary, or is it?"

Another problem dealt with the liability of the school districts for the students who live within their boundaries. Any problem there would have to be resolved in court, he said.

Officials from the three districts agreed to let students cross their boundaries to go to school, but they couldn't agree on what constituted voluntary and mandatory assignments.

Greenwald said the negotiations had been conducted in a spirit of friendliness with no outbursts of animosity between districts.

ARKANSAS DEMOCRAT   •   SATURDAY, NOVEMBER 12, 1983

PROFESSIONAL
PUBLISHING ASSOCIATES

RELOCATION PUBLICATIONS DIVISION
Dallas   Toronto

November 24, 1984

The Honorable Henry Woods
United States District Court
Eastern District of Arkansas
U.S. Post Office & Court House
P.O. Box 3683
Little Rock, Arkansas 72203

Dear Judge Woods:

I want you to know how much I appreciated your thoughtfulness in forwarding your most recent opinion in the Pulaski County school consolidation case. As I read the text, my mind's eye came upon many flashbacks to our mediation effort. How close they were to a joint accommodation that would have avoided the prolonged litigation that you so accurately foretold. I will always be convinced that the parties could and would have reached an agreement through the voluntary process had it not been for political considerations and, for some, an unwillingness to face reality and to show enlightened leadership.

Since you sent the case material to my home address, I can assume that you know that I retired from the Department on July 1st last. I don't clearly recall having advised you of that expectation, but apparently I did. In any case, I'm pleased that you sent the information to my residence. Otherwise, I would not likely have ever seen it.

I found your opinion to be consistent with my general reading of your position throughout the period of my involvement under your auspices. Your reputation for forthright adjudication is unblemished. I cannot help but reflect on the irony of a far more severe remedy than the plaintiffs were willing to consider during the final days of mediation. I can only imagine the gyrations that now follow your predicted "Draconian" alternative.

I noted in the text of your opinion that the expected Eighth Circuit appeal has been filed. No telling, I suppose, how much longer delay there will be.

I am indebted to you Judge, for the opportunity to have undertaken one of the more challenging cases of my career as a third party facilitator. I do not consider that we were unsuccessful. I honestly believe that the majority of those who participated in the mediation proceedings, from all three mediation teams, were in their minds capable of a rational compromise. But as I indicated earlier, too many of them were not emotionally ready to withstand the perceived consequences.

Best of luck and most sincere regards,

Bob Greenwald

10271 Better Drive   •   Dallas, Texas 75229   •   214-352-1872

–THE NEWS, Port Arthur, Texas   Thursday, January 30, 1975

City, CCPAA in talks

By LINDA WRIGHT
Of The News Staff

Questions ranging from what Port Arthur Police Department's present firearm policy is to what type report is required after a shooting incident are included in an agenda for negotiations that began Wednesday in the city.

Federal mediator Robert Greenwald Wednesday morning released the detailed agenda which will be discussed by negotiating teams from the city and the black community.

The negotiations began at 2:30 p.m. at the city's Operations Center.

Under the first issue — firearms policy and use of deadly force—there are eleven questions, around which discussion will center Wednesday and Thursday, Greenwald said.

Those questions are:

"What is the present policy of the Port Arthur police department (PAPD)? Is such policy reduced to writing? Is it sufficiently comprehensive to cover abuses which have been said to lead to unnecessary loss of life?

"Is it clear that deadly force must be used only under clearly limited and prescribed circumstances, as practiced by effective law enforcement agencies elsewhere in the nation?

"Are such restrictions, if they exist, clearly understood by police personnel and the public? What is the practical effect of the Texas Penal Code provisions on the use of firearms? Is there support for modification of that law if such need can be demonstrated?

"Is there evidence of concern by municipal administrators and law enforcement officials at policy-making levels for fair and reasonable safeguards against arbitrary or unwarranted use of deadly force?

"Precisely what type of report is required after an incident involving use of firearms? Do such reports and related departmental investigations assure full disclosure of the facts and an expectation of a completely fair and objective finding?

"Are the results of investigative findings related to a specific incident available to appropriately concerned parties?"

The agenda was prepared by members of the Concerned Citizens of Port Arthur Association (CCPAA), the group that is representing the black community in the negotiations with the city.

Discussion of the other three issues, "Effective police-community relations, arrest-detention procedures and minority recruiting and utilization," will follow in other sessions.

The mediator, who works for a division of the U.S. Department of Justice, said resource personnel may be brought in to aid in the negotiations, but it will depend on whether the teams feel the help is needed once the negotiations begin.

Beaumont Enterprise, Wednesday, Jan. 29, 1975

Police Firearms Policy Due Look

PORT ARTHUR — The police department's firearms policy and standards for officers' using deadly force will be the first issue to be discussed by negotiating teams representing the city government and the black community during negotiating sessions which begin today.

Black leaders and city officials have agreed to use the mediation services of the U.S. Department of Justice in working toward a resolution of racial discontent that followed the fatal shooting of a black jail escapee by police Dec. 29. The first joint meeting of negotiating teams for the black community and the city government is scheduled for 2:30 p.m. today at the city's operations center on Texas 73.

The Rev. Ransom Howard, chairman of the black negotiators, Tuesday made public the issues to be discussed today. The issues, listed in the order in which they will be discussed, are the police department's firearms policy and the use of deadly force by officers, effective police community relations, arrest and detention procedures and minority recruiting for the police department and training and promotion of black officers within the department.

Robert Greenwald, a mediator from the Justice Department's Community relations service, said technical assistance would be provided for either side when needed. He said he could not say when such assistance would be brought in or even if it would be needed until he saw what emerged from the meetings.

An example of technical assistance would be providing the firearms policies of other cities and national law enforcement groups to compare with those of Port Arthur, Greenwald explained.

In the area of community relations, Greenwald said specialists in setting up such programs might be brought in for consultation.

183

Black leaders feel elected official should be on city team

Port Arthur News

January 31, 1975

Members of the black community who began negotiations Wednesday with representatives of the City of Port Arthur feel there should have been elected officials on the city's negotiating team.

The Rev. Ransom Howard, chairman of the Concerned Citizens of Port Arthur Association and the black negotiating team, said Friday he sent a letter to the mayor and city council advising them of the feelings of the blacks.

In the letter, which was delivered Wednesday, Howard said, "In the sincere and profound interest of our city and its inhabitants, we are grateful you have seen fit to select a committee with which we may negotiate.

"However, we are of the most candid opinion that at least some of our honest, fair-minded policy makers should have been included on the committee."

The Rev. Howard said the CCPAA felt the mayor or a city councilman should have been in the city's group.

Appointees to the city's negotiating team, who were announced Jan. 20, are City Manager George Dibrell, City Atty. George Wikoff, Police Chief James Newsom, Director of Personnel and Civil Service Dave Brinson and Chairman of the Civil Service Commission Gene Cooksey.

Alternates included a member of the Civil Service Commission, two police officers and the assistant city attorney.

The Rev. Howard said it would be up to the city to redesignate delegates to the negotiations if they want to.

The city and black community are negotiating a number of issues concerning law enforcement, which came to the fore after the Dec. 29 shooting of escaping prisoner Clifford Coleman.

Beaumont Enterprise   February 1, 1975

NAACP Wants Probe Into Coleman Shooting

By JIM McMAHON
Staff Writer

PORT ARTHUR — The local chapter of the National Association for the Advancement of Colored People wants the civil rights division of the Justice Department to conduct an investigation of the Dec. 29 fatal shooting of a black jail escapee by police and of unrelated allegations of police misconduct.

Before asking for the investigation, the civil rights organization will give the city a second opportunity to respond to a NAACP request that Police Chief James R. Newsom fire three officers involved in the arrest and shooting of the escapee, Clifford Coleman.

Newsom earlier told the organization that "there is no basis for any type of suspension" of policemen because the grand jury has completely exonerated all officers involved."

During a press conference Friday, Amos Evans, president of the local NAACP branch, said. "We are in disagreement with the grand jury report which leaves a lot of questions unanswered." Evans indicated that he had read the statement of findings prepared by the district attorney's office based on the grand jury investigation.

In a letter to Newsom dated Thursday, the NAACP alleged that the arrest of Coleman was illegal. The letter also accused unspecified city officials of "conspiracy, misrepresentation of facts and civil and criminal negligence."

Copies of the letter to Newsom were sent to Mayor Bernis Sadler, Councilman Arthur Guidry, the civil rights division of the Justice Department in Washington, D.C., and the national and regional offices of the NAACP.

Evans indicated that his organization will first ask the city to request the Justice Department investigation. If city officials fail to respond appropriately to that request and the demand for the firing of the three officers, the local NAACP branch will seek the federal investigation, he said.

The officers the NAACP wants removed from the police department are Patrolmen Loddie Valka, Darrell Hendrix and George Woods. Newsom has said that Valka was the officer who fatally shot Coleman as he fled from the police station while Hendrix and Woods made the initial arrest for disorderly conduct by use of abusive language.

If the Justice Department does send investigators here, the NAACP wants an examination not only of the Coleman shooting and other actions by the Port Arthur Police Department but also of actions by other police agencies in Jefferson County, Evans said. The federal investigators should also examine what the NAACP considers to be other irregularities, including alleged racial discrimination in the selection of jurors, according to the branch president.

Evans noted during the press conference that city officials and some representatives of the black community are currently engaged in negotiations with a Justice Department mediator in an effort to iron out some police-community relations problems.

"We (the NAACP) have nothing to do with the mediation process which does not solve the present problem, although it may have value in the future." Evans said. The "problem" Evans referred to is the termination of the employment of the officers involved in the arrest and shooting of Coleman.

A federal mediator working with blacks and the city government in talks here has indicated that suspension of the officers is not a negotiable issue.

Port Arthur News   February 9, 1975

Weapon policy draws attention

When the negotiations resume between city of Port Arthur officials and representatives of local blacks over police matters, one issue will be the policy on use of weapons.

Robert Greenwald, federal mediator assigned to the negotiations growing out of the Clifford Coleman shooting, said the groups aren't able to proceed on other crucial matters until the weapons question is cleared.

Quoting Greenwald: "The Texas Penal Code sets forth the legal parameters under which a police department should operate . . . including use of firearms and deadly force. What relationship does that statute have to the discretion of local police departments in modifying firearms policies?" is the question posed for negotiations.

As he explained, one view is the state law is, in effect, the policy for all police departments, while another view is the law is only a guide beyond which a police department may go to establish policy at a local level.

From the interpretation of a story the other day in The News, it appears other police departments are adopting the attitude that the use of deadly force should, for the most part, be restricted to the protection of an officer's life or that of a third party.

The story told how guidelines for degrees of force necessary are often vague and imprecise. This led to an advisory board of the Texas Criminal Justice Council and the legal section of the International Association of Police Chiefs devising a manual which they say "combines the legal requirements and restraints of Texas law with sound principles of police practices."

Model rules of the Texas Criminal Justice Council, the story said, specifically prohibit the use of firearms under the following circumstances:

As a warning; if a person is 17 years or under; unless in defense of an officer's or another person's life; in any misdemeanor case, unless in defense of life; from a moving vehicle or at a moving or fleeing vehicle, except in defense of an officer or another person's life; and unless all other reasonable means of defense have failed.

Also, the rules prohibit use of firearms to affect the arrest of an individual attempting to escape, unless the person is attempting to escape from a murder, rape, robbery, burglary, theft or arson and "then only if there is a serious threat of immediate danger to the officer or third person, such as the use of firearms or hostages."

The story also outlined how the Port Arthur Police Department procedural manual published in 1971 says an officer may fire a pistol to defend his own life or others, to apprehend a fleeing felon, to kill a wounded animal with permission. Now the policy on fire arms use is being revised to reflect the new Texas Penal Code whereby officers may use "any force including deadly force" to stop a person from escaping jail.

Finding the answer to the firearms policy question won't be easy for the negotiating teams. But at least the Texas Criminal Justice Council has provided suggested guidelines that we find more restrained, more acceptable more humane and more professional than those of the Port Arthur Police Department.

—THE NEWS, Port Arthur, Texas   Monday, May 5, 1975

Police recruiting study okayed

By LINDA WRIGHT
Of The News Staff

A proposal for an outside survey of minority recruiting in the Port Arthur Police Department was approved Monday by the city council with the only questioning coming from Mayor Bernis Sadler.

The mayor said, "How in the devil are we going to be able to hire minority policemen when they can go out to industry and make twice as much money? I don't see how an outsider is going to come in and change that."

All six city councilmen favored the proposal which calls for a team from the Criminal Justice Center at Marquette University to study past minority recruiting procedures, as well as variables which effect minority recruiting.

The team may be in Port Arthur Wednesday through Friday.

The proposal came from negotiations between the city and the black community and was endorsed last week by the Civil Service Commission.

Sadler said he did not oppose the survey but emphasized he would not accept lower standards in the police department.

He also said he does not recognize the leaders of the Concerned Citizens of Port Arthur Association (CCPAA) as community leaders.

The CCPAA is the black organization with which the city is negotiating four issues which arose after the shooting of a black prison escapee Dec. 29.

Speaking of the CCPAA leaders, the mayor said, "They had their election," referring to the April city elections in which each incumbent had a black opponent. He called the CCPAA movement "purely political."

City Manager George Dibrell said the minority recruiting survey, which was suggested by U.S. Justice Department mediator Robert Greenwald, would not cost the city anything.

"It will be funded by the federal government through the Law Enforcement Assistance Association, he said.

He said the main thrust of the study would be in the police department but there would also be a look at the fire department.

The center's representative who met with the negotiating teams "was very implicit in that his organization comes in and tells it just like it is," Dibrell said.

Arthur Guidry, the city's only black councilman, emphasized the need for the community to know the current recruiting procedures and the results of the study.

He pointed out Texas A&M University set up the standards for police recruitment and the school has reviewed the exams to see if they might be biased against minorities.

He said currently police officers are encouraged to recruit minority officers through a system whereby any officer who recruits a black who makes the force is rewarded with a bonus.

Blacks-Port Arthur talks to end soon

Beaumont Enterprise

May 15, 1975

PORT ARTHUR — Negotiating teams representing city government and the black community may end their work by mid-June after meeting periodically since late January to resolve police-related issues that came to a head following the fatal shooting of a black jail escapee by police Dec. 29.

Bob Greenwald, a U.S. Justice Department mediator working with the negotiators, said Wednesday that he hoped the teams could wrap up their work by mid-June after three to five more sessions. The negotiators met for two and a half hours Wednesday and another session is scheduled from 5 p.m. until 7 p.m. today.

Negotiators Wednesday agreed to use the services of the National Association of Police-Community Relations Officers, a professional organization of law enforcement officers involved in community relations, provided the city council extends an invitation to the association. The city council will consider asking for the assistance at its next meeting May 27.

The city has already applied for a police-community relations grant which may be approved this summer. If the services of the national association are used, the organization would evaluate community relations needs as seen by policemen and segments of the entire city before assisting the city in setting up a program designed to improve relationships between officers and citizens.

The association of police-community relations officers has received a grant to assist in improving or creating programs in 10 cities, Greenwald said. The group can begin its evaluation in Port Arthur in July at no cost to the city if a council invitation is obtained, the mediator indicated.

A week or two would be needed to evaluate the community relations needs here, Greenwald said. Technical assistance in implementing a community relations program would be offered from time to time by the association.

Negotiators Wednesday met with Robert Barton, president of the association and director of the St. Louis, Mo., police-community relations program, and Major Leroy Swift, commanding officer of the patrol division of the Kansas City, Mo., police department. The two officers explained to negotiators the services the association is able to provide to Port Arthur, Greenwald said.

The mediator indicated that, barring unforeseen developments, further discussion of the police-community relations issue by the negotiators will not be necessary. Today the two teams will take up the question of the police department's arrest and detention practices, the last of four issues to come before negotiators.

Houston Post

Accord aimed at understanding

It's Saturday, August 2, 1975

PHIL HEVENER
Post Reporter

PORT ARTHUR — It's All-America designation seared firebombings and racial unrest last December, this Gulf Coast city has completed the first steps in an ambitious rebuilding of relations between its black and white communities.

"This is noteworthy nationally," stressed Robert Greenwald, the Justice Department's community relations mediator who guided the 13 sometimes stormy meetings exploring four basic issues over a period of about five months.

Each issue was grounded in the dissatisfaction of blacks with police department procedures. These included community relations, policies on the use of firearms and arrest and detention, and minority recruiting.

The talks involved Greenwald and two nine-member committees representing the city administrators and the black community.

A document dealing with each of the four items has been completed and is scheduled for consideration by the City Council Monday night.

Black leaders such as A.Z. McElroy, a former school board chairman who was vice chairman of the black committee, hope the document will become an official part of city policy.

"We hope it becomes a requirement, not just an unofficial guideline," he said.

"And it's not a black instrument. It's a very human document," he added.

But it was the slaying of a young black man, 22-year-old Clifford Coleman last Dec. 29, that blew the top off the simmering pot of race problems. Clifford was gunned down, as he tried to run from the police station following his arrest on a disorderly conduct charge.

Hundreds of young blacks roamed the city during the next couple of days and two lumber yards were burned during a spree of firebombing.

Black leaders demanded the firing of Police Chief James R. Newsom, a move refused by City Manager George Dibrell as unrealistic.

The Justice Department's community relations division read of the problems and approached local leaders with an offer of mediation services.

"We thought it was a good idea, something that would move the trouble off the street and to the conference table," Dibrell explained.

Blacks were even successful in forcing the cancellation

Please see Port Arthur/page 23A

Port Arthur document points toward harmony

From page 1

of ceremonies at which Port Arthur was to receive one of the All-America Cities awards presented by the National League of Municipalities.

"Tension was running high," Dibrell remembers.

And City Atty. George Wikoff, one of the city's committee members, conceded it was not easy to clear some of the emotional hurdles generated by the meetings of the two groups.

Newsom claims some blacks "on the committee thought a black officer couldn't even arrest a white."

"It was hard to get started because it seemed like nobody trusted anyone else," McElroy observed.

But the Rev. Ransom Howard, who headed the committee from the black community, insisted that even though "we were sometimes near to knocking heads," there was solid agreement on the need to "keep anything like this from happening again."

That interest was the thread linking the long series of closed meetings where the document which will be voted on Monday was hammered out.

The police department's current 25-pages of rules has only five lines devoted to the use of firearms. This was enlarged to five pages defining deadly force and when to use it.

The lack of blacks on the department will be changed with a stepped-up minority recruiting program. About 40 per cent of Port Arthur's population of about 60,000 is black, but only six blacks are members of the 91-member police department.

Civil Service Director Davis Brinson said such an effort must be aimed at overcoming a basic disinterest of blacks in becoming police officers.

"We have had very few minorities that would even come in and take the test," he said, adding the $759-a-month starting salary does not compare with what is available from nearby private industry.

Howard does not believe, though, the problem was only money. "Blacks have never got any respect."

He cited the case of a black officer who quit the police force because he could no longer put up with the "constant references to 'nigger this' and 'nigger that' and 'boy this' and 'boy that'."

The fourth negotiated point is community relations, a largely racial issue.

Greenwald cautions the agreements reached on these four points do not necessarily signal an end to racial problems in Port Arthur.

But he was equally quick to point out the significance of reaching such an agreement at the city level. The Justice Department's mediation services have been similarly successful only once before. That was Birmingham, Ala., in 1972.

"This is an instrument everyone is proud of," McElroy beamed.

"I wouldn't want to live in this city without something like it," Howard said. "If people read it carefully, they'll see there's nothing there but things that are going to help this city."

By GEORGE DIBRELL
City Manager
City of Port Arthur
Port Arthur, Texas 77640

MEDIATION

IN CIVIL RIGHTS ISSUES

The Port Arthur Experience

WHEN RACIAL UNREST over actions by the police department exploded in the southeast Texas city of Port Arthur (population 57,371) early in 1975, city fathers and black leaders alike anxiously puzzled over the best road to a solution ... Until — in the midst of a week filled with protest marches, arsons, and angry demonstrations — there appeared a representative from a little-known division of the U.S. Department of Justice, the Community Relations Service.

Having learned of Port Arthur's problems through news media accounts, a representative of the service arrived in the city and offered the division's mediation services to the opposing groups. Eight months and 13 negotiating sessions later, the Port Arthur City Council adopted a statement of agreement which initiated a new police department firearms policy, a new arrest and detention policy, and new programs for police-community relations and minority recruitment. A four-year-old federal program had succeeded in a unique way, and in doing so brought solutions to what could have been a tragic situation.

The train of events began in the early morning hours of December 29, 1974, when a 22-year-old black, while escaping from jail, was shot by a white police officer about a block from the police station. He was dead on arrival at a local hospital, felled by a single bullet.

In the black community, making up more than 40 percent of the city's population, there was rampant hostility in some quarters. Two separate investigations — one by the Port Arthur Police Department and one by the Jefferson County Grand Jury — were launched as old prejudices resurfaced among blacks and whites alike.

The New Year was given a rousing welcome with 300 black protesters meeting at a local church, two large lumber yards destroyed by fire thought to be arson, other arson attempts, and several cases of vandalism. Police forces were beefed up with all officers on overtime, and deputies from the sheriff's department stood on alert.

On January 2, protesters marched on the police station and city hall and demanded the suspension of the four police officers involved in the affair and, later, the resignation of Police Chief James R. Newsom. Meeting in an emergency formal session Mayor Bernis Sadler and the six-member city council heard the demands made to this city manager for the ouster of the officers and the police chief. Newsom

firmly refused to take action against the officers until the grand jury findings were released.

Within 24 hours, the black protest had shifted from the masses to a group of prominent black community leaders, including two black elected officials — a port commissioner and the school board president. That group, in a conference meeting with officials, repeated the demands for dismissal of Police Chief Newsom and the officers involved in the incident.

Their ultimatums were rejected, and instead a four-point proposal was presented which included creation of a grievance procedure for investigating complaints against the police department and a bi-racial committee for improving communications between the community and the police department. Blacks, in turn, rejected this proposal, but indicated portions of it were favorable and might be acceptable later.

There was only a hint of conciliation in the ensuing days as the grand jury verdict was awaited. The black man's death turned out to be the tip of an iceberg, as black citizens brought into the open a number of other community grievances that had been simmering beneath the surface.

It was into this situation that Community Relations Service representative Gustavo Gaynett walked. Determining that the problems fell within the realm of the division's work, Gaynett offered its mediation services to this city manager. After an investigation of the Community Relations Service's past record, the process was proposed to the city council, who authorized its initiation if blacks agreed.

Representative Gaynett then presented the mediation idea to the Concerned Citizens of Port Arthur Association (CCPAA), who endorsed the plan and publicly proposed the mediation arrangement to city officials. Thus the plan was under way.

Citizens complained of instances of discrimination and civil rights violations, some of them predating the shooting. City officials dealt with all complaints as they were received.

Throughout this fast-paced series of events, the ground was quietly being laid for peaceful solution through the mediation process. Five negotiators and four alternates were named by each side. The city council named the city's representatives, which included this city manager as chairman, city attorney, police chief, personnel director, and chairman of the civil service commission; and the CCPAA named the opposing group, comprised of leaders in the black community. Working under the coordination of federal mediator Robert Greenwald, the group in late January decided on four major areas for discussion: a firearms policy for police officers, recruiting of minorities for the department, police-community relations, and arrest and detention procedures.

Tension ran high in the first meetings, which were marked with frequent argumentative exchanges. The distrust, evidenced by the emotional outbursts, also caused problems in choosing a site for the negotiating sessions. As the distrust dissipated and the strong emotions calmed down, the two teams gradually got down to real problem solving. On June 26, both sides signed their "statement of understanding" which was ratified in August by the Port Arthur City Council. While compromises had been made on both sides and no one felt the document was perfect, all felt they had something which would build a more effective police department.

The major factors in the mediation which made the process so successful in developing a policy guide for the police department were its voluntary character and its non-adversary framework, differing in that respect from both a court proceeding and from arbitration.

"Mediation is a process of facilitating negotiations through a third party — hopefully a neutral party. It's nothing more than a way to communicate that most protesters are unaccustomed to," according to Mediator Greenwald. "It draws much less attention than public hearings or street demonstration."

Throughout their five-month duration, the Port Arthur negotiations retained a low public profile. Both teams agreed that all sessions would be closed to the press and public and that no one involved but Greenwald would make statements to the press. The Port Arthur case was the first in which substantive changes in police policies and practices were developed jointly by city and citizen committees through mediation. Likewise, it marked the first time in the United States that mediation resulted in a statement involved in changing policies on firearms and arrest procedures.

According to Greenwald, there are two additional reasons the Port Arthur case is unique in mediation history: the extent to which the negotiating teams drew on the outside resources and the consistency with which the teams devoted themselves to their task.

Greenwald made it clear from the beginning session that the teams could turn to outside resource persons as often as they felt they needed more information on a subject. People from throughout the country were drafted for help. Among the outside resources used were the Jefferson County district attorney, the Criminal Justice Division of the Texas governor's office, the International Association of Chiefs of Police (IACP), Marquette University's Criminal Justice Center, and the National Association of Police-Community Relations Officers. The groups relied heavily on the "Model Rules for Law Enforcement" prepared by the IACP for the Criminal Justice Department of Texas governor's office.

In addition to having excellent outside help, the groups consistently devoted themselves to the negotiating task. Seldom were more than two members of either team absent, even though members of the black team often had to miss work to be at the negotiating table.

The two conditions for mediation placed by the Community Relations Service on the blacks were (1) all street marches and protests would cease for the duration of the negotiations and (2) the firing of Police Chief Newsom and the four officers would not be a negotiable item.

Before negotiations got under way, the grand jury exonerated the officers involved in the shooting, after hearing testimony from numerous eyewitnesses. In a detailed report, which was released to the public, the grand jury found the black youth had been in the process of being booked into the city jail at the time he broke from custody. The report noted he had attacked police officers and briefly took hostage a citizen before running down the street to the place where he was shot by a pursuing officer. The Texas Penal Code upheld the officer's action.

The controversy, however, did not center on the legality of shooting the escaping prisoner so much as it did on the propriety of that action. Partisans argued that the victim was arrested in the first place on a misdemeanor charge (use of abusive language) and that officers knew where he lived and therefore did not need to shoot him to prevent escape.

It was generally conceded that the incident was not the real issue; and both sides were soon looking for the genuine problems that divided the community.

The city council did not wait for the negotiations to begin before taking steps to correct some apparent deficiencies. The city's legal department was asked to recommend a procedure for investigating "severe" citizens' complaints against city employees. A bi-racial committee "to look at Port Arthur's problems and give recommendations" was also appointed. A criminal justice grant of $69,000 was sought to develop in-service training and community education programs. The city council also approved hiring an additional assistant city attorney to serve as police legal advisor. Finally, a criminal justice professor from the Institute of Contemporary Corrections and Behavior, Sam Houston University, was invited to teach Port Arthur officers criminal justice courses.

The forces of dissent remained active, too. After the lumber yard fires and initial vandalism, there were other incidents. Arson was suspected in a fire that razed the home of an earlier protestor, rampaging vandals caused up to $5,000 in damage to establishments along the main downtown thoroughfare, and a bi-racial fight on a local high school campus involved 50 to 75 persons. Four fire bombs were later tossed into a predominantly black housing complex, in units that were unoccupied at the time while renovation was in progress.

Even as mediation teams were tackling the city's problems, there were continuing demands for the resignations of officers involved in the shooting incident. The local chapter of the National Association for the Advancement of Colored People (NAACP) disagreed with the grand jury findings and said the U.S. Department of Justice would be asked to conduct a separate criminal investigation.

Of the four points on which agreement was reached, the one dealing with firearms and deadly force by the police was most directly related to the original shooting incident. The final agreement provided specific guidelines to be followed in future incidents of this nature. Since for the first time policy was reduced to writing, negotiators felt they had provided a more definitive guide to police officers in the field as well as an aid in assessing the validity of their actions. The new policy spells out the conditions under which an officer may use deadly force, but it also stresses that such force must not be used unnecessarily. And — there should be more understanding on the part of the public as to whether proper guidelines are followed. Most conceded that a lack of communication was responsible for much of the turmoil triggered by the recent case.

Arrest and detention procedures were negotiated along the same lines as firearms policy. That finalized policy consisted of a common sense approach with reasonable guidelines spelled out to avoid misunderstandings in the future.

Considering the issues of minority recruiting and police-community relations, the negotiating teams recommended to the city council the services of two of their resource groups. As a result, a minority recruiting specialist from Marquette University and officials from the National Association of Police-Community Relations Officers (NAPCRO) were in the city several times throughout the summer months.

After conducting his own study, the Marquette University specialist recommended the city hire 30 more police officers, increase police salaries, step up recruiting of minority applicants, and provide tutoring for black applicants to help them pass the entrance examination. All but the final suggestion had been advocated earlier by the council and staff. With the help of the specialist, a campaign was mounted to recruit minority candidates for a July police examination; and a program was established to tutor the candidates in test-taking methods. While the recruiting drive was successful in that 19 minority candidates took the test, none of the minorities passed all of the required tests and checks to qualify as an officer.

Recruiters said they had difficulty in interesting qualified persons from minority groups in police work. In the past months, the city has improved its financial position to a point where officials hope higher salaries may be offered to attract more qualified minority applicants. In addition, a black counselor at a local secondary school has been hired as a minority recruiter to locate potential candidates. Stepped-up recruitment of minorities will continue, likewise, in the newly formed community relations unit of the police department. Recently, a very well-qualified black candidate has passed the police exam.

Using the grant money acquired from the Criminal Justice Council, and with the aid of NAPCRO officials, a three-man police-community relations unit was established with minority recruiting as one of its main concerns. In addition, the P-CR program will be aimed at informing the public about police activities, instilling confidence in the department, and encouraging citizens to become more involved in crime reporting and neighborhood crime prevention. Some of the specific projects under consideration for the program are self-defense training for women, a community-based rape counseling center, a property identification system, and community education courses for officers.

Many feel this program is the key to making all points of the mediation agreement work. It is designed not only to foster understanding among citizens, but also to encourage officers to better understand community problems.

With completion of the series of talks mediator Greenwald praised the black participants, but he said the key to successful negotiations of this type was the patient and objective handling of group members during emotional confrontations by the group chairman. A calm assessment of the various complaints and acknowledgment of the validity of some of them, Greenwald said, made it possible to separate emotion from fact and conduct realistic negotiations.

Full solution has not yet been found, to be sure. Both blacks and whites feel that the serious confrontation was well handled and that the community needs to heal its wounds and begin pulling together. A civil lawsuit concerning the young black's death was filed but was subsequently dismissed, and a Justice Department civil rights investigation produced no federal charges of any kind. However malcontents are still grumbling. But the dispute has been taken off the street and into the conference room — and a lot of people are seeing each other in a different light — thanks to mediation.

Mediation in the field of civil rights is a relatively young process — only about four years old, according to Greenwald. The work in the police-community conflict is even newer.

The Community Relations Service was set up eleven years ago under the Civil Rights Act of 1964. At that time, it was in the Department of Commerce but about a year later it was transferred to the Department of Justice. In its early days, the service was programmed primarily to prevent conflict, but about four years ago a large portion of the budget was cut and since then the work has been mainly remedial — with a major emphasis on mediation. The division's present staff of slightly more than 100 is located in Washington D.C., and ten regional offices.

The Community Relations Service has handled about 40 mediations in addition to other types of intermediary work. Among the trouble spots it has entered was Boston during the city's stormy periods of school desegregation.

In his closing remarks to the Port Arthur City Council on the day the agreement was presented, mediator Greenwald cautioned the city council and audience about thinking the successful mediation was a sign that race relations were as they should be in the city. "The mediation was simply a demonstration of a process which can provide a depth of communication where there was a lot of misunderstanding," he said.

Both city officials and black leaders agree, but both are looking toward a future where a better understanding of one another — initiated through mediation — will advance better race relations in the city.   ★

The News

Good evening!

Thursday, Dec. 13, 1979

82nd Year — No. 346

Coleman incident topic

Dibrell, Howard discuss '74 tensions

News Washington Staff

WASHINGTON — To hear City Manager George Dibrell tell it, the 1974 shooting of a black man by a Port Arthur policeman sparked frank, intense discussions between white city officials and the black community that finally produced "closer police-community relations than we have ever had."

To hear the Rev. Ransom Howard tell it, it was the intervention of the Department of Justice in the racially troubled situation which made city officials listen — truly listen — to what black citizens were telling them about the police department.

"Without the availability of federal observation...we would have found ourselves at a dead end," said Howard. "All our labors would have proved futile."

Both men spoke Tuesday at a unique, three-day nationwide conference on safety and force in Silver Spring, Md., a suburb of Washington. Billed as "an opportunity for police-minority community cooperation" — the first of its kind — the conference is sponsored by the Department of Justice community relations service, the National Urban League and the League of United Latin American Citizens.

The 1974 Port Arthur incident, which Dibrell said is "constantly with me," was one of four case studies described in a panel discussion of successful community-police conciliation efforts. Others were in Ft. Lupton,

See COLEMAN, page 3A

From page 1A

Colo., San Jose, Calif., and Seattle, Wash.

Dibrell recalled the night he got a phone call telling him a Port Arthur policeman had shot and killed Clifford Dexter Coleman, who was being booked at the police station, escaped and ran down the street.

It was Howard who told conference participants the circumstances of Coleman's arrest: He had been sprayed with Mace after refusing to cooperate with officers who sought to question him.

There were four areas of discussion: Police firearms policy, arrest and detention procedures, minority recruitment and effective police-community relations. Initially, the discussions were "very emotional — the tensions were great," said Dibrell. But after five months, participants agreed on a policy paper that addressed all four issues.

"The problem is not only devising the policy but carrying it out," he said, but added that the experience "completely said" procedure.

"Because of the assistance of the Department of Justice, we were able to adequately handle our problem," said Howard.

The shooting aroused "substantial anger and hostility" in the black community, said Dibrell, and there were protest marches in the days that followed. Howard led a large group of protestors to city hall to sit in the various offices. When the mayor tried to get them to leave, Howard said he told him that city hall belonged to the people, and they "just wanted to stop by for the morning."

Black leaders demanded that the police chief and the four officers involved in the Coleman incident be fired. City officials refused to do that, but proposed a counter offer, which included making a "full report" of the incident when the grand jury completed its investigation. The chief would also take "appropriate action" against any police officer indicted by the grand jury. The grand jury eventually no-billed the officers involved, but ordered that the report be written.

Meanwhile, the Department of Justice's community relations service agreed to enter the case and help initiate discussions between the city and representatives of the black community. The department insisted on conditions, said Dibrell: That protestors would agree to "come off the streets to the negotiating table" and that dismissal of the police chief would not be a negotiable item.

Hispanic-police meeting brings unusual action

Saturday, September 23, 1978

By ERIC MILLER

An unprecedented meeting between representatives of the Mexican-American community and the police chiefs of five Texas cities brought some unusual action Friday.

They agreed to agree.

The participants in the 2½-hour closed session, reportedly brought about by the deaths of 16 Mexican-Americans while in police custody during a 16-month span, agreed to form a steering committee to explore the possibility of a regional conference dealing with the controversial subject of police brutality and minorities.

The meeting was planned by the community relations section of the U.S. Department of Justice with the intent of easing police-minority tensions that have been building in recent months.

The principal objective was to decide whether these issues can be discussed profitably," federal mediator Robert Greenwald said.

He said "one or more" additional meetings will be held.

The most significant aspect of Friday's session, Greenwald said, was about 30 Mexican-Americans and Mexican-American leaders — some of whom have become activists on the touchy subject — could gather in the same room.

All of those invited to the meeting were present.

They included police chiefs Donald Byrd of Dallas, William Banner of Corpus Christi, Frank Dyson of Austin, Emil Peters of San Antonio and Andres Vega of Brownsville.

Also attending were Ruben Bonilla, state director of the League of United Latin American Citizens; Rep. Paul Moreno, D-El Paso, chairman of the Mexican-American Caucus; Jose Garcia, state chairman of IMAGE; Jose Cano, state chairman of the American GI Forum; Juan Perez of the Brown Berets; and Joaquin Avila, associate counsel of the Mexican-American Legal Defense and Education Fund.

Justice Department representatives included Greenwald, Maurelio Ortiz, regional director of the department's community relations service, and Fred Toler, head of the Texas Commission on Law Enforcement.

Perez, contacted after the meeting, reportedly said his attendance in no way represented his organization's official sanction of the meeting.

He also was quoted as saying he was hesitant to endorse the idea, although be basically supported the meeting with police.

"My position there was to be an observer, to see that there would be no hanky-panky," Perez said. And, he added, his organization would be careful "when there's a situation like this when we would, in a sense, commit ourselves."

Bonilla was quoted as saying he believes the most immediate effect of the meeting will be to unite support from the Mexican-American community — "from grass-roots organizations like the Brown Berets to established groups like LULAC."

The Dallas Morning News

The News, oldest business institution in Texas, was established in 1842 while Texas was a Republic

Editorial Page

Jim Wright, Editorial Director

TUESDAY, SEPTEMBER 26, 1978

Police Brutality:

Discussions Should Begin

Police administrators from six major Texas cities and Mexican-American leaders have agreed to explore the possibility of a regional conference on police brutality and minorities. This is good news.

Mexican-Americans have been distressed at the number of hispanics who have been killed while in police custody in the state during the past 16 months. The Dallas meeting was set up by the U.S. Justice Department community relations section to ease the tensions that have been building in recent months.

This exploratory session was itself extraordinary. Too often minorities and law officers exchange views by shouting at each other in the media. Rational discussion of differences in views could lead to better understanding between the groups.

Unfortunately Texas leads the nation in the number of civil rights complaints filed with the U.S. Justice Department and many of them deal with police brutality. Whether the complaints are valid or not isn't the point. They are considered so by many citizens, and this suspicion, justified or not, poisons law officers' relations with many Texans.

Any steps toward better communication between law-enforcement officials and minority groups should be encouraged and promoted.

Corpus Christi Caller

THURSDAY, SEPTEMBER 28, 1978   PAGE 16A

Hopeful beginning

It's a beginning.

Police Chief Bill Banner and LULAC director Ruben Bonilla both agree that last week's meeting in Dallas between Texas police chiefs and Hispanic leaders set the stage for improved understanding between the two groups they represent. The problems which have plagued Texas, involving allegations of police mistreatment of minorities, particularly Mexican-Americans, were of course not solved at the gathering. But at least each side now knows of the other's concerns; it is evidence, as Bonilla observed, of "a spirit of unity and cooperation that is long overdue."

Most hopeful of all is that the conference is expected to spawn more such gatherings, involving greater numbers of police chiefs in the process. There is a basic mistrust and misunderstanding at work between law enforcement and members of minority groups; any contact which can help break through that barrier can do more to bring about a change in attitudes than any amount of street-corner confrontation or impassioned speech-making.

At bedrock, both law enforcement and offended minorities are in pursuit of the same goal: a just and safe society. Unfortunately, fear and mistrust on both sides cloud the issue. Neither side has a lock on all the good or all the bad in the relationship; each must come to recognize that fact, and work together to weed out the bad apples.

Not all allegations of police brutality are in fact incidents of untoward violence or racial abuse. Neither are all law enforcement officers fit to wear a badge. Clearly, a better screening process is needed in hiring police officers (although no system can reach perfection) and those on the force need to be given intensive training in understanding minorities and the perception minorities have of them. Likewise, minority group leaders need to establish and maintain close relationships to law enforcement officials, and to impart to their people the feeling of trust which should develop.

The meeting last week was a beginning, and a hopeful one. No Texan, no American should fear for abuse from law enforcement; no law enforcement official should tolerate abusive behavior by those under his command. With cooperation and communication, we can hope to reach that goal.

San Antonio EXPRESS-NEWS—Saturday, October 21, 1978

Plans begun for meeting between Hispanics, police

By DICK MERKEL
Chief, Express-News Capitol Bureau

AUSTIN — Initial steps were taken Friday toward a possible historic meeting in San Antonio involving Hispanic leaders and top-level law enforcement officials from across South Texas.

The initial plan was formulated during a two-hour, closed-door session of a committee appointed last September in Dallas during a meeting between Hispanic leaders and Texas police chiefs.

The Committee — described by one participant as "strictly ad hoc" — met in the offices of Austin Police Chief Frank M. Dyson.

Attending were Ruben Bonilla, executive director of the Texas League of United Latin American Citizens from Corpus Christi; Joaquin Avila, associate counsel for the Mexican American Legal Defense and Educational Fund, San Antonio, and State Rep. Paul Moreno, El Paso, chairman of the Mexican-American Caucus of the House of Representatives.

Others

Also on the committee and attending were Dyson; Don Byrd, Dallas Chief of Police; William C. Banner, Corpus Christi Chief of Police; J. T. Alley, vice president of the Texas Association of Police Chiefs, Lubbock; and Kieth Collier, president of the Texas Association of Sheriffs.

The meeting was chaired by Robert F. Greenwald, mediator with the U. S. Justice Department's community Relations Service regional office in Dallas.

After the meeting, Greenwald said the committee had voted to conduct a survey of a "all police jurisdictions in an area from Del Rio to San Antonio, to Houston.

Survey

"The survey will be to determine if there is enough interest among top-level law enforcement officials to justify a conference.

"If there is, then a conference could be held after the first of the year and the most likely place would be, of course, San Antonio."

He said the goal of the conference would be to gather about 200 people evenly divided between law enforcement officials and Mexican American leaders."

The entire aim of the conference, as well as the meetings which will have preceded it, Bonilla said, "is to provide a vehicle to facilitate maximum communications between the two groups."

Greenwald viewed the San Antonio plan as "a pilot program. If such a meeting is held, as far as I know it will be the first of its kind in the nation.

"It could lead to other such sessions, not only in Texas but in the nation."

Whether or not the conference is held will depend "strictly on what kind of participation we can get from both groups."

Monday, October 23, 1978 □ THE DAILY TEXAN

Chicanos, police chiefs meet
Leaders discuss problems

A group of Texas police chiefs and Chicano community leaders met in Austin Friday to try to narrow differences between Mexican-Americans and police throughout the state.

Bob Greenwald, a federal mediator from the Justice Department who helped organize the meeting, said the conference was in response to a variety of Mexican-American protests and demonstrations concerning excessive police force against Hispanic Texans.

"There is a need for vastly improved communication between the two groups," Greenwald said. Previously, Chicano and police arguments were exchanged, somewhat unsuccessfully, through the media, he said. The Justice Department Community Relations Service is trying to get the two factions to work out the problems themselves "without resorting to lawsuits or court action."

"We could be breaking new ground here," Greenwald said. "We feel that if police and Hispanic community leaders are willing to address this problem in a civilized manner in Texas, the rest of the country will be interested."

However, Greenwald said he recognized the limitations of workshops. "We could fall flat on our faces," he said.

"We are making headway," said Lubbock Police Chief J.T. Alley, vice president of the Texas Police Chiefs' Association. "Anytime people can sit down and discuss problems in a rational manner, it's a step in the right direction."

Ruben Bonilla, executive director of the United League of Latin American Citizens described the meeting as "historic."

"We are not only optimistic but we predict the success of the meetings to be of benefit to the total community," Bonilla said.

"Hispanic representatives are lending unequivocal support to the concept and planning of the meetings," he said.

LULAC is seeking legislative reform accompanied by a uniform written policy dealing with excessive police force and police use of firearms, Bonilla said.

The Austin meeting was just preliminary, Greenwald said a number of items, including the project's funding, still have to be resolved. The group's immediate goal, he said, is to set up a series of statewide meetings to discuss police relations in Hispanic communities.

Greenwald said the first major meeting will probably be held in San Antonio during January and will focus on problems in the South Texas area.

The Austin conference was a follow-up to a Sept. 20 meeting in Dallas.

STEERING COMMITTEE ON TEXAS
LAW ENFORCEMENT AND COMMUNITY RELATIONS

November 13, 1978

MEMBERS

Ruben Bonilla, Jr. (Co-Chair)
State Director
League of United
 Latin American Citizens
Corpus Christi

Frank Dyson, Chief (Co-Chair)
Austin Police Department

J. T. Alley, Chief
Lubbock Police Department

Joaquin Avila
Associate Counsel
Mexican-American Legal Defense
 and Education Fund
San Antonio

William C. Hanner, Chief
Corpus Christi
 Police Department

Donald A. Byrd, Chief
Dallas Police Department

Keith Collier, Sheriff
Scurry County, Snyder

Hon. Paul C. Moreno, Chairman
Mexican-American Caucus, Texas
 House of Representatives
El Paso

RESOURCE

Fred Toler, Executive Director
Texas Commission on
 Law Enforcement & Education
Austin

COORDINATOR

Robert F. Greenwald
Community Relations Service
U.S. Department of Justice
1100 Commerce St., Rm. 13B37
Dallas 75242
214.749.1535

To: South Texas Law Enforcement Agency Administrators

Subject: Proposed Intergroup Communication Conference

Threat or opportunity?

Over the past several years there has been a number of rallies, demonstrations and other forms of protest charging brutality or other wrongdoing on the parts of various law enforcement agencies. A majority of the more recent of these occurances have involved largely Hispanic leadership and participation. Houston, Dallas, Austin, Plainview, Laredo, Corpus Christi, Odessa/Big Spring, San Antonio and Lubbock were among the locations at which these events took place. Some were relatively small and poorly organized. Some drew substantial community interest and were carefully planned in cooperation with local officials.

The Community Relations Service of the U.S. Department of Justice, after having played a third party role in various of these events, called a meeting in Dallas last September 22 to examine the matter of police-community confrontation. Six law enforcement administrators and six spokesmen for Mexican-American statewide constituencies were invited to discuss prospects for a constructive approach to moderate the problem. Among the conclusions reached was that any impact on the deteriorating relationships would require reasonably wide involvement from both quarters. Perspectives would have to be shared openly and honestly.

A steering committee was subsequently formed (as shown on this letterhead) to plan one or more regional conferences within the state, the first of which has been tentatively scheduled for early 1979 in San Antonio. But before we proceed much further, we decided to sample law enforcement executives as to their willingness to participate in such a conference. Attendance would be limited only to heads of agencies. A maximum of approximately two hundred conferees would be invited, half from police and sheriff's departments, half from community-based organization leadership (such as LULAC, American GI Forum and IMAGE, among others).

Most of you have had no direct involvement in connection with citizen reaction to an incident in which a fatality or serious injury resulted from action taken by an officer in your organization. But it can happen anywhere. There will be other incidents, inevitably. The question is whether or not communication and understanding can be improved between law enforcement professionals and those minority citizens, and others, who are prone to condemn us whenever they think

Page 2. Intergroup Communication Conference

we've failed in our duty or misused our authority. We need to hear them, first hand, and they need to hear us.

We intend to conduct a conference that has carefully built-in controls to avoid useless rhetoric, to use our time judiciously, and to assure a productive result. There will be no discussion of specific incidents in terms of the guilt or innocence of any peace officer.

The conference is likely to be a day and a half in length. There will be only a modest registration fee, if any, to cover costs (we're going to try to get funding that will cover all expenses, thereby eliminating any fee to participants).

We know you can't make a definite commitment at this point since no dates have been set. We simply want to know what percentage of heads of law enforcement agencies are likely to support our effort and, given no urgent conflict in time priorities, would be apt to attend the conference in San Antonio. Please use the enclosed self-addressed envelope and the survey card to indicate your reaction. We will appreciate hearing from you no later than November 27.

If you have any questions or need for clarification, don't hesitate to call me at 512-476-3541, or Bob Greenwald, our committee coordinator, at 214-749-1525 (collect, if necessary).

I am enclosing a few selected press clippings, from among the many published, to give you some further idea of developments to date.

Best regards,

Frank Dyson
Co-Chair

Encl: Selected press clippings

A SYMPOSIUM ON CONTEMPORARY ISSUES IN TEXAS POLICE-COMMUNITY RELATIONS

TWO PERSPECTIVES - ONE RESOLVE

March 23-24, 1979   El Tropicano Hotel   San Antonio, Texas

P R O G R A M

Friday, March 23

10:00 A.M. - 12:45 P.M.   Registration, refreshments, informal visiting

Continental
Ballroom Foyer
Third Floor   Presiding: Symposium Co-Chairmen

                          Ruben Bonilla, Jr., State Director
          League of United Latin American Citizens, Corpus Christi
                          Frank Dyson, Chief of Police
                               Austin Police Department

1:00 - 1:15 P.M.   OPENING SESSION: Preliminary remarks

Continental   INVOCATION
Ballroom   Rev. Dermot N. Brosnan

                    WELCOME
                        E.E. Peters, Chief of Police, San Antonio

1:15 - 1:30 P.M.   OF THE BEGINNING

                        Robert F. Greenwald, Symposium Coordinator

1:30 - 1:40 P.M.   THE TEXAS CONNECTION
                        Gilbert G. Pompa, Director, Community Relations
                             Service, U.S. Department of Justice, Washington, D.C.

1:40 - 2:15 P.M.   KEYNOTE
                        Donald W. McEvoy, National Program Director, National
                             Conference of Christians and Jews, New York City

2:15 - 2:35 P.M.   Break

2:35 - 4:05 P.M.   EXCESSIVE FORCE: ITS USE AND CONTROL
                    Panel Presentations
                        Glen R. Murphy, Director, Bureau of Governmental
                             Relations & Legal Counsel, International Association
                             of Chiefs of Police, Gaithersburg, Maryland
                        Amitai Schwartz, Legal Director, Northern California
                             Police Practices Project, San Francisco

4:05 - 5:15 P.M. Continental Ballroom	SELECTION AND TRAINING Panel Presentations 　　Dr. Guadalupe Quintanilla, Assistant Provost 　　　　University of Houston 　　Dr. Stephen Wollack, President 　　　　Wollack Associates, Greenwood, California

6:30 - 7:30 P.M.　　　Hospitality, cash bar

Terrace Ballroom

7:15 - 9:30 P.M.　　　Dinner

Continental
Ballroom

THE NEWS DILEMMA - ROLE AND RESPONSIBILITY OF THE MEDIA
Panel Chairwoman
　　Ms. Marian Pfrommer, Assistant Professor of Journalism
　　　　Communications Center, Trinity University,
　　　　San Antonio
Panel Presentations
　　Bob Rogers, News Director
　　　　KENS Television, San Antonio
　　Rone Tempest, Metropolitan Editor
　　　　Dallas Times Herald
Panel Reactors
　　William C. Banner, Chief of Police, Corpus Christi
　　Fernando Perez-del-Rio, Director of Spanish Programming,
　　　　Texas State Network, Ft. Worth

Saturday, March 24

8:00 - 8:50 A.M.　　　Refreshments

8:50 - 9:00 A.M.　　　Announcements

9:00 - 10:00 A.M.　　COMPLAINT PROCESS/INTERNAL INVESTIGATION
Continental
Ballroom

Panel Presentations
　　A.J. Brown, Chief of Police, Ft. Worth
　　J.A. "Tony" Canales, United States Attorney, Houston
　　Ruben Sandoval, Civil Rights Attorney, San Antonio

10:00 - 11:00 A.M.　ROLES FOR COMMUNITY ORGANIZATIONS
Panel Presentations
　　Harry Caldwell, Chief of Police, Houston
　　Honorable Henry Cisneros, City Councilman, San Antonio
　　Ms. Lorrine Cunningham, Chairperson, Ad Hoc Group on
　　　　Police-Community Relations, Memphis, Tennessee

11:10 - 12:10 P.M.　CONCURRENT WORKSHOPS

Continental
Ballroom

Group A EXCESSIVE FORCE: ITS USE AND CONTROL
Moderator
　　Rev. Dermot N. Brosnan, President & Executive Director,
　　　　The Patrician Movement, San Antonio
Resources
　　Glen R. Murphy
　　Amitai Schwartz

River Room   <u>Group B</u> SELECTION AND TRAINING
Street Level   Moderator
                        Dr. <u>Lawrence S. Schoenfeld</u>, Associate Professor,
                            Department of Psychiatry, Division of Psychology,
                            University of Texas Health Science Center/San Antonio
           Resources
                        Dr. <u>Guadalupe Quintanilla</u>,
                        <u>Dr. Stephen Wollack</u>

Fontana Room   <u>Group C</u> COMPLAINT PROCESS/INTERNAL INVESTIGATION
Street Level   Moderator
                        Dr. <u>James L. Greenstone</u>, President
                              Southwestern Academy of Crisis Intervenors, Dallas
           Resources
                        <u>A.J. Brown</u>
                        <u>J.A. "Tony" Canales</u>
                        <u>Ruben Sandoval</u>

Hemisfair Room   <u>Group D</u> ROLES FOR COMMUNITY ORGANIZATIONS
Street Level   Moderator
                        Dr. <u>Louis John Tomaino</u>, Dean & Professor of Social Work,
                              Our Lady of the Lake University, San Antonio
           Resources
                        <u>Harry Caldwell</u>
                        <u>Henry Cisneros</u>
                        <u>Ms. Lorrine Cunningham</u>

12:10 - 12:40 P.M. Break, final check-out

12:40 - 1:50 P.M.   Luncheon
                   INTRODUCTIONS
Terrace Room   REMARKS
Third Floor   Honorable <u>Mark White</u>, Attorney General, State of Texas

2:00 - 3:00 P.M.   CONCURRENT WORKSHOPS (repeated/rotated)

                   <u>Group A</u> SELECTION AND TRAINING
                   <u>Group B</u> COMPLAINT PROCESS/INTERNAL INVESTIGATION
                   <u>Group C</u> ROLES FOR COMMUNITY ORGANIZATIONS
                   <u>Group D</u> EXCESSIVE FORCE: ITS USE AND CONTROL

3:10 - 4:10 P.M.   CONCURRENT WORKSHOPS (repeated/rotated)

                   <u>Group A</u> COMPLAINT PROCESS/INTERNAL INVESTIGATION
                   <u>Group B</u> ROLES FOR COMMUNITY ORGANIZATIONS
                   <u>Group C</u> EXCESSIVE FORCE: ITS USE AND CONTROL
                   <u>Group D</u> SELECTION AND TRAINING

4:20 - 5:20 P.M.   CONCURRENT WORKSHOPS (repeated/rotated)

                   <u>Group A</u> ROLES FOR COMMUNITY ORGANIZATIONS
                   <u>Group B</u> EXCESSIVE FORCE: ITS USE AND CONTROL
                   <u>Group C</u> SELECTION AND TRAINING
                   <u>Group D</u> COMPLAINT PROCESS/INTERNAL INVESTIGATION

5:30 - 5:45 P.M.   WRAP-UP

Continental
Ballroom

Chicanos, law officers meet to 'open minds'

By DOUG BLDELL
Staff Writer

SAN ANTONIO — In what was characterized as a "precedent-shattering" meeting, about 200 Mexican-American leaders and Texas law enforcement officers met face-to-face Friday for discussions designed to quell the rising resentment over alleged police brutality against Chicanos.

In the past three years, at least 10 Mexican-Americans have died while in the custody of Texas law enforcement officers, sparking civil rights investigations by the U.S. Justice Department and a report by former state Atty. Gen. John Hill that officially called three of the deaths "unjustified."

In speeches marked by cautious optimism, community relations experts from across the country Friday urged the two groups to ease their bickering and enter a roundup of workshops today with open minds.

"We feel you cannot afford to fail," said Gilbert G. Pompa, director of the Justice Department's Community Relations Service (CRS), which has cosponsored the two-day symposium.

"The entire nation has a stake in your success."

Ruben Bonilla, symposium co-chairman and state director of the League of United Latin American Citizens (LULAC), told the El Tropicano Hotel ballroom audience that it was part of "an historic gathering — the first of its kind ever.

"We have an opportunity to demonstrate to all Texans and all Americans that we have the capacity, the intellect and the will to solve our problems."

The format of the convention was developed late last year by a committee of 12 Mexican-American leaders and law enforcement officials. Dallas CRS mediator Robert F. Greenwald arranged the meeting after protests were raised by Mexican-Americans across the state denouncing the deaths of Mexican-Americans at the hands of Texas law enforcement officers.

These preliminary comments between the groups recalled in the first joint discussions of their differences, Greenwald said. Eventually, they led to the symposium structure, which will

See CHICANOS on Page 3

> 'We have an opportunity to demonstrate to all Texans and all Americans that we have the capacity, the intellect and the will to solve our problems.'
>
> Ruben Bonilla

DALLAS TIMES HERALD

Saturday, March 24, 1979

Chicanos, law officers meet to 'open minds'

Continued from Page One

feature small group discussions on subjects ranging from methods of controlling the use of excessive police force to the role of community groups in changing police policies.

"I think we have the makings here for success," Greenwald said in his opening remarks. "It could be a disaster. Who knows?"

Greenwald's warning was echoed by another expert in police-community relations, Donald W. McEvoy, program director for the National Conference of Christians and Jews.

"Don't expect too much," he said in his keynote address. "The problems with which we are dealing have been a long time in the making and will take a long time to correct.

"Law enforcement has made great strides in the past decade, but the gap between community standards and those of today's police forces is still at least 10 years wide. McEvoy said.

"But that's only for too little progress either," he said. "The Hispanic and the police have a number of things in common — one of which is your minority status.

"In every community in which you live, each of you is being used. And when you're being used, the best thing to do is force a coalition."

After the general statements of Greenwald, the delegates were prepared for today's small group sessions by two panels — one made up of authorities on the legal aspects of regulating excessive police force, the other of community organizational experts.

Glen H. Murphy, director of the Bureau of Governmental Relations and legal counsel to the International Association of Chiefs of Police, said the best way to control the use of deadly force is not by drawing up new statutes, but through internal department policies.

The community should have input in the formulation of the guidelines, "but they can't be made in periods of conflict. We believe there should be community participation in department policy making before the problems arise.

"That way, everybody knows the rules of the game before the game starts."

With the number of lawsuits rising every year, he cautioned the audience against overly restrictive rules governing when force may be used. If the new regulations are too limiting, Murphy said, officers may find themselves being sued by citizens for inmate breaches of the department's rules.

Murphy also faulted the press for "speculative journalism" in cases of alleged police brutality.

Houston Chronicle   Saturday, March 24, 1979

Two groups confer in San Antonio

Mexican-Americans, police urged to end rift

BY GORDON HUNTER
Chronicle Staff

SAN ANTONIO — Mexican-Americans and the police in Texas should form a political coalition to fight the power structures that pit them against each other, a police-community relations specialist told representatives of the two groups here Friday.

Donald McEvoy, national program director for the New York-based National Conference of Christians and Jews, said that "in every community, police and Hispanics are being used."

"Get sophisticated and get together," he urged those attending the two-day conference of about 200 Mexican-American community leaders, police chiefs and sheriffs from South Texas and the Houston area attending a conference sponsored by several Mexican-American groups, including the League of United Latin American Citizens and the Texas Police Association, which is paying more than 90 percent of the costs.

"The smartest thing to do" McEvoy said in the conference's first major address, "is form a coalition and work together," using what he labeled "political log-rolling."

McEvoy was director of the national group's police-community relations section for seven years, ending in 1975.

While there are no "long-range plans" made by the politically powerful, McEvoy said, many Texas police agencies are used to stymie the economic and political advancement of Mexican-Americans. He said the police and Mexican-Americans "tend to be pitted against each other, both tend to be victimized by the power structure."

In presenting his case for a coalition, McEvoy listed several similarities between the two groups. Both, he said, share easy identification, the police officer with his uniform or badge, the Mexican-American with his ethnic traits. Both share public stereotyping, he said.

McEvoy said law enforcement in the United States over the past two decades has undergone a "radical revolution," making greater change than any other institution in the country.

"But as they have changed, public expectations have also risen," he said, "and the gap is still there and never will be closed."

Part of the conference deals with the role of community groups with the police, and McEvoy said that for many years he advocated civilian review boards holding police directly accountable for their actions.

"It hurts me to say it, because I pushed it for so long, but that's never been successful," he said.

Instead, McEvoy said, community groups should try to influence police policy decisions "by building trust and talk" with the police. It is preferable, he said, to influence attitudes that may prevent a police brutality case, rather than review such a case after it happens.

Houston Police Chief Harry Caldwell, also speaking on the role of community groups and police policy, said backing from these groups can sometimes make a police chief's decision easier.

He said Houston has a very stringent firearms policy, and without the help of the Coalition for Better Law Enforcement (a Houston Mexican-American group), it could not have been adopted.

Another speaker, Glen Murphy, legal counsel for the International Association of Chiefs of Police, said there is a "serious legal problem" if police departments establish gun control rules for their officers that are more stringent than rules passed by state legislatures.

He said there has been a "tremendous" increase in lawsuits against police for alleged acts of violence involving guns, and that the more stringent local rules can be admitted in court as evidence.

This results in a police chief, who has instituted the stronger rules, placing his men and the local government in more liability, he said.

"But police chiefs should not be dissuaded by this (increased liability with stronger rules)," he said.

Ruben Bonilla, LULAC's state director and co-chairman of the conference with Austin police chief Frank Dyson, called the meeting a "historic and precedent shattering conference."

The conference was largely organized by Bob Greenwald, head of the U.S. Department of Justice's Community Relations Service in Dallas, who said the idea of the meeting started about 10 months ago after Mexican-American leaders expressed "a high-level, intense feeling of frustration" with police and alleged cases of brutality against members of their community.

"If this (conference) is worth it, we may try it again," possibly in West Texas, Greenwald said.

Corpus Christi Caller

A page of opinion

WEDNESDAY, MARCH 28, 1979

Police, Hispanics established rapport

The historic meeting held last weekend in San Antonio between Mexican-American leaders in the state and law enforcement officers will not assure us that another Joe Campos Torres case will not occur sometime in the future, but the chances certainly have been reduced.

The discourse was frank, sometimes sharp, in the closing session on Saturday, a rather distinct improvement over the somewhat restrained opening session on Friday.

There is yet a long way to go and much work to be done before a final solution to what the Mexican-Americans have called police brutality, in the worst context, or insensitivity to the rights of minorities while in police custody, in the best.

Attorney Ruben Sandoval of San Antonio, an outspoken critic of police handling of minority prisoners, said he was encouraged by reaction to his straightforward speech from law-enforcement officials.

Suggested at a number of workshop sessions were a state civil rights law, guidelines for use of force and use of firearms in cases involving fleeing felons, adoption of arrest procedures and written internal review policies in cases of alleged police brutal-ity, referral to a grand jury in cases in which law enforcement officers are accused of a crime, establishment of internal affairs divisions in law enforcement agencies with written and publicized procedures, and formation of a civil rights unit in the state attorney general's office.

Important as the specific recommendations are, the most significant aspect of the meeting seemed to be the rapport between the delegates. True, it was not all peaches and cream, but the representatives of police departments, sheriffs' offices and other law enforcement agencies apparently came away with a better understanding of the complaints Mexican-American leaders are voicing.

Atty. Gen. Mark White said he was "embarrassed" that Texas ranks first in civil rights complaints filed with the federal government. He promised strong support of changes in the state laws pertaining to police brutality.

The session was a giant step toward solution of a problem that on several occasions in recent years has been an embarrassment to the entire state of Texas. More meetings of this kind should be scheduled for the future, particularly at the local level.

Monday, January 28, 1980   Houston Chronicle

Follow up

Police, minority attitudes change

Follow up is a weekly feature that provides updated information about people or events formerly in the news.

BY RAUL REYES
Chronicle Staff

Last March, about 200 Texas police chiefs, sheriffs and Mexican-American leaders met in San Antonio to try to establish lines of communication between law enforcement agencies and minority communities.

Officials on both sides hoped the meeting would lead to some practical solutions to problems left untended for decades.

Now, about a year later, officials say attitude changes have led to a better understanding of each other's problems.

But the praise is cautiously tempered.

Ruben Bonilla Jr., national president of the League of United Latin American Citizens, said the conference in San Antonio has led to "visible progress.

"Police chiefs, to a one, have been sensitized to the unique problems of minorities and their communities."

But the same can't be said about all the state's sheriffs despite the efforts of Harris County Sheriff Jack Heard to improve relations, Bonilla said.

Baytown Police Chief R.H. "Bo" Turner, cochairman of the Police Community Council, basically agrees with Bonilla's assessment.

"It was kind of enlightening," Turner said of the conference, "to see we wanted to do the same things, but we were referring to it by different terminology."

The council Turner co-chairs is a direct result of the conference. The council is composed of area minority leaders and law enforcement officials. Similar councils have been formed in other areas.

Another co-chairman of the council, LULAC District 8 director Johnny Mata, said, "Some police departments are now

really serious about cleaning house and we're finding that we can help each other solve some problems."

Bob Greenwald, a mediator with the U.S. Justice Department in Dallas, said there has been "a dramatic decline (since the conference) regarding the number of incidents which could be classified as excessive force and which drew an adverse reaction from a community."

But, Greenwald said, the decline does not mean fewer incidents are occurring, but rather that community reaction is more restrained and channeled toward achieving long-term changes.

James Hammett, a Justice Department mediator here, said the council could eventually resolve some of the gaps, such as recruiting minorities as peace officers.

Methods of encouraging minorities, he said, would be to begin recruiting at the high school level and offer bonus and specialized training programs similar to those offered by the Army.

But while Mata and others praise some of the conference byproducts, no one will deny that tension still exists between minorities and police.

Just saying things have improved is not enough, Bonilla said.

"Regardless of what some of the so-called Hispanic leaders say," he said, "there is always a vacuum between the leadership and the members of the community who are the victims.

"Due to the residue of mistrust, it's hard to overcome."

Bonilla also said that, despite active recruiting in communities, there has been no significant increase in the hiring of minority peace officers.

But as Chief Turner said: "We haven't got all the answers. But we've got the basis for it. If we just work out some of the organizational problems, we'll get things done."

Bonilla   Turner

U.S. DEPARTMENT OF JUSTICE
COMMUNITY RELATIONS SERVICE
SOUTHWEST REGIONAL OFFICE
1100 COMMERCE STREET
DALLAS, TEXAS 75242

April 15, 1982

To: Statewide task group on citizen complaint processing

Subject: The final product

If you're like me, there were times when you wondered whether we would ever see this pamphlet in print. I hope it meets your expectations.

Copies will soon be sent to virtually all law enforcement agencies in the state, courtesy of Fred Toler's TCLEOSE mailing list. Then, as soon as possible, we will arrange for selective mailings to minority organization contacts.

It is our hope that initiatives will be taken by various departments and community groups to use this document as a basis for local workshops or other dialogue facilitation. That is, after all, the reason we created it. Chief Curtis Harrelson, Wichita Falls PD, has already had preliminary discussions with the local human relations commission there to jointly sponsor such an event. Tentatively, that will be a gathering of law enforcement agencies and community representatives from throughout the Council of Governments (COG) jurisdictions in that area. In Lubbock next week, another "cluster workshop" on police-community relations will also make use of this material. There too, representation is expected from a wide radius around the host city.

I'm sending two copies to each of you. We will have an ample supply in a week or two, so don't hesitate to notify me of any needs you have for a larger quantity. We want to be careful to distribute them in a way that will assure effective useage. Those of you on the task group that helped develop the publication, of course, have first priority.

Some of you invested a good deal of thought and time in this effort. Many of you traveled at your own expense to attend meetings and to assure a worthwhile result. We are grateful to each of you for your contributions and early recognition of the merit of the project. Special thanks is due the Dallas Black Chamber of Commerce and its executive director, Adolph Hauntz, for arrangements made for a corporate donor to cover printing costs (see letter attached).

We hope these guidelines will be seen by all who use them as a well balance presentation of a difficult and sensitive problem that needs and deserves our attention.

Best regards,

Robert F. Greenwald
Task Group Coordinator

Attachments: "Texas Law Enforcement Agencies and Citizen Complaints" (2 copies)
            Letter to Doyle E. Rogers, dtd 4/13/82

RFG:s

U.S. DEPARTMENT OF JUSTICE
COMMUNITY RELATIONS SERVICE
SOUTHWEST REGIONAL OFFICE
1100 COMMERCE STREET
DALLAS. TEXAS 75242

June 28, 1982

To: Texas LULAC Council Presidents

Subject: Citizen Complaint Processing by Texas Law Enforcement Agencies

Attached are three copies of a recently published reference document for police agencies and community organizations on an important and sensitive subject. It is the result of more than a year of dedicated effort to satisfy a need that has been too long unmet.

Your names were provided to this office by your State Director, Oscar Moran. He was enthusiastic about the prospect of local LULAC councils using this booklet as a tool in addressing the police-community issue in a new and constructive way. We think you will find after a careful reading of its content that it can be used effectively as a basis for dialogue with law enforcement officials in your community. Copies were mailed last month to every police and sheriff's department in the state.

If you think we can be helpful in guiding or assisting with arrangements for a mini-workshop with police and citizen participants, we would be pleased to explore that possibility with you. A number of communities have already made and/or executed such plans.

Should you decide you would like to distribute a larger number of these booklets to more members, or to others outside your organization, simply let us know how many you need and we'll be pleased to send them to you promptly. You can call here, collect, at 214-767-0824 to expedite such requests.

Some of you know that much of the impetus for this undertaking arose out of the 1979 Texas symposiums on police-community relations held in San Antonio and Fort Worth. Ruben Bonilla, you will recall, then Texas State Director for LULAC, served as co-chairman of those two historic events and continues today to support efforts to carry on follow-up activities.

Don't hesitate to be in touch if we can be of any further service.

Muchas gracias,

JOHN G. PEREZ
Regional Director

Robert F. Greenwald
Regional Mediator

Attachments (3): "Texas Law Enforcement Agencies and Citizen Complaints" with
                  original cover letter to police agencies

Copies: Oscar Moran, LULAC State Director
          Tony Bonilla, LULAC National President

RFG:s

P.O. Box 1431

September 21, 1982

To: Selected Texas and Oklahoma Law Enforcement Officials, Media and
    Organization Representatives

Subject: Wichita Falls Forum on Police-Community Relations

You are invited to take advantage of a rare opportunity!

    Late last month you will recall having received an announcement regarding a
forum on current issues in police-citizen relations, to be held on Saturday,
October 16th, in the Fine Arts Building, Midwestern State University, Wichita
Falls.

    This will be a unique occasion in several respects. For the first time, to
our knowledge, a significant number of law enforcement administrators/legal ad-
visers/trainers, minority organization representatives, news media professionals,
and human relations agency officials, from designated sections of Oklahoma and
Texas, will convene and address two very sensitive and important contemporary
issues--the use of extreme force by peace officers, and citizen complaint processing. Together, we will explore problems and perceptions that persistently erode
a healthy law enforcement environment in many communities across the land. We
expect no cure-all remedies to emerge. We do look forward to honest dialogue and
open communication. We will avoid discussing details of specific past conflict
incidents (except perhaps to illustrate a problem or circumstances). There will
be no debate regarding the guilt or innocence of any parties alleged to have committed wrongful acts.

    The attached program draft sets forth topic and schedule details. We think
you'll agree that our featured speakers are especially well qualified to present
useful information and insights.

    This invitation letter is addressed, for the most part, to professionals and
volunteer leaders of agencies and organizations in north-central Texas and south-
central Oklahoma who are likely to be interested in the topics to be presented.
Each is welcome to register several associates to attend. PLEASE BE SURE TO MAIL
YOUR PRE-REGISTRATION FORM (attached) AS EARLY AS POSSIBLE AND NOT LATER THAN
THURSDAY, OCTOBER 7th. We need advance registration information to provide sufficient lead time for campus meal preparation and other arrangements.

    A map is enclosed that should save you time in finding your way to the Fine
Arts Building on Midwestern campus if you are unfamiliar with the area. For those
who will be traveling considerable distances and who choose to come into Wichita
Falls Friday night, the 15th, there are several motels in or near the downtown
area, not far from the campus. Motel information is shown in the map insert.

Page 2.
Wichita Falls Forum on Police-Community Relations

Reservations should be made directly by those who desire such accommodations.

There is no registration fee. The only expense will be the noon meal ($6.00), payable when you pick up your name tag upon arrival.

If you have any questions or need for further clarification, don't hesitate to contact the forum coordinator, Bob Greenwald, at the address shown on the return envelope (or if you prefer, telephone collect, 214-767-0824). We hope to see you on the 16th of next month in Wichita Falls!

Sincerely,

Lee D. Cary

Dr. Lee D. Cary, Co-Chairman
Convener, Forum Planning Committee
Wichita Falls Human Relations Commission

C.R. Harrelson

Curtis R. Harrelson, Co-Chairman
Chief, Wichita Falls Police Department

Attachments:

1. Tentative program draft
2. Pre-registration form and self-addressed return envelope
3. Map with directions to forum site

AGREEMENT BETWEEN THE CRYSTAL CITY SCHOOL BOARD AND THE NEGOTIATING COMMITTEE OF STUDENT BOYCOTT SPOKESMEN AND REPRESENTATIVE PARENTS

January 4, 1970

The parties to this document agree to the following:

ISSUE: I.   CONDITIONS UNDER WHICH STUDENTS ARE TO RETURN TO SCHOOL

ACTION:

A. Grades established before December 9th shall remain in tact.

B. Grades missed by students on walk-out during December 9-19 will not be used, with the exception of 3-weeks tests and 6-weeks tests.

C. Students who attended classes may drop an equal number of grades as those missed by students who participated in the boycott. This does not include 3-weeks tests or 6-weeks tests.

D. Students participating in the boycott will be given the opportunity to take the 3-weeks and/or 6 weeks tests during regular class time while non-affected students are given study periods. Teachers will ~~unconditionally~~ cooperate with walk-out students in providing subject matter covered during December 9-19.

E. The practice of applying a two-point-per-day penalty for unexcused absence will not apply.

F. Time lost in connection with Driver Education classes can be made up, if possible, during regular class periods. Otherwise, students will be allowed to make their own financial and time arrangements with qualified personnel. Cooperation from faculty will be expected in order to reach these alternate objectives

ISSUE: II.   ESTABLISHMENT OF GRIEVANCE PROCEDURE TO FACILITATE EFFECTIVE COMMUNICATION

ACTION:

A ten-member parents' advisory committee will be formed. It will be composed of eight Mexican-Americans and two Anglos to be selected by high school students. The recently formed local "churchmen's group", chaired by Dr. Robert Stauber, will prepare a proposal for consideration and approval by both parties to this agreement. In addition, the establishment of an "ombudsman" function to facilitate effective communication between the advisory group and school authorities will be developed and included in said proposal. The target date for completing and submitting this proposal is January 31, 1970.

Page 2.   AGREEMENT BETWEEN PARTIES

ISSUE: III.   EXPLORATION OF BI-CULTURAL AND BI-LINGUAL PROGRAMS TO BE IMPLEMENTED IN ACCORDANCE WITH RECOMMENDATIONS FROM COMPETENT EDUCATIONAL AUTHORITIES MUTUALLY AGREED UPON BY THE PARTIES HEREIN NAMED

ACTION:

Contacts with the Texas Education Agency (TEA), already partially in-itiated by Crystal City school authorities, will be vigorously pursued in order to facilitate the availability of qualified **education** specialist(s) to help establish an acceptable program, subject to **funding** availability.

ISSUE: IV.   UTILIZATION OF PROFESSIONAL CONSULTANTS TO EVALUATE CERTAIN TEST-ING PROCEDURES AND TO RECOMMEND CHANGES WHICH WOULD OVERCOME ALLEGED INEQUITIES

ACTION:

The school board acknowledges the probable existence of inequities in the administration of tests designed to measure school-entry readiness. In seeking a remedy to this problem, the TEA will be requested to provide suitable technical assistance. Any specialist(s) assigned to this task will consult with parents and students who represent the original complaint issue. The most competent available resources will be sought and utilized, as recommended by the state agency.

ISSUE: V. IDENTIFY AND APPLY METHODS OF OVERCOMING PATTERNS OF ETHNIC ISOLATION

ACTION:

Contact will be made with the appropriate resource at the University of Texas (TAC) and/or the TEA to seek corrective measures. Problem identi-fication will include attention to the allegation that Anglo children in certain grades are not found in lower achievement sections, contributing to patterns of artificial ethnic separation.

ISSUE: VI. REVISION OF METHODS BY WHICH CERTAIN STUDENT POSITIONS ARE DETERMINED

ACTION:

A. Most Representative Student--The designation for this position will be changed to "Faculty Student Representative".

B. Cheerleaders--Procedure will be changed to provide for election by student body.

C. Baseball Sweetheart--Provide for only one such honoree (instead of two).

Page 3.   AGREEMENT BETWEEN PARTIES

to be nominated and elected by members of the team.

D. Prom Servers--Provide for election by junior class from one list of all sophmore students without regard to ethnic grouping.

E. Twirlers and Drum Major--Provide for selection by the CCISD school superintendent four non-resident band directors (or other similarly qualified persons) and four band members (elected by the band) to judge and select candidates by a point system. Mechanics of such a system will be constructed in a manner which will best assure impartial and independent selections.

ISSUE: VII.   COMPLAINTS AGAINST CERTAIN SCHOOL PERSONNEL

ACTION:

Specific complaint substance was noted by the board and will be given appropriate consideration at the time of contract renewal. Such related problems, requiring improved sensitivity to cultural diversity, will be included for attention by previously noted consultants.

ISSUE: VIII.   CONSIDERATION OF THE NEED FOR ADDITIONAL COUNSELING PERSONNEL

ACTION:

Availability of additional counseling personnel will be explored. If funds are available, through Title VI, Sec 8910, or otherwise, a qualified bi-lingual candidate will be recruited and employed.

ISSUE: IX.   APPROPRIATE SCHOOL-WIDE OBSERVANCE OF SEPTEMBER 16 (DIEZ Y SEIS)

ACTION:

Observance of this holiday will provide for a suitable assembly program (during the last regular class period of the day for the high school). Students will be permitted to select speakers and/or program content, subject to approval by the school administration. Such assemblies will include participation by the total junior high and senior high student bodies.

ISSUE: X.   INEQUITABLE ETHNIC DISTRIBUTION OF STUDENTS REGARDING SIZE OF CLASSES

Page 4.   AGREEMENT BETWEEN PARTIES

ACTION:

Superintendent will examine the extent and nature of the problem. Particular attention will be given to alleged disparities in classes in which driver education, civics and English are offered. Such technical assistance as may be indicated will be sought from previously identified resources in order to implement corrective measures. Such remedies as are found to be in order will be applied to take effect not later than September, 1970.

ISSUE: XI.   INADEQUACY OF SHOWER FACILITIES

ACTION:

The school board acknowledged the problem as a high priority need among facility improvements under consideration. It was agreed that the stated condition would be carefully evaluated as to costs involved, etc., and that the most feasible action would be taken, within the limitations of available funds.

ISSUE: XII.   ACCESS TO SCHOOL FACILITIES DURING OFF-HOURS

ACTION:

Said facilities will be open for student use on Monday, Tuesday and Thursday of each school week, between the hours of 7:30 P.M. and 9:30 P.M. Access areas will include the library, typing room, one or more classrooms as needed. Supervision during such hours will be provided by school personnel.

ISSUE: XIII.   ALLEGED PRESSURES ON FACULTY MEMBERS DESIGNED TO INHIBIT EXPRESSION OF VIEWS OR PARTISAN SUPPORT IN CONNECTION WITH CONTROVERSIAL ISSUES

ACTION:

Both parties agreed that it could be anticipated that this problem would likely be resolved through the establishment of an effective grievance procedure as has been set forth under issue II.

ISSUE: XIV.   CRITICISMS OF EXISTING STUDENT NEWSPAPER AND SUGGESTIONS FOR CRITICAL IMPROVEMENTS

ACTION:

The school board will take appropriate action to assure that the student

Page 5.   AGREEMENT BETWEEN PARTIES

newspaper (The Javelin Herald) reflects the highest possible standards of professional journalism, including the regular presentation of divergent viewpoints and generally meaningful content with likely appeal to a wide cross-section of the student population.

ISSUE: XV.   REVIEW AND UP-DATING OF DRESS CODES

ACTION:

The student council will be requested by the school administration to examine present student handbook provisions and to recommend to the board suitable revisions in keeping with currently acceptable styles and fashions. Such revisions will apply to both junior and senior high school levels.

ISSUE: XVI.   PROVISION OF TRAINING FOR TEACHER AIDES

ACTION:

Resolution had already been accomplished, a fact previously unknown to the protest group.

ISSUE: XVII.   REVIEW OF PRACTICES IN CONNECTION WITH STUDENTS PERFORMING CUSTODIAL DUTIES

ACTION:

Physical Education students will be given an option as to whether they will participate in the regularly scheduled P.E. activity or choose to assist in clean-up activity on the athletic field and elsewhere on school property.

For the Student/Parent Negotiating Committee   For the CCISD School Board

For the Community Relations Service
U.S. Department of Justice

Observer-Witnesses

212

San Antonio EXPRESS/NEWS — Sunday, Jan. 4, 1970

Boycott To Continue Unless Demands Met

CRYSTAL CITY, Tex. (AP)— Boycotting Mexican-American pupils and their parents met with the school board Saturday night for a second round of talks with one day remaining in the Christmas vacation.

Earlier Saturday, more than 800 Mexican-American young-sters and parents were reported in favor of continuing the boycott of public schools here Monday, first day of school after the holidays.

School Supt. John Billings indicated another meeting on the dispute would be held soon if Saturday night's meeting went well.

Two Justice Department officials served as mediators at the session, aimed at halting a boycott that began Dec. 9 after the school board refused to discuss a group of pupils' demands for policy changes.

The pupils, charging the school district discriminates against the predominantly Mexican-American student body, demanded such changes as bilingual education, Mexican-American counselors, and revisions in selection of class representatives.

The boycotters' number grew to more than 1,000 at times and included students in grades one through 12.

José Angel Gutierrez, a local Mexican-American leader in close touch with the boycotters, said about 950 pupils and parents braved cold weather Saturday afternoon to vote to resume the boycott Monday—and continue until the demands are met.

Gutierrez has said previously that he expects the school board to meet the pupils' demands.

Saturday's vote came at a rally at a local park in honor of teachers from TEAM, Texans for the Educational Advancement of Mexican-Americans, who tutored the boycotters during the holidays.

Gutierrez said he understood an agreement had been reached at the first negotiation session here Wednesday on the demonstrators' demand for amnesty against scholastic penalties.

Both sessions were closed to the public and school officials declined to comment on the proceedings.

Gutierrez predicted the meetings will make little headway until Monday, when school authorities check for absentees.

Tuesday, January 6, 1970   The Dallas Morning News

Crystal City Students Agree to End Boycott

CRYSTAL CITY, Texas (AP) — Boycotting Mexican-American pupils began returning to school Monday for the first time in four weeks, halting a walkout that drew federal investigators and saw more than 1,000 pupils on strike.

Hundreds of Mexican-American pupils and parents overwhelmingly approved agreements negotiated by the boycotters' representatives and the school board.

School Supt. John Billings, saying "only time will tell" what effect the agreements will have on the school district, said some pupils returned to class at 1 p.m. Monday.

The others, boycotting since Dec. 9, were expected to return to school Tuesday, he said. Monday was the first day of school after the Christmas holidays, which began Dec. 19.

The boycotters, claiming those with Spanish names are discriminated against in the public schools of this predominantly Mexican-American town, had demanded such policy changes as bilingual education.

Most of the district's 2,950 pupils are Mexican-American.

In three marathon negotiation sessions, representatives of the pupils and their parents thrashed out agreements on 17 demands. Two U.S. Justice Department officials mediated at the negotiations. The final session, held Sunday night, lasted 10 hours.

The agreement was signed by both sides Monday.

It states that the school board will "explore" bicultural and bilingual education programs.

They would be implemented "in accordance with recommendations from competent educational authorities."

The agreement also protects the boycotters against scholastic penalties, provides for grievance procedures and establishes three week nights for use of school facilities for study purposes.

The negotiators agreed to introduce a special assembly for the full student body on Sept. 16, Mexico's independence day, with speakers to be selected by the pupils and approved by the administration.

Dallas Times Herald

LEE J. GUITTAR
Chairman of the Board

THOMAS R. McCARTIN
Publisher

KENNETH P. JOHNSON
Editor

WILL D. JARRETT
Managing Editor

JON T. SENDERLING
Editorial Page Director

22—A   Wednesday, June 3, 1981

Politics vs. public interest

One of the most frivolous episodes of this year's legislative season in Austin occurred in the waning days of the 67th session when Rep. Bill Ceverha and four fellow-Republicans put political pettiness before public interest and blocked a good piece of legislation simply because they did not like its sponsors.

Rep. Ceverha, a North Dallas Republican, and his allies — Reps. Jim Horn of Denton, Ken Riley of Corpus Christi, J. H. Reynolds of Floresville and Jerry Cockerham of Monahans — took advantage of a House rule to knock the bill off the local and consent calendar, thereby sealing its doom.

The measure, sponsored by Sen. Oscar Mauzy, D-Oak Cliff, and Rep. Craig Washington, D-Houston, both considered to be "liberals" by the five Republicans, would have permitted Dallas County and other counties of more than 500,000 population to establish centers to mediate minor civil disputes, saving time for judges and legal and court costs for the individuals involved.

Ironically, the bill was strongly supported by several Dallas County organizations and was a pet project of Republican County Commissioner Nancy Judy. Rep. Chris Semos, D-Oak Cliff, chairman of the Dallas County legislative delegation, interceded on the bill's behalf, and Gov.

William P. Clements Jr. put an emergency tag on the legislation in a last-minute attempt to save it. But by that time, the Texas House had become involved in a debilitating orgy of retaliation and partisanship, and the bill was killed.

Rep. Ceverha attempted to justify his pettiness by arguing that one of the bill's sponsors, Rep. Washington, "fights every law-and-order bill that comes through the House." He pouted that county officials should pick the sponsors of their legislation more carefully. But that, we think, is a lame excuse for unstatesmanlike conduct that ignores the best interests of the state and its citizens. Also, the bill in question, we might point out to Rep. Ceverha, involved civil law, not criminal law.

Declared Rep. Washington: "This is a hell of a way to run a railroad, when you kill a bill off the calendar and you don't even know what it does." We agree.

Former State Rep. Jim Clark of Dallas once referred to the Texas Legislature as "the greatest time-wasting machine ever devised by man." Clark may have been exaggerating somewhat. For the Legislature does manage to fulfill its main purpose each session and pass an appropriations bill to finance state government for the next two fiscal years.

But some legislators, sadly, still insist on trying to make a farce out of the process.

DISPUTE MEDIATION SERVICE OF DALLAS

August 11, 1981

COORDINATING
COMMITTEE

Judge George Allen
Justice of the Peace

N. Alex Bickley
Executive Vice President
Dallas Citizens Council

Judge Oswin Chrisman
44th Civil District Court

Judge B.F. (Bill) Coker
County Court at Law #1

Carl Flaxman
Criminal Justice Committee
Greater Dallas Community
of Churches

Honorable Nancy E. Judy
Dallas County Commissioner

Calvin B. Massmann
Senior Manager
Price Waterhouse & Co.

Dr. William L. Pharr
Executive Director
National Conference of
Christians & Jews

Wallace H. Savage
Director
Lakewood Bank & Trust Co.

Louis J. Weber, Partner
Jenkens & Gilchrist
Attorneys at Law

TEMPORARY STAFF

Robert F. Greenwald
Coordinator
Community Relations
 Service
U.S. Department of Justice
Suite 15B35
Dallas 75242
214-767-0824

James Coplin
Secretary

To: Planning Council Members of Record and
     Board of Directors
     Dispute Mediation Service of Dallas

Subject: Final Update Pending Start-up Operations

This summary of current developments is directed to the approximately one hundred Dallas citizens who made known over the past 18 months their interest in and support for the establishment of a dispute resolution program in Dallas. Some have asked simply to be informed of progress, unable to take part directly in planning activities. Others have attended meetings, served on committees, responded to requests for special needs, contributed time, energy and talents. Thirteen now serve on a recently created board of directors.

Nine months of concept formulation and support building, five months of fund-raising, and finally, another four months of organization preparation, are now behind us. On Monday of this week, the principal staff officer of the Dispute Mediation Service (DMS), Richard Evarts, was on board and several assistants hired. Administrative preliminaries are under way. The first case processing is projected for early October.

Mr. Evarts has been the Executive Director of the Center for Dispute Resolution in Denver. He spent almost three years with that program, having provided staff leadership from the outset, including the development and implementation of a very effective training component for volunteer mediators. He has the determination, the energy and the capacity for making the Dallas center a model for the nation.

Those of you who intend to remain connected with DMS will want to meet Richard Evarts soon. I am confident you will agree that the screening committee made an outstanding choice and that we are truly fortunate to have him share in the leadership. I urge you to contact him at the newly established DMS headquarters:

Dispute Mediation Service of Dallas
1310 Annex at Live Oak, Suite 203 (75204)
(new extension to the Dallas Community Chest Trust Fund
     building)
Phone: 821-4380

If you are interested in joining the first mediator training sessions, tentatively planned for mid-September, please complete and forward the attached application form (if you have not already submitted one) to the above address. There are already over 20 applications in hand and others pending. The "charter" mediator training group will likely be limited to no more than 30 participants, all of whom will be carefully screened and evaluated before acceptance. If you wish to take some other part in the program, your interest and counsel will be welcome.

Final DMS Update
Page 2.

Most of you are aware by now that our first year's funding has been fully committed. A contract with the Texas Department of Community Affairs (TDCA) has been executed. Interagency coordination meetings are pending. Half the 1981-82 budget (approximately $65,000) was given by The Meadows Foundation and half by TDCA. The Pollock Foundation provided another $2,000 to help with unanticipated start-up contingencies.

Prospects for long-term funding are promising, to say the least. Some of you are familiar with the unfortunate developments related to the dispute resolution bill introduced before this year's state legislature. The attached newspaper clippings and letter from Rep. Ceverha to Governor Clements reflect the nature of those circumstances. We have reason to be assured that a similar measure will be enacted into law during the 1983 session. Meantime, another year and a half of operating funds will need to be raised. In that connection, we are pleased to inform you that the Texas Industries Foundation, through the response of its President, Mr. Ralph B. Rogers, has already contributed $10,000, the first grant toward the second year fund.

It has been a genuine privilege to have served as temporary coordinator of this organizational undertaking. The rewards have been many. The response of this community to the concept paper first circulated early last year was nothing less than phenomenal. Subsequent support from individuals, organizations and corporate institutions with a broad range of interests and resources likewise has been far beyond expections.

There is an opportunity for Dallas to excel in this emerging and exciting new field of nonadjudicative conflict resolution. Many talents and strong commitments are needed. If you wish to take an active part in the Dallas program, be sure to let the DMS staff know of your interest and availability.

With best wishes,

Robert F. Greenwald
Temporary Staff Coordinator (retired!)

Attachments:

1. Mediator training application
2. Dallas Times Herald editorial (6/3/81)
3. Dallas Times Herald letter to the editor (6/18/81)
4. Letter from Rep. Ceverha to Governor Clements (7/1/81)

RFG:s

A Selected List of Institutions of Higher Education Offering Degree or Certificate Programs in Mediation/Conflict Resolution

The following is a partial list of North American colleges and universities (137) offering some of the most prominent degree/certification programs related to mediation and conflict resolution. It is estimated that the total number of institutions of higher learning nationwide providing courses in peace/conflict resolution is well over 300. Some, however, do not grant corresponding degrees or certificates. Increasingly, parallel higher education curricula are found on campuses throughout the world. These educational facilities are exclusive of the hundreds of non-academic institutions and organizations that offer parallel training programs, and others devoted solely to research and/or community services:

INSTITUTION/LOCATION	ACADEMIC PROGRAMS
Abilene Christian University Conflict Resolution Abilene, Texas	MA in Conflict Resolution and Reconciliation; two Graduate Certificates
American University Washington, DC	PhD in International Relations with Concentration in International Peace & Conflict Resolution; MS, same
Antioch University The McGregor School Program in Conflict Resolution Yellow Springs, Ohio	MA in Conflict Resolution; Professional and Graduate Certificates
Antioch University of Seattle Seattle, Washington	Graduate Certificate in Conflict Resolution
Arcadia University Glenside, Pennsylvania	MA in Peace and Conflict Resolution
Arizona State University School of Justice Studies Tempe, Arizona	PhD in Justice Studies with Concentration in Dispute Resolution; MS, same
Associated Mennonite Biblical Seminary Elkhart, Indiana	MA in Peace Studies; MDiv in Theology Studies with Concentration in Peace Studies
Bethany Theological Seminary Richmond, Indiana	MA in Theology with Emphasis on Peace Studies; MDiv, same
Bethel College Kansas Institute for Peace & Conflict Resolution North Newton, Kansas	BA in Global Peace & Justice Studies; Certificate in Conflict Resolution
Boston University School of Law Boston, Massachusetts	JD with Concentration in Litigation and Dispute Resolution
Brandeis University Waltham, Massachusetts	MA in Coexistence and Conflict
Bryn Mawr College Bryn Mawr, Pennsylvania	Graduate Certificate in Conflict Resolution
California State University Behavioral Science Program Dominquez Hills, California	MA in Conflict Management; Graduate Certificate, same

California State University/Long Beach Long Beach, California	Certificate in Peace Studies
California Western School of Law Center for Creative Problem Solving San Diego, California	JD with Concentration in Creative Problem Solving
Cambridge College Cambridge, Massachusetts	Graduate Certificate in Business Negotiation and Conflict Resolution
Capital University Law School Center for Dispute Resolution Columbus, Ohio	JD with Certificate in Dispute Resolution
Carleton University Ottawa. Ontario, Canada	PhD in Cultural Mediation; Graduate Certificate in Conflict Resolution
Chapman University Orange, California	BA in Peace Studies
City University of Los Angeles School of Law and Legal Studies Los Angeles, California	LLM in Conflict Resolution
City University of New York Dispute Resolution Consortium John Jay College of Criminal Justice New York, New York	Dispute Resolution Certificate
Clark University Worcester, Massachusetts	MS in Professional Communication with Concentra- tion in Conflict Management and Resolution; Graduate Certificate in Conflict Mgmt.
Colgate University Hamilton, New York	BA in Peace and Conflict Studies
Columbia College Columbia, South Carolina	MA in Human Behavior and Conflict Management Graduate Certificate, same
Columbia University Teachers College New York, New York	EdD in Int'l Educational Development with Specialization in Peace Education; MA in Organizational Psychology with Concentration in Conflict Resolution; Graduate Certificate, same
Cornell University Institute on Conflict Resolution Ithaca, New York	MA in Industrial & Labor Relations with Concentration in Conflict and Dispute Resolution; Certificate in Conflict Resolution; 2 PhDs, 2 Masters in Regional Planning or Economics with major or minor in Peace Science
Dalhousie University Halifax, Nova Scotia, Canada	Graduate Certificate in Negotiation and Conflict Management
Dallas Baptist University Dallas, Texas	MA in Organizational Management with Concentration in Conflict Management
Depauw University Greencastle, Indiana	BA in Conflict Studies
Duquesne University Graduate Ctr for Social and Public Policy Pittsburgh, Pennsylvania	MA in Social and Public Policy with Concentration and Certificate in Conflict Resolution & Peace Studies
Eastern Mennonite University Harrisonburg, Virginia	MA in Conflict Transformation; Graduate Certificate, same

Earlham School of Religion Richmond, Indiana	MA in Religion with Emphasis in Peace & Justice
Faulkner University Thomas Goode Jones School of Law Institute for Dispute Resolution Montgomery, Alabama	Certificate in Dispute Resolution
Florida State University Tallahassee, Florida	Interdisciplinary Graduate minor in Dispute Resolution
Fordham University Bronx, New York	MA in Pastoral Ministries with Sub-Concentration in Education for Peace and Justice; MS, same; Professional Diploma, same
Fresno Pacific University Ctr for Peacemaking & Conflict Studies Fresno, California	MA in Conflict Management and Peacemaking; Five Certificates, same
George Fox University Center for Peace and Justice Newberg, Oregon	3 Undergraduate minors in Peace Studies, Certificate, same
George Mason University Inst for Conflict Analysis & Resolution Arlington, Virginia	PhD in Conflict Analysis & Resolution; MS, same; BS/BA, same; Graduate certificate, same + same, for health professionals
Georgetown University Center for Peace and Securities Studies Washington, DC	MA in Conflict Resolution
George Washington University School of Law Washington, DC	LLM in Litigation and Dispute Resolution
Golden Gate University San Francisco, California	Graduate Certificate in Conflict Resolution
Goshen College Goshen, Indiana	BA in Peace, Justice and Conflict Studies; Certificate in Conflict Transformation for Teachers
Goucher College Towson, Maryland	MEd with Specialization in School Mediation; Graduate Certificate, same
Gustavus Adolphus College St. Peter, Minnesota	Undergraduate minor in Peace Studies
Guilford College Greensboro, North Carolina	BA in Peace and Conflict Studies
Hamline University School of Law Dispute Resolution Institute St. Paul, Minnesota	Certificate in Alternative Dispute Resolution
Harvard Law School Program on Negotiation Massachusetts	Certificate of Participation in Continuing Legal Education; seminars, research, clearinghouse and Cambridge, special projects
Humboldt State University Institute for Study of Alternative Dispute Resolution Arcata, California	Certificate in Mediation
Iliff School of Theology Justice and Peace Studies Program Denver, Colorado	MA in Special Ministries with Concentration in Justice and Peace Studies; MDiv, same

Illinois Institute of Technology Program in Litigation and Dispute Resolution	JD Certificate in Litigation and Alternative Dispute Resolution
Indiana State University Resolution Program Department of Sociology Terre Haute, Indiana	MS in Conflict Resolution; Graduate Certificate of Conflict Mediation
Indiana University Indiana Conflict Resolution Institute Bloomington, Indiana	Graduate Certificate in Conflict Management
James Madison University Inst for Conflict Analysis & Intervention Harrisonburg, Virginia	BA/BS in Communication Studies with Concentrations in Conflict Communication and Intervention
John F. Kennedy University Orinda, California	Graduate Certificate in Conflict Resolution and Organizational Conflict Management
John Marshall Law School Center for Advocacy & Dispute Resolution Chicago, Illinois	JD in Advocacy and Dispute Resolution
Juniata College Huntingdon, Pennsylvania	BA major or program of emphasis in Peace and Conflict Studies
Kent State University Center for Applied Conflict Management Kent, Ohio	BA in Conflict Management; Undergraduate Minor same
Kennesaw State University Department of Political Science and International Affairs Kennesaw, Georgia	MS in Conflict Management; Certificate in Alternative Dispute Resolution
Lesley University Cambridge, Massachusetts	MEd in Curriculum & Instruction with Specialty in Conflict Resolution and Peaceable Schools; MA in Intercultural Relations with Specialization in Inter-Cultural Conflict Management; Graduate Cert, same
Marquette University Center for Dispute Resolution Education Milwaukee, Wisconsin	MA in Public Service with Specialization in Dispute Resolution; Graduate Certificate in Dispute Resolution
Menno Simons College Winnipeg, Canada	BA in Conflict Resolution Studies
Montclair State University Department of Legal Studies Upper Montclair, New Jersey	MA in Legal Studies with Concentration in Dispute Resolution for non-lawyer professionals in the legal field.
North Central College Naperville, Illinois	Undergraduate Minors in Professional Conflict Resolution and Community Conflict Resolution
Northland College Ashland, Wisconsin	BA in Peace, Conflict and Global Studies
Northwestern University Kellogg Graduate School of Management Dispute Resolution Research Center Evanston, Illinois	Certificate in Negotiation Teaching; Post-Doctoral Fellowships in Dispute Resolution and Negotiations
Nova Southeastern University Dept. of Conflict Analysis and Resolution Fort Lauderdale, Florida	PhD in Dispute Resolution; MS, same; Graduate Certificate, same; Graduate minor in Conflict Resolution Studies

Ohio State University Moritz College of Law Columbus, Ohio	JD with Certificate in Dispute Resolution
Oklahoma City University School of Law Center on Alternative Dispute Resolution Oklahoma City, Oklahoma	Post-JD Certificate in Client Representation in Alternative Dispute Resolution
Oregon State University Corvallis, Oregon	Graduate Certificate of Peace Studies
Pepperdine University School of Law Straus Institute for Dispute Resolution Malibu, California	LLM in Dispute Resolution; Master, same; Joint Master with Public Policy; Graduate Certificate in Conflict Resolution
Portland State University Portland, Oregon	MA/MS in Conflict Resolution
Royal Roads University Victoria, British Columbia, Canada	MA in Conflict Analysis & Management
Saint Ambrose University Davenport, Iowa	Interdisciplinary Minor in Peace and Justice
Saint Edwards University Austin, Texas	MA in Human Services with Specialization in Conflict Resolution
Saint Joseph College West Hartford, Connecticut	BA in Religious Studies with Concentration in Justice and Peace; Certificate, same
Saint Paul University Canadian Institute for Conflict Resolution Ottawa, Canada	MA in Conflict Studies
Saint Thomas University Institute for Pastoral Ministries Miami, Florida	MA in Pastoral Ministries with Specialization in Peacemaker of the Community; Graduate Certificate, same
Saint Xavier University Chicago, Illinois	Graduate Certificate in Conflict Resolution
Salisbury University Center for Conflict Resolution Salisbury, Maryland	BA in Conflict Analysis and Dispute Resolution
Saybrook Graduate School San Francisco, California	Certificate in Peace and Conflict Resolution Studies
School of International Training Brattleboro, Vermont	MA in Conflict Transformation
Sonoma State University Rohnert Park, California	Certificate in Conflict Resolution
Southern California University for Professional Studies Santa Ana, California	MSL with Specialization in Dispute Resolution
Southern Methodist University Center for Dispute Resolution and Conflict Management Dallas, Texas	MA in Dispute Resolution; Graduate Certificate, same
Southern Oregon University Ashland, Oregon	Undergraduate minor in International Peace Studies

Stanford University Martin Daniel Gould Center for Conflict Resolution Programs Stanford, California	Four broad interdisciplinary dispute resolution programs for law and graduate students
Sullivan University Louisville, Kentucky	MS in Conflict Resolution; Graduate Certificate, same
Syracuse University Program on the Analysis and Resolution of Conflicts Syracuse, New York	PhD in Social Science with Concentration in Conflict Resolution and Peace Studies; 4 Graduate Certificates in related studies; interdisciplinary undergraduate minor in Non-violent Conflict and Change
Temple University Philadelphia, Pennsylvania	PhD in Communication Sciences and MA in Applied Communication with Specializations in Conflict Processes
Texas State University San Marcos, Texas	MA in Legal Studies with Concentration in Alternative Dispute Resolution
Texas Woman's University Denton, Texas	Certificate in Conflict Resolution
Trinity College & Seminary Newburgh, Indiana	MA in Pastoral Ministry with Concentration in Conflict Management
Tufts University Medford, Massachusetts	BA in Peace and Justice Studies; Certificate, same
Union Institute & University Cincinnati, Ohio	Interdisciplinary PhD with Concentration in Peace Studies
Universidad Autonoma del Estrada de Mexico Toluca, Mexico	Master's Programme in Studies for Peace and Development
University of Alaska Anchorage, Alaska	Certificate in conflict Resolution
University of Baltimore Center for Negotiations & Conflict Mgmt. Baltimore, Maryland	MS in Negotiations and Conflict Management
University of California Berkeley, California	BA in Peace and Conflict Studies; undergraduate minor, same
University of Cincinnati The Urban Center for Peace Research Cincinnati, Ohio	Graduate Certificates in Urban Education and in Peace Education
University of Connecticut Storrs, Connecticut	BA in Interdisciplinary Peace Studies
University of Denver Conflict Resolution Institute Denver, Colorado	MA in Conflict Resolution; MS in Applied Communication with Concentration in Alternative Dispute Resolution; Certificate in Alternative Dispute Resolution
University of Hawaii at Manoa Honolulu, Hawaii	PhD in Political Science with Specialization in Conflict Resolution; MS, same; Graduate Certificate in Peace Studies
University of Houston/Clear Lake Clear Lake, Texas	MA in Cross-cultural Studies with Specialization in Mediation and Alternative Dispute Resolution
University of Houston Law Center College of Business Administration Houston, Texas	Basic Mediation for law students; Graduate Certificate in Conflict Resolution

University of Idaho Martin Institute Center for Peace Studies & Conflict Resolution Moscow, Idaho	BA/BS in Interdisciplinary International Studies; MA/MS, same
University of Maine Peace Studies Program Orono, Maine	Undergraduate Minor in Peace Studies
University of Maryland Center for International Development & Conflict Management College Park, Maryland	Undergraduate minor in International Development & Conflict Management
University of Massachusetts Program on Negotiation/Harvard Boston, Massachusetts	MA in Dispute Resolution; Graduate Certificate, same
University of Massachusetts/Amherst Amherst, Massachusetts	PhD with Concentration in the Psychology of Peace and the Prevention of Violence
University of Minnesota/Twin Cities Minneapolis/St. Paul, Minnesota	Graduate minor in Conflict Management
University of Missouri Columbia School of Law Center for the Study of Dispute Resolution Columbia, Missouri	LLM in Dispute Resolution
University of New Haven New Haven, Connecticut	MA in Industrial Organization with Concentration in the Psychology of Conflict Management
University of New Mexico Albuquerque, New Mexico	MA in Public Administration with Concentration in Dispute Resolution; Graduate Certificate, same
University of North Carolina/Greensboro Greensboro, North Carolina	MA in Conflict Resolution
University of North Dakota Grand Forks, North Dakota	BA/BS in Interdisciplinary Peace Studies
University of Notre Dame Mendoza College of Business South Bend, Indiana	MA in Peace Studies; Executive Certificate in Negotiation
University of Oregon School of Law Eugene, Oregon	MA in Conflict and Dispute Resolution
University of Prince Edward Island Charlottetown, PE, Canada	Certificate in Conflict Resolution Studies
University of San Diego Joan B. Kroc Institute for Peace and Justice San Diego, California	MA in Peace and Justice Studies
University of San Francisco San Francisco, California	Interdisciplinary Undergraduate Minor in Peace and Justice Studies
University of South Carolina Spartanburg, South Carolina	Three undergraduate minors in Conflict Resolution
University of South Florida Mediation Institute Tampa, Florida	Certificate in Mediation Skills

University of Tennessee College of Law Knoxville, Tennessee	JD with Concentration in Advocacy and Dispute Resolution
University of Tulsa College of Law Tulsa, Oklahoma	JD with Certificate in Dispute Resolution
University of Utah Salt Lake City, Utah	Graduate Certificate in Conflict Resolution
University of Victoria Victoria, British Columbia, Canada	MA interdisciplinary in Dispute Resolution
University of Waterloo Conrad Grebel University College Waterloo, Ontario, Canada	Interdisciplinary Undergraduate Program in Peace and and Conflict Studies
University of Wisconsin Milwaukee, Wisconsin	Graduate Certificate in Mediation and Negotiation; Certificate in Peace Studies
Villanova University Center for Peace & Justice Villanova, Pennsylvania	BA concentration or minor in Peace & Justice Education
Wayne State University Center for Peace & Conflict Studies Detroit, Michigan	Joint JD/MA in Dispute Resolution for law students; MA, same; Graduate Certificate, same; co-major BA, Peace and Conflict Studies
Wellesley College Wellesley, Massachusetts	BA in Peace and Justice Studies
West Chester University West Chester, Pennsylvania	Undergraduate Minor in Peace and Conflict Studies
Willamette College of Law Center for Dispute Resolution Salem, Oregon	Graduate Certificate in Dispute Resolution
Wilmington College Wilmington, Ohio	Certificate in Conflict Resolution
Woodbury College Montpelier, Vermont	MA in Mediation and Applied Conflict Studies; Graduate Certificate in Conflict Skills
Yeshiva University law Benjamin N. Cardozo School of Law New York, New York	Certificate in Dispute Resolution for JD students; train students to serve as mediators
York University Toronto, Ontario, Canada	Graduate Certificate in Alternative Dispute Resolution

A Partial List of Non-Academic Conflict Resolution Training/Education
Resources for Professional Practitioners, Volunteers and Others Seeking
Dispute Settlement Competence[1]

Primary Activity Codes (founding dates in parenthesis):
    [NP]: nonprofit
    [FP]: for profit
    [M]: requires membership
    [G]: government agency

A.A. White Dispute Resolution Center, Houston, TX (n/a)
    [NP] www.law.uh.edu/blakely/aawhite
Academy of Management/Conflict Management Division, Briarcliff Manor, NY (1936)
    [NP/M] www.aomonline.org/cm
ADR Institute of Canada, Toronto, Canada (1974) [NP] www.amic.org
Alabama Center for Dispute Resolution, Montgomery, AL (1994)
    [NP] www.alabamaadr.org
Alberta Arbitration & Mediation Society, Edmonton/Alberta, Canada (1982)
    [NP/M] www.aams.ab.ca
Alliance for Education in Dispute Resolution, Ithaca, NY (1998)
    [NP] www.ilr.cornell.edu/alliance
Alliance for Mediation & Conflict Resolution, Katonah, NY (1992)
    [FP] www.mediate.com/amcr
Alternatives to Violence Project, Houston, TX (1975) [NP] www.nal.usda.gov
Alternatives to Violence Project, St. Paul, MN (1975) [NP] www.avpusa.org
Alternatives to Violence Project in New Hampshire, Peterborough, NH (1975)
    [NP] www.avpnh.org
American Arbitration Association, New York, NY (1926) [NP] www.adr.org
American Bar Association, Section of Dispute Resolution, Washington, DC (1993)
    (NP/M) www.abanet.org/dispute
Arbitration & Mediation Institute of Manitoba, Winnipeg/Manitoba, Canada (1989)
    [NP] www.amim.mb.ca
Association for Conflict Resolution, Washington, DC (2001)[2]
    [NP/M] www.acrnet.org
Association of Family & Conciliation Courts, Madison, WI (1963)
    [NP/M] www.afccnet.org
British Columbia Arbitration & Mediation Institute, Vancouver/BC, Canada (1980)
    [NP] www.amibc.org
Canadian Bar Association/National Alternative Dispute Resolution Section, Ottawa,
    ON, Canada (1994) [NP/M] www.cba.org/CBA/Sections/Adre
Canadian International Institute of Applied Negotiation, Ottawa/Ontario, Canada (n/a)
    [FP] www.ciian.org

---

[1]Excludes community-based resolution centers shown in a separate roster
[2]Merger of Academy of Family Mediators (AFM), Society for Professionals in Dispute Resolution (SPIDR),
and Conflict Resolution Education Network (CREnet)

CDR Associates, Boulder, CO (n/a) [NP] www.mediate.org/index
Center for African Peace & Conflict Resolution, Sacramento, CA (1996)
    [NP] www.csus.edu/org/capcr
Center for Dispute Settlement, Washington, DC (1971) [NP] www.cdsusa.org
Center for Nonviolent Communication, La Crescenta, CA (1984) [NP] www.cnvc.org
Children's Creative Response to Conflict, Nyack, NY (1972)
    [NP] www.planet-rockland.org/conflict
Coast to Coast Mediation Center, Encinitas, CA (1982) [FP] www.ctcmediation.com
Colorado Council of Mediators, Littleton, CO (n/a)
    [NP/M] www.coloradomediation.org
Common Ground Mediation Center, Lafayette, CO (1992)
    [FP] www.commongroundmediation.com
Concur, Santa Cruz, CA (1987) [FP] www.concurinc.com
Conflict Management Initiatives, Evanston, IL (1990) [NP] www.cmi-salem.org
Conflict Research Consortium, Boulder, CO (1988) [NP] www.colorado.edu/conflict
Conflict Resolution Catalysts, Montpelier, VT (1987) [FP] www.crcvt.org
Conflict Resolution Center/University of North Dakota, Grand Forks, ND (1988)
    [NP] www.und.nodak.edu/dept/crc
Conflict Resolution Network Canada, Waterloo/Ontario, Canada (n/a)
    [NP/M] www.crnetwork.ca
Consensus Building Institute, Cambridge, MA (1994) [NP] www.cbuilding.org
Council of Better Business Bureaus/ADR Division, Arlington, VA (n/a)
    [NP] www.dr.bbb.org
Crisis Prevention Institute, Brookfield, WI (1980) [FP] www.crisisprevention.com
CPR Institute for Dispute Resolution, New York, NY (1979)
    [NP/M} www.cpradr.org
CRU Institute, Seattle, WA (1987) [NP] www.cruinstitute.org
Education for Conflict Resolution, North Manchester, IN (1989)
    [NP] www.workitout.org
Family Mediation Canada, Guelph/Ontario, Canada (1985) [NP] www.fmc.ca/index
Federal Mediation & Conciliation Service, Washington, DC (1947)
    [G] www.fmcs.gov/internet
Florida Conflict Resolution Consortium, Tallahassee, FL (1987) [NP]
    www.consensus.fsu.edu
Georgia Office of Dispute Resolution, Atlanta, GA (n/a) [G] www.godr.org/adr
Global Futures-Business Environmental Conflict, San Francisco, CA (1995) [NP]
    www.globalfutures.com
Harvard Mediation Program, Cambridge, MA (1981) [NP]
    www.law.harvard.edu/students/orgs/hmp
Indian Dispute Resolution Services, Sacramento, CA (1990)
    [NP] www.indiandispute.com
Indiana Association of Mediators, Noblesville, IN (1992)
    [NP/M] www.mediation-indiana.org
Institute for Environmental Negotiation, Charlottesville, VA (1980)
    [NP] www.virginia.edu/ien
Institute for International Mediation and Conflict Resolution, Washington, DC (1996)
    [NP] www.iimcr.org
Institute of World Affairs, Washington, DC (1924) [NP] www.iwa.org

International Association of Facilitators, St. Paul, MN (1994) [NP/M] www.iaf-world.org
International Institute for Conflict Prevention & Resolution, New York, NY (1979)
  [NP/M] www.cpradr.org
Iowa Association for Dispute Resolution, Ames, IA (1994) [NP/M] www.iowaadr.org
Just Solutions, Louisville, KY (1991) [NP] www.just-solutions.org
Key Bridge Foundation, Washington, DC (n/a) [FP] www.keybridge.org
Lombard Mennonite Peace Center, Lombard,IL (1983) [NP] www.lmpeacecenter.org
Massachusetts Office of Dispute Resolution, Boston, MA (1985)
  [G/M] www.umb.edu/resolution
Mediation Matters, Bethesda, MD (1984) [FP] www.mediationmatters.com
Mediation Network of North Carolina, Siler City, NC (1985) [NP/M] www.mnnc.org
Mediation Research & Education Project, Chicago, IL (1980) [NP] www.mrep.org
Mediation Training Institute International, Mission, KS (n/a)
  [FP] www.mediationworks.com
Mediation Works, Inc., Boston, MA (1994) [FP] www.mwi.org
National Association for Community Mediation, Washington, DC (1993)
  [NP/M] www.nafcm.org
National Center for Conflict Resolution Education, Urbana, IL (1997
  [FP] www.nccre.org
National Coalition Building Institute, Washington, DC (1984) NP] www.ncbi.org
National Conflict Resolution Center, San Diego, CA (1983) [NP] www.ncrconline.com
New Jersey Association of Professional Mediators, Hillsborough, NJ (n/a)
  [NP/M] www.njapm.org
New York State Dispute Resolution Association, Troy, NY (1985)
  [NP/M] www.nysdra.org
Northern California Mediation Center, San Rafael, CA (1981)
  [NP] www.ncmc-mediate.org
Northern Virginia Mediation Service, Fairfax, VA (1988) [NP] www.nvms.us
Ohio Commission on Dispute Resolution & Conflict Management, Columbus, OH
  (1989) [G] www.disputeresolution.ohio.gov
Ohio Mediation Association, Reynoldsburg, OH (1989)
  [NP/M] www.mediation.com/ohio
Oregon Mediation Center, Eugene, OR (1983)
  [FP] www.to-agree.com
Partners for Democratic Change, Washington, DC (1989) [NP] www.partnersglobal.org
Peacemaker Ministries, Billings, MT (1982) [NP] www.peacemaker.net
Peninsula Conflict Resolution Center, San Mateo, CA (1986) [NP] www.pcrcweb.org
Public Conversations Project, Watertown, MA (1989) [NP] www.publicconversations.org
Resolution Forum, Houston, TX (n/a) [NP] www.resolutionforum.org
SERA Learning, San Francisco, CA (1992) [FP] www.sera.com
Southern California Mediation Assn, Beverly Hills, CA (1989)
  [NP/M] www.scmediation.org
South Carolina Council for Conflict Resolution, Columbia, SC (1985)
  [NP] www.scmediate.org
State Bar of Texas, Alternative Dispute Resolution Section, Dallas, TX (n/a)
  [NP/M] www.texasadr.org/drtexas
Texas Association of Mediators, Dallas, TX (n/a) [NP/M] www.txmediator.org

The Balanced & Restorative Justice Project, Ft. Lauderdale, FL (1993)
[NP/G] www.barjproject.org
The Conflict Center, Denver, CO (1987) [NP] www.conflictcenter.org
The Dispute Resolution Ct/Woodbury College, Montpelier, VT (n/a)
[NP] www.woodbury-college.edu/drc/index
The Forum on Restorative Community Justice, Broomfield, CO (1998)
[NP] www.coloradorestorativejustice.org
The Negotiation Institute, New York, NY (1966)
{NP] www.negotiation.com
Peace Center, Langhorne, PA (1982)
[NP] www.thepeacecenter.org
U.S. Arbitration and Mediation, Seattle, WA (1984)
[FP] www.usam.com
U.S. Dept of Justice, Office of Dispute Resolution, Washington, DC (n/a)
[G] www.usdoj.gov/odr
U.S. Institute for Environmental Conflict Resolution, Tucson, AZ (1999)
[G] www.ecr.gov
Victim-Offender Mediation Association, St. Paul, MN (1997)
[NP] www.voma.org
Washington Mediation Association, Seattle, WA (1982)
[NP] www.washingtonmediation.org
Western Justice Center Foundation, Pasadena, CA (1985)
[NP] www.westernjustice.org
Workplace Violence Research Institute (n/a)
[FP] www.workviolence.com

Web Site Information

www.adrr.com
www.jca.apc.org
www.mediate.com
www.CRinfo.org

Note: It is estimated that there are almost 200 *campus* mediation centers at colleges and universities in North America (in which on-campus disputes are handled), yet another category of dispute intervention programming.

SUGGESTED READING

A History of Alternative Dispute Resolution: The Story of a Political, Social, and Cultural Movement
    Jerome T. Barrett and Joseph Barrett, Jossey-Bass, 336pp (2004)
Basic Skills for the New Mediator
    Allan H. Goodman, Solomon Publications, 110pp (2nd ed, 2004)
Beyond Machiavelli: Tools for Coping with Conflict
    Roger Fisher et al., Harvard University Press, 160pp (1996)
Beyond Neutrality
    Bernard Mayer, Jossey-Bass, 336pp (2004)
Bridging Cultural Conflicts: A New Approach for a Changing World
    Michelle LeBaron, Jossey-Bass, 353pp (2003)
Communicating Across Cultures
    Stella Ting-Toomey, The Gilford Press, 310pp (1999)
Conflict Resolution
    Daniel Dana, McGraw-Hill, 169pp (2000)
Essentials of Negotiation
    Roy J. Lewicki et al., McGraw-Hill Higher Education, 274pp (3rd ed, 2003)
Getting Past No: Negotiating Your Way from Confrontation to Cooperation
    William L. Ury, Bantam Books, 208pp (1993)
Getting to Resolution: Turning Conflict Into Collaboration
    Stewart Levine, Berrett-Koehler, 226pp (2000)
Getting to Yes: Negotiating Agreement Without Giving In
    Roger Fisher and William Ury, Penguin Books, 224pp (2nd ed, rev 1993)
Managing Public Disputes: A Practical Guide for Professionals in Government, Business and Citizens' Groups
    Susan L. Carpenter, Jossey-Bass, 314pp (2001)
Mediating Dangerously: The Frontiers of Conflict Resolution
    Kenneth Cloke, Jossey-Bass, 272pp (2001)
Mediation Career Guide: A Strategic Approach to Building a Successful Practice
    Forrest S. Mosten, Jossey-Bass, 320pp (2001)
Resolving Conflicts at Work: Eight Strategies for Everyone on the Job
    Kenneth Cloke and Joan Goldsmith, Jossey-Bass, 272pp (2nd ed, 2005)
Resolving Racial Conflict
    Bertram Levine, University of Missouri Press, 262pp (2005)
Settling Disputes: Conflict Resolution in Business, Families, and the Legal System
    Linda R. Singer, Westview Press, 212pp (1994)
Social Conflict: Escalation, Stalemate and Settlement
    Dean Pruitt and Sung Hee Kim, McGraw-Hill Higher Education, 307pp (2003)
The Dynamics of Conflict Resolution
    Bernard Mayer, Jossey-Bass, 263pp (2000)
The Eight Essential Steps to Conflict Resolution
    Dudley Weeks, Penguin Group, 304pp (1994)

The Mediation Field Guide
    Barbara Ashley Phillips, Jossey-Bass, 352pp (2001)
The Mediation Process
    Christopher W. Moore, Jossey-Bass, 624pp (3rd ed. 2003)
The Mediator's Handbook
    Jennifer E. Beer, New Society Publishers, 176pp (1997)
The Process of Mediation: The Transformation Approach to Conflict
    Robert A. Baruch and Joseph P. Folger, Jossey-Bass, 304pp (2004)
The Third Side: Why We Fight and How We Can Stop
    William L. Ury, Penguin Books, 272pp (2000)

REFERENCES

Conflict Research Consortium (CRC), University of Colorado (2004). *The conflict resolution information source: Education and Training Information.* http://www.gradschools.com/program/peace-studies.html

Cook, Royer F. et al. (1980). Neighborhood Justice Centers Field Test Report 2.

Fee, Thomas (1988). Introduction to National Institute on Dispute Resolution Forum, The Status of Community Justice.

Hart, Barry (2001, April). *Conflict Prevention and Resolution Forum.* Faith-Based Peacemaking: The Role of Religious Actors in Preventing and Resolving Conflict Worldwide.

Warters, William C. (1999, May). *The Online Journal of Peace and Conflict Resolution.* Graduate Studies in Dispute Resolution: A Delphi Study of the Field's Present and Future.

INDEX

Printed in the United States
201968BV00003B/1-52/P